JOY IN OUR WEAKNESS

JOY IN OUR WEAKNESS

A Gift of Hope from the Book of Revelation

———

REVISED EDITION

Marva J. Dawn

William B. Eerdmans Publishing Company • *Grand Rapids / Cambridge*
Lime Grove House Publishing Ltd • *Sydney / Aukland*
Regent College Publishing • *Vancouver*

Published jointly 2002 by

Wm. B. Eerdmans Publishing Co.

255 Jefferson Ave. S.E., Grand Rapids, Michigan 49503 /

P.O. Box 163, Cambridge CB3 9PU U.K.

www.eerdmans.com

and by

Lime Grove House Publishing Ltd

PO Box 37-955, Parnell, Aukland, NZ

and by

Regent College Publishing

an imprint of Regent College Bookstore

5800 University Boulevard, Vancouver, B.C. V6T 2E4

www.regentpublishing.com

Printed in the United States of America

07 06 05 04 03 02   7 6 5 4 3 2 1

Eerdmans ISBN 0-8028-6069-9

Lime Grove House Publishing ISBN 1 876798 84 X

Regent College Publishing ISBN 1-55361-050-4

Dedicated to all those who suffer
from chronic and terminal illness,
from handicaps and impairments and age,
from loneliness and fears and misfortunes,
and from the misunderstandings and mis-statements
of the well-meaning,

and especially to Linden and Tim
and to our spouses, Brenda, Debbie, and Myron

Contents

Preface   x

1. We Do Not Have to Be Afraid of The Revelation   3

2. The Gift of Weakness   12

3. God Is God, and We Are Wee   19

4. 1:1-3 and 9-11 — A Vision to Sustain Us in Suffering:
   The "Mysterious" Purposes of God   26

5. 1:5-8 — Who Is Christ for Our Suffering?   33

6. 1:12-20 — Who Is the Son of Man?   39

7. Chapters 2–3 — Flaws and Virtues   46

8. 2:1-7 — Ephesus: Losing Our First Love   52

9. 2:8-11 — Smyrna: Limitations of Suffering   57

10. 2:12-17 — Pergamum: The Importance of the Word   63

11. 2:18-29 — Thyatira: True Authority   71

Contents

12. 3:1-6 — Sardis: The Call to Renewal — 78

13. 3:7-13 — Philadelphia: An Open Door — 83

14. 3:14-22 — Laodicea: Whatever Our Limitations
We Don't Have to Be Tepid — 89

15. 4:1-11 — The First Reason for Praise: The Gift of Life — 96

16. 5:1-14 — The Second Reason for Praise:
The Lamb Who Saves by Suffering — 103

17. 6:1–7:8 and 19:11-21 — Don't Forget the First Horse
of the Apocalypse! — 109

18. 6:9-11 and 7:9, 13-15 — Endurance:
The Meaning of Biblical Patience — 116

19. 7:9-17 — The Third Reason for Praise: Hope for the Future — 123

20. 8:1-6 — Skills to Read The Revelation:
Silence and Trust in God's Vindication — 129

21. 8:6–9:21 — The Persistence of Sin and the
Immensity of Grace — 135

22. 10:1–11:13 — Asking the Right Questions in Our Suffering:
How Long? and Meanwhile? — 141

23. 11:14–12:17 — 42 Months, 1,260 Days, and 3½ Years — 149

24. Chapters 12–13 — Taking the Presence of Evil Seriously — 156

25. Chapter 14 — Songs, Proclamations, and Harvests — 163

26. Chapters 15–16 — We Wouldn't Want Love without Holiness — 169

27. Chapters 17–18 — Fallen! Fallen Is Babylon the Great! — 176

28. 19:1-21 — Preludes and Wedding Songs — 184

Contents

29. 20:1–21:8 — The Ultimate Defeat of the Powers of Evil
    and the Present Reign of Christ   190

30. 21:9–22:7 — The Beautiful City: An Agent of Healing   199

31. 22:8-21 — "Come!": Living Now in the Coming Victory   207

    EPILOGUE: Qualities for a Theology of Weakness:
    Perspectives from The Revelation on Suffering   214

    For Further Consideration   218

Preface

This is not a book for scholars. I write this book instead for you, for me, and for all of us who together make up the Body of Christ and who need the book of Revelation to learn how to find Joy[1] in every circumstance of our lives, especially in our trials and sufferings.

I write as one who is weak but not weak enough. I struggle with physical handicaps enough to know their great benefits for the Christian life, but I am not weak enough yet to accept their pain gladly. My brittle diabetes defies all the rules for taking care of its rapid blood-sugar swings. It is scary, life-threatening, immobilizing. A crippled leg, frequent foot wounds and hand surgeries, constant intestinal pain from nerve dysfunction and the scar tissue after an intussusception, a blind eye and the threat of hemorrhages in the other, a deaf ear, cancer, kidney deficiencies, and other deteriorations keep reminding me of a doctor's words a decade ago: "Let's face it. You have debilitating diseases; you've had them a long time. It is downhill from here . . ." How can people with chronic illness cope?

---

1. In this book I am capitalizing the word *Joy* to refer specifically to the Joy that is ours because our relationship with God fills us with security, confidence, and hope. I use the capitalized form in order to invite readers to pause and be reminded that Joy is the deep sense of God's sustaining presence, the realization that divine light is greater than any darkness that might temporarily assail us. Thus, Joy does not mean "happiness," which is dependent upon human circumstances. This distinction is elucidated more thoroughly in chapter 12 of my book on the Psalms, *I'm Lonely, Lord — How Long?* (Grand Rapids: Wm. B. Eerdmans Publishing Co., 1997).

Obviously I am weak, but physical handicaps alone do not suffice to teach me how weak I truly am. At times I am deeply aware of the feebleness of my Christian life, and yet far too often I fall into the trap of thinking that somehow by my own great effort I can accomplish the purposes of God.

Because I am weak and not weak enough, this book is written from two sides. As one who is handicapped, I plead for all of us to learn better to care for and listen to each other, and especially those who struggle with particular physical, emotional, and mental challenges. On the other hand, my calls to repentance are written by one who needs this prodding.

A theology of weakness emphasizes that each of us is helpless and hopeless in our sin and desperately in need of God's grace. However, because we have so many physical and mental capabilities, we are usually unable even to recognize — much less to acknowledge — how helpless we are. We need a theology of weakness to remind us that our relationship with God is utterly dependent upon the Triune One's infinite grace and mercy. Only through total reliance upon that grace are we able to live as God's servants in the world.

Consequently, a theology of weakness also realizes that those who accept their weakness and acknowledge their dependence can teach us best about the grace that invades all of our lives. Therefore, this theology challenges our churches to encourage the gifts and teaching potential of those who suffer and to become more truly a Christian community that cares deeply about each person.

This book is also about "The Revelation of Jesus Christ" (the title in the original Greek for the last book of the Bible). This title reminds us that by grace God revealed through the seer and servant John the truth about the Lordship of Jesus to comfort people who were powerless against various persecutions. Many people are uncomfortable with The Revelation for the very reason that it is filled with the paradox of weakness, in contrast to our world's emphases on efficiency and usefulness, position and power. We don't want to face the weaknesses in ourselves or cope with the weaknesses of others.

Furthermore, many people find The Revelation difficult because it cannot be analyzed scientifically. In our technological craving for facts and fixes, we can hardly understand a book that is flooded with images, memories, symbols, and mysteries. Consequently, we miss some of God's best promises and the comfort that Christ would give us through this wonderful book of hope.

Our culture needs the gift of hope more than any of the other theological virtues. The Revelation is a book that overwhelms us with hope — but it is accessible to us only if we can acknowledge our weakness, and that is awfully hard for us. We don't want to shed our facades, our pretentiousness.

Finally, some people avoid the book of Revelation because they are frightened by the grotesque stories of supernatural warfare that are sometimes overaccentuated or falsely elaborated in anticipation of the end of time. While some Christians claim to know exactly how to pin down the explicit meaning of each symbol in The Revelation, others ignore the last book of the Bible in order to stay away from the fray over its contents. The whole business is too disruptive and too mysterious.

Participants in my classes and retreats on The Revelation have urged me to write a commentary on the book, but good ones already exist.[2] Instead, this is a book about suffering — using The Revelation as a text to invite everyone, Christian and non-Christian alike, to explore the value of its message for the twenty-first century.

Many retreat participants have offered perspectives and criticisms, arguments and questions, to clarify my thinking as we explored this unique message together. Please do the same. Pass this book around to all your friends, discuss it over lunch at your job, struggle with its questions for your own spiritual disciplines, consider its theology and application to your personal and social and religious life (whatever form the latter might take). The Revelation contains questions that apply to that dimension of everyone's existence that is manifested in our allegiance to something — anything — with an ultimate commitment.

The value of The Revelation for everybody is that it portrays the Lordship of Christ. One of its great themes (often missed) is that Christ reigns especially in the midst of our suffering.

In my experience, some of the Christians who have understood best what that reign means have been disabled people or people with other limitations that force them to live out of weakness. In their suffering they have learned enormous lessons usually ignored by a culture that focuses on power and success. People who have learned to trust God in their physical

---

2. An excellent guide to The Revelation, accessible to laypersons, is Craig R. Koester's *Revelation and the End of All Things* (Grand Rapids: Wm. B. Eerdmans Publishing Co., 2001).

challenges or other struggles, therefore, often render us all a great service by teaching us a theology of weakness sometimes lost in a triumphalistic gospel.

The Revelation invites us to learn a theology of weakness. My desire is that all of us in Christ's Body could learn that theology better by receiving the wisdom that our own suffering brings us and by valuing more thoroughly the contributions that those who suffer bring to our communities. This book thus has a double reason for existence: it pleads with churches to discover the gifts of the weak among us, and it offers encouragement to all of us both to recognize the importance of dependence in our sufferings and to offer those insights and perspectives freely to deepen the faith of our communities.

This book is dedicated to two people who have especially taught me from their weakness. Linden, who suffers from quadriplegia, and Tim, who lives by means of three weekly sessions on a kidney dialysis machine, are two of the most strongly gentle men I've ever known. (My precious husband is a third.) I can see Christ's reign in their lives. I owe them an enormous debt of gratitude for their input when I wrote the first draft of this book almost twenty years ago, for their wise and supportive friendships, for their profound (and unromanticized) love and affection, for their gutsy courage in encountering the world.

As representatives of many other physically challenged people who have been a part of this book, I thank especially these two: Connie Kramer, who, out of her visual impairment, gave me a story of grace when I was depressed about possible amputation of my foot; and Karyl Groeneveld, who, in spite of severe pain from chronic back problems and sudden widowhood, uses her expert linguistic and computer skills to research details for me. For example, she provided information on *tephillin* for chapter 24 of this book.

I also give great thanks to my former secretary, Sandy Drees, who first gave me space and time in her home and heart to get excited about the possibilities of this book and to begin fleshing out its contents; to Leonard and Odessa Johnson, who gave me refuge (literally, since a tornado came frighteningly close) to finish the first draft; to Holy Trinity Lutheran Church, Elmira, New York, which hosted a teaching conference on The Revelation and provided financial aid to give me a month off from teaching to begin working on revisions for the book's first appearance; and to Samuel Eerdmans and to my superb editor, Jennifer Hoffman, who made it possible for this newly revised edition of the book to be published for the sake of those who suffer and for the whole Church.

MARVA J. DAWN
The Day before Easter

The praises
of the sick
and the
broken
excuse the
silence of
the healthy
and
whole.

RABBI MOSHE HAKOTUN

Remember Your word to Your servant,
in which You have made me hope.
This is my comfort in my distress,
that Your promise gives me life.

PSALM 119:49-50
(NRSV, ALTERED)

CHAPTER 1

We Do Not Have to Be Afraid
of The Revelation

The lecturer had everything pinned down. On that day twenty years ago, he knew exactly what events of world history were prophesied by which images in the book of Revelation so that he could plot on a timeline exactly how close we were to the end of the world. His perspective fit in well with the contemporary situation of nuclear madness and economic chaos, so his listeners were both terrorized and strangely comforted by his predictions. Though the tribulation would be ghastly (Armageddon in terms of nuclear holocaust), at least Communist evil would finally be punished and American justice would prevail. Meanwhile, he insisted, the job of Christians was to tell others that noticeable events, such as the eruption of Mount St. Helens and the severe droughts of previous summers, were signs of the imminent end, to which the world ought to pay attention in order to repent.

A careful study of The Revelation will demonstrate that this is *not* the book's primary message. Rather, because God is the focus, its symbols and images affirm the truth that victory lies in receiving divine grace for our weakness. Such an interpretation invites us to turn to the Bible's last book when things are hard — when we are struggling with illness or harassment at work, with financial shortages or family difficulties. Such a perspective really offers profound comfort and hope.

The Revelation itself invites our careful study. It is the only biblical book that both begins and ends with a promise to those who pay attention to its message. At the beginning the seer John testifies that everything he saw is

3

truly the Word of God and the testimony of Jesus Christ, and then he proclaims, "Blessed is the one reading and those hearing the words of the
prophecy and heeding the things which are written in it, for the time is near"
(Rev. 1:3).[1] Similarly, at the book's end, the One who is coming soon gives
this promise: "Blessed is the one heeding the words of the prophecy of this
book" (22:7). Certainly these promises invite us to search for insight into this
precious, mysterious book. Its visions will give us a new understanding of
life and suffering and the significance of our religious yearnings.

In an interesting experiment conducted before *glasnost* and the break-
down of the Soviet empire, U.S. school children were shown pictures of
tree-lined streets and asked why Russians planted trees like that. The children responded, "So people won't be able to see what's going on beyond
the road" and "to make work for prisoners." When asked why American
roads have trees beside them, the same children said, "for shade" or "to
keep the dust down." Everything depends on perspective!

Most important for a careful study of The Revelation is the basic perspective with which we view it. At the outset, these four guidelines will allow our approach to preserve the book's artistic and theological integrity.

1. A Historical Perspective

The first rule for understanding any piece of literature is to know in what
time period it was written — to clarify what it might have originally suggested to those who first read it. The most obvious flaw of many interpretations of the Bible is that they begin with the twenty-first century and
move backwards. Starting with particular events of our times, these interpretations claim to find "prophecies" that predicted them.

Of course, statements in the Scriptures are often fulfilled in times after
they were written. Indeed, much of the Christian understanding of who Jesus was and what He[2] did comes from recognizing the significance in His

---

1. Unless otherwise noted, the translations in this book are the author's own.

2. In this book I will be capitalizing all of the pronouns that refer to God. This will
be especially important when the divine pronouns refer to Jesus since Christ's Lordship
is the point of both Revelation and this book. How easy it is to slip back into our all-
too-human perspectives and to forget that God is here and that the risen Christ reigns
eternally!

As much as literarily possible, I try to avoid third-person pronouns for God, life of certain passages from the First Testament.[3] However, this is the second level of meaning for those Hebrew passages. Honest interpretation of the Christian Scriptures must begin with the Hebrew perspectives of the ones who wrote and of their Jewish readers. Anyone reading the previous illustration, for example, would have to keep in mind the pre-1989 hostilities between the U.S.S.R. and the U.S. to interpret it appropriately.

Therefore, to be faithful to the text, we must begin by understanding the historical situation in which The Revelation was written. Even though scholars disagree about many particulars of that situation (such as whether the John who wrote the book was the disciple of Jesus and whether the author actually saw the visions or dreamed them), all scholars agree that the book was written during a time of persecution against the early Christians — perhaps the fulminations of Nero, around A.D. 64, or of Domitian, between A.D. 81 and 96, but more probably local persecutions.[4]

To begin with the first century as opposed to the twenty-first makes a

---

though I have always understood the pronouns *He, His, Him,* and *Himself* to be gender-neutral — and yet personal — when used in connection with God. However, I am beginning to think that a larger problem in our theological vocabulary is that Jesus is being reduced to humanly understandable dimensions. He was, indeed, human and male — not that the Triune God is, but that God's human incarnation took that particular form. But Jesus was also the incarnation of *God,* which is especially emphasized in the book of Revelation; throughout its history the Church has confessed Him to be both God and man.

3. I join many other scholars and pastors in calling the first three-fourths of the Bible the "First Testament" to avoid our culture's negative connotations of the name *Old Testament* and to emphasize both the consistency of God's grace for all people and the continuity of God's covenants in the Bible first with Israel and then in addition with Christians.

4. The debate over the kind of persecution suffered by the recipients of The Revelation is a good example of the diversity of scholarly opinion concerning the book's setting. Craig Koester (*Revelation and the End of All Things* [Grand Rapids: Wm. B. Eerdmans Publishing Co., 2001]), who is convinced (along with the majority of scholars) that John the disciple of Jesus did not write the book, also rejects the notion that the believers suffered from persecution originating with the emperor and extending throughout the region. He recognizes the persecution more as a family fight concerning who are the true Jews (pp. 63-66). Edwin Walhout, in *Revelation Down to Earth: Making Sense of the Apocalypse of John* (Grand Rapids: Wm. B. Eerdmans Publishing Co., 2000), accepts the early Church's conviction that the disciple John was the author and the theory that the persecution was that unleashed in the area by the Emperor Domitian (p. 2).

huge difference in the ordering of our theological work — and, therefore, in its faithfulness. From the book itself we listen to the narrative details and hear the hope the text gave to the people at the time of its writing, and thereby we are formed to deduce more authentically what implications that message might have for us. Such an approach deals more truly with the text than an approach that begins with our situation and then forces twenty-first-century perspectives onto first-century minds. To study the Scriptures with historical integrity means to judge them in their own time and place and to take literally their original message for the original readers.

Our approach in this book, then, will be to hear a passage along with the earliest Christians, to be formed by that narrative to be a Christian people, and only then to think about that text in relation to our present society.

2. Literary Purposes

This aspect naturally follows from the preceding. If we are looking at The Revelation for what it said in a historical situation of persecution, we will search for what we can perceive about the reasons why, and the way in which, it was written.

In a conference on The Revelation I asked the participants to gather with other members of their families to talk about some situation of great fear in which its resolution taught them an important lesson about God's love. Then they were to prepare a sentence to intrigue the rest of us and to remind their own family of the event's meaning.

One family delighted us all with this summary: "Don't worry! The police will bring him back." Everyone in the room couldn't wait to hear the story.

One day their toddler had wandered away from home during rush hour, safely crossed one of the busiest highways in their city, and was found about two miles from home by a policeman who was able to return him because of the brand-new identification bracelet on his wrist. Can you imagine that family's immense relief when the policeman brought him unharmed to their door and told them where he had been found? The symbolic message, "Don't worry! The police will bring him back," reminded that family of an instance of God's immense care — and now, a score of years later, still fills me with wonder and comfort.

The same literary purposes are operating in the book of Revelation. The writer addressed Christians confronting an agonizing situation. They were being persecuted — perhaps tortured, thrown to lions, burned, or suffering economic consequences — because they clung to the Lordship of Christ. How could they have the courage to go on in the face of such suffering? How could they find hope in the midst of such terror?

The writer of The Revelation responds carefully. He, too, is a prisoner for his faith. According to his testimony, he was imprisoned on the Isle of Patmos, where Roman authorities sent political captives. Those who thought him subversive for his verbalization of "the word of God and the testimony of Jesus" were wise (humanly speaking) to put the eminent leader John there. To make John a martyr would only have increased the influence of his witness. So he was sent away into exile and perhaps slave labor. Perhaps his letters were censored by the powers who had arrested him.

How, then, could he communicate with Christians back in Asia Minor? How could he offer them hope and comfort without his letters being destroyed by the officials who guarded him?

He wrote stories and visions. They might seem like crazy and bizarre stories — perhaps the work of a lunatic. But they overflowed with images identifiable to the family, to those who knew the family history, for The Revelation is filled with stories and images from the First Testament and from the oral traditions of Jesus' teachings maintained in the early Christian community. Its pictures come from the traditions of Israel; they symbolize the ways in which God took care of the weak and despised Hebrews and made them a covenant people.

The original readers of The Revelation would immediately recognize those images as well as the larger biblical passages from which they came. They would have known, for example, that the writer was not just mentioning a lamb that was slain, but that he referred to the entire context of that image as it began in the Passover sequence of Exodus 12. The Israelites observed that festival (as well as the Day of Atonement, which significantly used instead a lamb that was not slain) to remember God's promises of protection and reconciliation and hope for a covenant land. Just as the retreat participants' phrase suggested a lovely story of divine protection and human care, so these images from the First Testament and from oral traditions about John the Baptizer and Jesus implied the sovereignty of the LORD and the community of God's people.

This is the literary framework in which we will look for the central thrusts of the message in The Revelation. From these purposes we can improvise our responses as God's people in our present times.[5]

3. The Study of Literature

We all read various kinds of literature in daily life with skills appropriate to their respective literary genres. For example, we don't read comic strips with the same seriousness as editorials or cookbook directions. Similarly, when we read the Bible we use different skills to study poetry, prophecy, apocalyptic literature (defined below in Chapter 4), narrative, sermons, history, or liturgy. Whereas some books are easy to understand because they might contain only one type of literary form, The Revelation contains all seven. Although we will comment on various aspects of these literary styles throughout the course of this book, at this point we must address particularly the problem of prophecy.

That word has distorted connotations in our times because of many who claim to be foretellers of the future. Long ago a famous visionary, Jeane Dixon, predicted that President John F. Kennedy would be assassinated. Those who believed her forecasts forgot that she also missed on some major issues, such as whether or not he would be elected, if Pope Paul would enjoy good health (he died), and if the roof of the gymnasium at the University of Georgia would collapse (my brother registered there safely). Prophecy is usually defined in our modern world as foretelling the future by means of paranormal abilities. In contrast, we understand biblical prophecy less as a prediction of the future than as an inspired speaking of God's Word or a recognition of where the present course is leading.

This ties in with the second principle above concerning literary purposes, for the writer of The Revelation was not at all foretelling far-distant events (other than the final victory of God) to comfort his friends in their present suffering. Moreover, as our first historical principle stresses, his words must certainly be applied first to that very situation of persecution

---

5. For a more thorough discussion than is possible here of my primary understanding of biblical application to our times, see Marva J. Dawn and Eugene H. Peterson, *The Unnecessary Pastor: Rediscovering the Call* (Grand Rapids: Wm. B. Eerdmans Publishing Co., 1999), chapter 2, section 5, "Improvising the Missing Act."

and then, secondarily, to our times. Saint John was clarifying for his original readers where present events or behaviors were leading and how they should respond to the crises. Thus, our third point is that, in a literary perspective, prophecy in The Revelation is a critical reflection on the meaning of first-century events in light of the eternal purposes and Word of God.

This is not to say, let me hastily add, that The Revelation might not also give us some perspective on events of our time. However, our perception of this must come after, and not before, the recognition of the original and primary purpose of biblical prophecy. When we have done a thorough job of ferreting out possible meanings for a persecuted people in Asia Minor at the end of the first century, then we can draw some conclusions about living these meanings in the twenty-first.

4. The Fundamental Point of View

It is necessary to remove ourselves from ordinary present-day ways of thinking in order to recognize the vast difference between contemporary anthropocentrism and the theocentrism of the first century. Our times are characterized by patterns of mind which begin with ourselves as the focus. These anthropocentric perspectives make humankind (the Greek word is *anthrōpos*) their center.

The Scriptures do not arise from such a perspective. They are written by people who began their thinking with the voice of God (*theos* is the Greek word for divinity). Notice how often throughout the Bible the writers include such notations as "thus says the LORD" or "declares the LORD." Notice also how often God is the one speaking, constantly repeating "I . . . I . . . I . . ." with various verbs of action. Anyone who carefully reads the Scriptures cannot miss this constant refrain of God speaking, God creating, God directing, God transforming, God intervening, God declaring divine purposes, God loving. Everywhere the perspective is God's, so it is with the LORD's viewpoint that we must read the literature. This makes an enormous difference in the way we read The Revelation. When we view it theocentrically, we read it to learn what it says about God, not about us, and about God's timing and purposes rather than ours.

Yet it is not necessary to believe in God to read it this way, just as we don't have to become like the idiot to accept his perspective in *One Flew Over the Cuckoo's Nest*. However, by the end of that book we find ourselves accepting the latter for who he is and the transformation that has been wrought. I think that The Revelation (properly explained) is a good book for non-believers to read in order to discover the character of the God who claims to be the Lord of everything.

I emphasize this point because far too often Christians do not realize how subtly we are dissuaded from the theocentric perspective that should characterize faith. We live in an age of super-subjectivism, in which how we are experiencing things determines their reality. Subjectivism is evident in such slogans as "If it feels good, do it." Not so evident is the way subjectivism distorts our society's approach to religious phenomena.

Postmodern interpretations of scriptural accounts center on the perceptions of the disciples rather than on what Jesus was teaching about His kingdom, or on the experience of the children of Israel rather than on what *YHWH*[6] was showing them about covenant purposes and faithfulness. Last Sunday I heard a sermon that focused primarily on dimensions of life that bend women over, but hardly mentioned anything about the Jesus who healed a deformed woman (Luke 13:10-17).

Because the twenty-first-century mind is characteristically inward-turned, this subjectivism has invaded our theology, as can be seen in much of contemporary Christian ethics, as well as Christian music. Several years ago a large dramatic Easter pageant shocked me and awoke me to the dangers of this invasion when the words from Handel's *Messiah,* "and the glory of the LORD shall be revealed," were changed to "when we shall see his glory." That shift might not seem so drastic, but think of the dichotomous difference of perspective it indicates. Now the emphasis is on how

---

6. As you have probably noticed, this book follows the customary practice in Bibles of capitalizing all the letters in the words *LORD* and *GOD* when the Hebrew word to be translated is the name *YHWH*, often vocalized as *Yahweh* (formerly as *Jehovah*). The original Hebrew noun, composed of the four consonants Y H W H, related to the root of the verb "to be." Since Orthodox Jews honor God's name by not saying it aloud (for fear that they might blaspheme it) and since the original Hebrew manuscripts were written with only consonants and not the vowel points, scholars are not sure how to say the word. Rather than make it readable, I will use *YHWH* occasionally in this book and hope that this will cause you to reflect upon its mystery and God's unreachable majesty. Throughout the First Testament the name *YHWH*, the LORD, implies the faithfulness of God, especially in delivering the covenant people from captivity. We, too, need to learn the glory of the LORD's constant covenant faithfulness and Christ's effective deliverance of His people from all their captivities.

we, subjectively, are (or are not) seeing God's glory, rather than on the objective fact of *YHWH*'s revelation.

In order to analyze properly a piece of literature, we simply must study it from the point of view from which it was written — and the Scriptures declare themselves to be God's own revelation. The Revelation (notice that the word is singular) literally begins as follows in the original Greek:

> The revelation[7] of Jesus Christ, which God gave to Him, to make manifest to His bond-servants the things which must necessarily take place shortly; and He communicated [these things], having sent [them] through His angel to His bond-servant John, who bore witness to the word of God and to the testimony of Jesus Christ, even to all that he saw.

In this one sentence the theocentric perspective (which includes the testimony of Jesus, clearly recognized in the book as divine) is mentioned four times.

This last element of perspective is one of the main reasons I feel compelled to write this book, for it seems to me that much of the flabbiness of contemporary Christianity derives precisely from this failure to approach things from God's perspective and to recognize the objectivity of the Triune revelation.[8] Later we will consider the validity of that revelation and the meaningfulness of such a perspective in a world where everyone wants to begin with him- or herself. But for now let us simply agree to look at The Revelation from the perspective of its author, who states unequivocally that he has written not his own thoughts and ideas, but the very words of God and the testimony of Jesus. This leads us to some incredible results, to be noted in the next chapter.

---

7. The Greek word *apocalypse,* translated "revelation," will be defined more thoroughly in Chapter 4.

8. A superb book focusing on this theological crisis is *Reading the Bible in Faith: Theological Voices from the Pastorate,* ed. William H. Lazareth (Grand Rapids: Wm. B. Eerdmans Publishing Co., 2001).

CHAPTER 2

The Gift of Weakness

Now that we have clarified the basic foundational perspective with which we enter into the book of Revelation, we can focus in this chapter on overviewing the main three-part theological message that the book conveys. In the next introductory chapter we will look more closely at our participation in that truth by acknowledging and valuing our weakness.

God's message to us in the book of Revelation is that in the present we are not always going to win; our lives will not always be characterized by triumph. That is a lesson hard to accept — in fact, impossible — except that it is balanced on the opposite side with this hope: eventually we will win because Christ reigns. These poles stand in a dialectical tension and cannot be brought together because of the intervening reality of opposition from all the powers of evil.

These three parts — the ultimate, cosmic Lordship of God in Christ; the present opposition of the powers of evil; and the resultant suffering on the part of God's people — lead to this other important aspect of the theology of The Revelation: meanwhile we can endure our weakness with patience. The hope of God's ultimate dominion sustains our long-suffering.

Many twenty-first-century Christians find these convictions almost impossible to accept. Instead they have espoused a theology of "victory, healing, luxury, and blessedness" that The Revelation does *not* teach. God does not promise us a rose garden — at least not one without legions of thorns.

And though there are, of course, many roses in life, they fade, too — with the promise that they will come again next season. Life has its rhythms and fragrances.

We have to keep our worldview genuinely realistic. We cannot ignore that we live in a world dominated by sin and not by the purposes of God. All the talk about the progress of the human race is verifiably an illusion, as we discover when we correctly read the Scriptures and human history. We see over and over again that power corrupts, leaders deceive, persons hurt each other for their own gains, dreams die — or, perhaps more precisely, are usually killed. This is not just gloomy pessimism.[1] In fact, Christian realism is much more optimistic than shallow illusions about humankind's goodness because this genuine realism recognizes that God is working still in spite of evidence to the contrary. Divine, covenant purposes will prevail in the world in spite of all the gunk and muck.

But the gunk and muck are there — and we do great disservice to those who suffer if we gloss over it and dump on them a mindlessly "hopeful" gospel of pablum victory over their pain. The Revelation teaches that God always gives victory eventually, but that the meanwhile entails suffering.

This message is crystal clear in many passages of The Revelation, such as 2:10-11. It is a message that we could more easily embrace if we paid better attention to those in our midst who understand the grace of weakness.

Let's start with the fact of evil. The letter to the Ephesians declares that we are battling "against the rulers, against the powers, against the world forces of this darkness, against the spiritual *forces* of wickedness in the heavenly *places*" (Eph. 6:12).[2] The book of Revelation describes these forces

---

1. See chapter 5, "On Christian Pessimism," in *Sources and Trajectories: Eight Early Articles by Jacques Ellul That Set the Stage,* trans. and ed. Marva J. Dawn (Grand Rapids: Wm. B. Eerdmans Publishing Co., 1997).

2. Since I have explicated this passage in numerous ways and places, I will not repeat that work here. See especially chapter 1 of Marva J. Dawn, *Powers, Weakness, and the Tabernacling of God* (Grand Rapids: Wm. B. Eerdmans Publishing Co., 2001); *Is It a Lost Cause? Having the Heart of God for the Church's Children* (Grand Rapids: Wm. B. Eerdmans Publishing Co., 1997); "The Concept of 'the Principalities and Powers' in the Works of Jacques Ellul," Ph.D. dissertation, The University of Notre Dame, 1992 (Ann Arbor, MI: University Microfilms, #9220614), and chapter 5 of Marva J. Dawn and Eugene H. Peterson, *The Unnecessary Pastor: Rediscovering the Call* (Grand Rapids: Wm. B. Eerdmans Publishing Co., 1999).

in terms of dragons, beasts, prostitutes, and the warriors of Armageddon. No matter what names we call the powers of evil, if we do not acknowledge their reality in the world we very foolishly deceive ourselves.

The narratives in Genesis 3–11 make this point unequivocal: human beings, fallen from their created purposes, are no longer capable of fulfilling God's intentions for them. Moreover, human rebelliousness has let loose all sorts of other evils in the world. Though that fall has been counteracted by the work of Christ, the restoration has not yet been completed. The letter to the Colossians declares that in our suffering we are completing Christ's work. Of course, we do not participate in the work of redemption itself, which has been thoroughly finished at the cross and empty tomb. Rather, we "fill up what is lacking" in the work of creating the community of God's people (Col. 1:24). Even as Colossians equates involvement in that work with the processes of our suffering, so The Revelation comforts those who undergo suffering and even martyrdom in order that the work of the kingdom of God might be continued in spite of, and in opposition to, the evil that assails it.

Furthermore, the evil that dominates the world seems at times to be out of God's control. We certainly cannot know why God allows the results of sin to be manifest in such things as terminal illness, the destructive forces of nature (like the tornado that totally demolished a town twenty-five miles from where I was first writing this book), or the demonic oppressions and destructions of tyrants. Moreover, we ought to be a little bit afraid of anyone who gives too simplistic an explanation for these phenomena. Nor should we trust those who say that God must not be powerful enough to stop such evil, but is still in the process of becoming almighty. That contradicts the constant refrain of the Scriptures that *YHWH is* the "Lord of hosts," that Christ *reigns* now as King of kings and Lord of lords, that the Trinity's purposes eventually *will prevail* and *are prevailing* now.

Of course, these assertions do not advocate a blind faith that merely says, "Well, it doesn't look true, but we just have to believe it." We certainly do not need to sacrifice our intelligence to believe in a God who is both all-loving and all-powerful. We do, however, have to acknowledge that, since our intelligence is vastly inferior to God's, we simply cannot yet know all that there is to know.

All the arguments declaring that God could not be both all-good and all-powerful and still allow such evil in the world are anthropocentric arguments.[3] If we begin instead with the covenant LORD and acknowledge the Trinity's infinite love and power and wisdom, then we must admit that we are not yet able to figure everything out. Our response to the problem of theodicy (God's justice in the face of evil) must be, as we will explore in the following chapter, that God is God and we are wee.

Beware of any answer that claims to be a total answer. Usually such approaches wind up trying to be God.

Though we cannot escape the horrendous amount of evil in the world, the good news of the gospel is that God will not let us be defeated at the hands of sin, evil, and death. Part of the meaning of the resurrection of Jesus is that God has triumphed through Christ's suffering and is continuing to go about the business of restoring this world to its original design and purposes. Though we might have to undergo intense suffering in our present times of trouble, yet after the death comes the resurrection. As Paul so wonderfully proclaims in 1 Corinthians 15, since Christ is raised we know that we too shall rise. Death and grave, sin and evil have all lost their sting.

Yet we remain in a meanwhile time beset with the problems of sin and the results of evil. We must face those ills realistically, truthfully.

Many people try to convince those of us who are handicapped that prayer will undoubtedly restore those parts of the body that are debilitated by accident or chronic disease. I know personally — and theologically — that we are better helped by a more realistic approach. For example, Rev. Bill Vaswig conducted a healing ministry for many years under the "Life Institute for Prayer," which aroused my deep respect because he was so very compassionate. He both acknowledged the reality of evil in the world and was able to free many people from various physical ailments in his wholistic approach to healing. In his conversations on the physical benefits of prayer, he listed several kinds of illness for which he had prayed and the positive results he had seen. However, he readily admitted that in some particular problems he had never seen improvement. This experienced person of prayer with a profound ministry of confirmed healing acknowledged that healing doesn't always occur.

I do not doubt God's power. Jesus still can grant complete healing if that is His perfect purpose. However, sometimes other, more important aspects of His work are involved than just our release from physical limita-

---

3. An excellent book that responds to various arguments is Peter Kreeft's *Making Sense Out of Suffering* (Ann Arbor, MI: Servant Books, 1986).

tions. Perhaps God can use us much more effectively in our limitations than if we were dependent upon our own powers. It would be too easy, if life were too simple for us, to take the credit for that which is, of course, always the Spirit's work through us.

Why is my friend Linden still in a wheelchair? Why is Tim still on dialysis? The answer is not that God is not capable of restoring these gifted men to perfect health (for someday the Lord will), but that the Spirit is using them more thoroughly in their physical limitations. Neither of them would object at this point to God's purposes, even though at times they struggle with frustrations and doubts.

None of us has given up on healing. We still pray for each other's total recovery. But, more important, we pray for each other's "meanwhiles" — how we are coping with the situations we are in and how we can enjoy them to the hilt, in spite of the obstructions. (Most interestingly, since I wrote the first draft of this book, all three of us have married wonderful people, and Linden and his wife have adopted a delightful Chinese daughter, whom they named Kimberly Dawn.)

During my four years in graduate school in Indiana, my prayers for physically challenged friends often arose while I rode the bus to the university. My visual handicaps necessitated this mode of transportation, but the daily bus trips were made easier by the frequent presence of a cheerful blind girl, who brought bright smiles and jokes wherever she went. What a lovely model she provided of a person who has seized the meanwhile. We all need to learn this lesson from the weak in our midst (see the following chapter).

The value of our weakness is that it teaches us to wait for God's timing, to overcome evil with love, to respond with gentleness instead of violence. In our world people often try to overcome limitations with power, but power always causes resistance. We can't force someone to believe in Christ, to love us, or to think as we do. Sometimes I hear people pray as if they were twisting Jesus' arm to force Him to live up to His promises to heal. Certainly we can't accomplish Christ's purposes through power or trying to force His hand.

One morning I awoke with stabbing pain in my eye. It felt like something was poking it, but several persons looked and could find nothing. All efforts to force whatever was causing the irritation to come out led to greater pain and more watering. I spent the entire day trying to avoid those movements that intensified the poke, and my eye chose to water all day long — while I gave the morning Bible study at camp, ate meals, and traveled by car from Iowa to Wisconsin. Finally somehow, somewhere, at some time, the irritant was finally dislodged. All the tears had gently done their work.

We can see the same process in model human relationships. Someone acts as an enemy, but the one opposed continues to be caring and gentle. In spite of badgering, mockery, hostility, even brutality, the gentle love of God through that individual persists, until finally grace prevails and the relationship is restored. Suffering love overcomes more effectively than power.

Yet too many Christians persist in using power. We try to control governmental policies. We try to barrage with brilliance and wealth. We try to force Christianity on others and make them buy our values. We try to win the success race with other churches.

The Revelation will teach us another way. It will help us discover and understand the victory of weakness, a discipline of willingness to suffer. In our post-Christian age we are very much like the believers for whom John wrote The Revelation. Christianity is not really in charge in our culture anymore, so it must be lived in the postmodern world from a minority position. We are all part of a society that forgets original sin, heaven and hell, the cross, and the absolute sovereignty of God. Consequently, we cannot simply assert what we believe and compel the rest of the world to believe it, too. But the Christian community can gently continue to live as the people of God and offer a viable alternative to the rat-race, smash-your-neighbor, greedy, violent society that surrounds us. We can live out the gospel in peaceful, caring ways that manifest the alternative way of life of those who follow Jesus Christ.[4]

That model attracts me because it genuinely follows the Jesus who brought healing to those who suffered and who demonstrated what it meant that God's kingdom had come near. Then He sent out His disciples to bring the same healing and message about the kingdom to the world in which they moved. Now The Revelation asserts in several places (such as 1:6 and 5:10) that He has made us a kingdom and priests, that our work in the world is to continue to model His alien values in a power-grabbing society.[5]

Such a perspective acknowledges, too, that there is sin in our midst. We

4. See Marva J. Dawn, *Truly the Community: Romans 12 and How to Be the Church* (Grand Rapids: Wm. B. Eerdmans Publishing Co., 1992; reissued 1997).

5. For examples of moral aspects, see Dawn, *Is It a Lost Cause?*

are not always going to be successful at modeling the alternative life in Christ. At those times we model other, core dimensions of our faith — the gift that we are forgiven, the care of the Christian community to restore those who have erred, and the opportunity to work together as a people to learn anew what it means to follow Jesus. Thus, we model in our failures what to do with sinful weakness — namely, forgive it, treat the sufferer with compassion, and work for restoration and reconciliation and wholeness.

The healing strength of such an approach was impressed upon me at a time when things seemed disastrous in my life. Newly arrived at Notre Dame, I felt overwhelmed by the brilliance of my colleagues in the Ph.D. program; the textbooks I needed to prepare for the Greek exam were lost by the moving company; mice invaded my apartment; an injury to my foot made me hobble for three weeks; too much stress affected my eyes so that I could not read for eight days; I lost my identification paper; my thermos bottle fell off the desk and broke; poor people were sleeping in cars in the parking lot beneath my bedroom window, and I grieved for their situation in life and felt helpless to aid them; I missed desperately all my friends on the West Coast from which I had moved; and I had a week to proofread the galleys for my book on the Psalms. I was overwhelmed by it all and did not have any close friends yet to whom I could turn.

One gentle act helped me find hope and strength to go on in my weakness. One person who noticed that I was close to tears pulled out a clean, white handkerchief and invited me to talk about whatever was troubling me. That touch of gentle kindness freed me to cry and then to go on with the struggle.

Similarly, in the turmoil and doubts brought on by our limitations and illnesses and sufferings, it is not necessarily a hyped-up promise of healing that will enable us to overcome. Usually the one who gently stands beside us, who touches us with caring, empowers us most and frees us to grow. I become more depressed when people who pray for healing harangue me about my lack of faith which prevents it, but I find new, wholistic healing when a friend asks for God's embrace in my life.

We will best overcome hostility against us by loving. Jesus overcame the hostility of the Roman empire, the Jewish religious leaders, and the aggravated crowds by submitting to their execution and forgiving their ignorance.

If we really want to follow Him, we must learn His methods for overcoming evil. And the persons from whom we can best learn those lessons are those who begin from a position of weakness.

CHAPTER 3

God Is God, and We Are Wee

G randma's eyes always twinkled in amusement over my failure to get
German pronunciation and phrasing right. Yet she patiently put up
with my slowness and helped me practice the language. Her confident repetition of favorite hymns and prayers, especially in the hours before her
death, inspired me when we were together and comfort me now as I remember the strength of her hope.

Grandpa, who died at age 101, continued for years to build birdhouses
and recipe holders. He rescued all sorts of junk from garbage cans and
converted it into useful items. He would gather stale bread from various
grocery stores in order to feed hundreds of ducks in the wintertime. Any
eggs left without mothers because of teenagers vandalizing the nests were
always brought immediately to his basement for hatching under a light
bulb, and Grandpa gently cared for the ducklings until they could make it
on their own in the river.

These beloved grandparents and many others like them demonstrate
the countless contributions of senior citizens to the well-being of our society. Yet many "senile" patients in convalescent centers have been discarded
by their families as worthless.

Studies have shown that senility (as distinguished from Alzheimer's
disease) is aggravated by abuse — that those who are treated as old people
are much more likely to develop the illnesses of age. They have been forgotten, and their deadened spirits are reflected in their bodies' inability to
cope.

We stand aghast at the abandonment of people in our society, and yet, to some extent, all of us are guilty. We have relegated the weak and infirm and mentally deficient and aged to places of insignificance.

Today, as arguments about abortion, euthanasia, racism, sexism, and ageism swirl around us, we who claim to be God's people must do some major rethinking about the place of the weak and helpless in our society and our churches. How much of a part do the handicapped, the retarded, the aged, the infants play in our Christian communities? How much do we welcome children into the world? How much do we value the contributions of the old instead of wishing they wouldn't be so traditional? To our great loss, in such antagonism we lose track of moral truths the elderly are trying desperately to preserve — the loss of which has led to great corruptions in our society.

The Bible is always on the side of the oppressed. The prophets in the First Testament rage against those who sell the needy for a pair of sandals (Amos 8:6), those who add house to house and join field to field (Isa. 5:8), thereby robbing the poor. Throughout the Scriptures God's people are warned against such harmful actions toward the unprotected and vulnerable, for the kingdom of God is made up of the poor, the humble, the weak, those who suffer.

This is made especially clear in the twelfth chapter of Luke. There Jesus' words, "Sell your possessions and give mercifully," are recorded right after He said, "Do not fear, little flock, for your Father took delight to give you the kingdom" (vv. 33 and 32). In sharing the life of the poor we most richly experience the kingdom of God.

The fact that God is on the side of the oppressed is an important truth rediscovered again by liberation theologians from the Two-Thirds World and by feminist and black theologians in the First World.[1] However, this

---

1. There has not been much emphasis, however, on "liberation" for the handicapped and elderly. Though both Jean Vanier and Henri J. M. Nouwen work/worked with, and write/wrote of, the mentally and emotionally handicapped, they have not developed a systematic theology of weakness. Their books are to be heartily recommended for their wonderful insights into the grace of God and the gifts of the infirm. See, for example, Nouwen's *In the Name of Jesus: Reflections on Christian Leadership* (New York: Crossroad, 1989) and Vanier's *The Heart of L'Arche: A Spirituality for Every Day* (New York: Crossroad, 1995). In addition, especially valuable is Stanley Hauerwas's excellent collection of essays, *Suffering Presence: Theological Reflections on Medicine, the Mentally Handicapped, and the Church* (Notre Dame: University of Notre Dame Press,

truth about God's care for the weak and helpless can be easily distorted if theologies do not remain biblical and when they advocate resorting to violence to accomplish their purposes. The peaceable kingdom of God can never be brought in by violence. If we want others to know its meaning, we must introduce them to its ruler: the Lamb who was slain. If we want to follow Jesus, then we must take up our cross — which does not mean to suffer some minor inconvenience, but to shoulder the crosspiece upon which we will die.

We can learn best about the redemptive power of suffering from those who can accept it even if it is imposed upon them without their choice. One of my goals in this book is to encourage us all to value the gifts of the infirm instead of trying to change them. How can we as the Body of Christ learn better to welcome them into the community and encourage them to offer their gifts?

Tim and Linden and I have often laughed at how many times people say to us that our physical situations could be changed if we would just learn to pray "right" or if we had stronger faith. I spent years trying to "grow" my faith so that it could convince God to grant me healing in response to my frequent petitions. I do believe in miraculous healing, for I experienced it twenty years ago when my intestine had intussuscepted and strangled itself. The nurses couldn't believe how rapidly my body recuperated — but that speedy healing and the prayers of many friends around the country both seemed to me to be miracles. Other physical situations have revealed to me the power available in God's timing and in the caring support of God's people along the way. But God's best plan has not been to grant me total release from my health problems — even as Christ's response to Paul included the retention of the thorn in the flesh.[2]

The problem has been much worse for friends whose physical limitations are more obvious. Countless times Linden has been approached by people who insist that he could get out of his wheelchair if he would just submit to their prayers (as if they had some sort of magic touch). How obnoxious!

Though he has not given up on the possibility of a miracle, Linden told

---

1986), which deals with many of the ethical issues related to the care of the mentally handicapped.

2. See 2 Corinthians 12:7-10 and chapter 2 of Marva J. Dawn, *Powers, Weakness, and the Tabernacling of God* (Grand Rapids: Wm. B. Eerdmans Publishing Co., 2001).

me several years ago that he greatly longed for his pastor (at that time) to stop praying in public worship for his healing. Such a practice enforced the attitude in the whole congregation that he was not acceptable in their midst until he was changed. He seemed to represent a failure on their part to claim God's power sufficiently, and so they could not tolerate this weakness that reminded them of their own.

Imagine how much more helpful it would have been for him — and for them — if instead they could have learned how to pray for his life in the chair in the meanwhile, as he waits for the final victory over sin and pain that is indeed coming. If they could have prayed for his strength and ability to cope, then they would have learned how to be a community of support for this time. Concurrently, they could have begun to learn more readily from Linden all that he has to teach about God's power in our suffering and the victory that can come only through weakness and limitations. They might have learned from him what it means to depend totally upon God and to learn the sufficiency of Triune grace. (See Chapter 18 for a more thorough explication of the biblical concept of God's grace and human patience.)

Similarly, the nature of our times makes it critically important to learn from the aged. As the values of our culture shift so much and so fast, our youth grope for something steady to hang on to. At a retreat a few years ago for senior citizens, we focused on the book of Malachi and the many principles it contains that have been lost in some contemporary churches — God's absolute prohibition against divorce,[3] the desirability of the tithe, the importance of leaders being faithful to God's Word and not seeking positions for personal gain. As I looked at the faces of the sixty senior citizens before me — all of them devoutly committed to their Lord — I was over-

---

3. I realize that some instances necessitate divorce, but research is conclusively showing that divorce is much more harmful than our idealistic society theorized. See Judith S. Wallerstein, Julia M. Lewis, and Sandra Blakeslee, *The Unexpected Legacy of Divorce: A 25-Year Landmark Study* (New York: Hyperion Press, 2000). Though this book is not written from a religious perspective, it demonstrates clearly that divorce almost always leads to deterioration in the quality of parenting a child receives. The children of divorced parents, even when they are deeply cherished by them, still suffer long-term consequences. See also Don S. Browning, Bonnie J. Miller-McLemore, Pamela D. Couture, K. Brynolf Lyon, and Robert M. Franklin, *From Culture Wars to Common Ground: Religion and the American Family Debate,* 2nd ed. (Louisville: Westminster/John Knox Press, 2000).

whelmed by the potential for clear instruction of youth if our churches could tap the wisdom of these folk.

Youth certainly are begging for such instruction. I am constantly surprised at how many youth thank me for offering them a better alternative than do the media when I speak about sexual relationships and advocate both the old-fashioned policy of sexual intercourse only within the covenanted security of lifelong marriage and also responsible tenderness in our affectionate relationships before marriage.[4] Many teenagers in personal discussion say that they wish their parents, grandparents, or pastors had talked with them about the positive values of these biblical principles.

Every time I see announcements of anniversary parties for couples who are celebrating fifty years together, I weep with both delight and sadness. What a treasure to see in them the model of devoted steadfastness, of suffering love that has put up with all their struggles for all these years. I rejoice that their relationships are indeed golden. And I weep for youth today and even for my generation, for very few people in our present society are willing to put up with the suffering long enough to refine their relationships into gold.

So what do all these comments mean for God's people? Most importantly, we must get back to scriptural formation, to recognize as did the believers for whom the book of Revelation was written that we live in an alien world with alien values and that we are involved in spiritual warfare against beasts and dragons and the spiritual hosts of wickedness in the heavenly places, embodied in various contemporary temptations. Secondly, we can pay more attention to those who might be able to teach us about steadfastness and commitment and longsuffering and strength in weakness, those who have battled limitations and survived.

I will never forget the first day I visited with Linden at his office in the alcohol treatment center where he was a counselor. He met me in the lobby, and, as we traveled down the hall to his office, I was impressed that he chose then not to have a motorized chair in order to force himself to exercise as he pushed his way from place to place. When we reached his office, I was suddenly shocked as he willingly bashed his arm against the wall to stop and turn his chair so that he could push his way into the room. That was just my first experience of his enormous courage and inner strength.

---

4. See Marva J. Dawn, *Sexual Character: Beyond Technique to Intimacy* (Grand Rapids: Wm. B. Eerdmans Publishing Co., 1993).

Shortly thereafter he decided to live on his own, hiring a helper to come in only to get him up in the morning and to put him to bed at night. In the between times he did his own cooking, played computer chess, read theological works voraciously, and even developed prize-winning nature photographs — all with the limitations of only biceps muscles and fingers that curl into his palms. However, in those times of caring for himself he also experienced long hours of work to pick something up, to struggle to find a way to turn a piece of meat in the frying pan, or to eat it without being capable of cutting it.

In his presentations to congregations, Linden often asks the participants to try shaking hands with a neighbor while their fingers are all curled in, so that they can experience what it is like to feel people withdrawing from them. More than anyone, people like Linden can teach us about total acceptance of other persons. He knows more deeply than most theologians what it means not to discriminate on the basis of any sort of limitations.

How could our churches become better equipped (in both our facilities and our attitudes) to welcome into our communities people with physical and mental challenges? Perhaps we could invite an articulate handicapped person such as Linden to teach some classes for us. A committee could discover what barriers our facilities pose to persons with limitations; a task force could investigate the possibility of using someone to sign our worship services or the cost for devices to aid the hearing impaired. For numerous years until her death, my great aunt taught a special Sunday school class for her own mentally impaired son and a bunch of his friends, provided transportation for them, and took them home for Sunday dinner.

How might our churches become havens of comfort for the lonely? It seems often that bars have taken over the Christian community's job of providing companionship for those who are alone. Perhaps we can be more deliberate about inviting singles to join small group Bible studies; couples could be more intentional in including those who live alone in family dinners and activities. Our churches could sponsor support groups for those who are sorely depressed in their loneliness. Instead of making single people feel left out, our vitally necessary emphasis on strengthening family life can be widened to stress that the family of the Christian community includes everyone in every station of life.[5]

5. See Rodney Clapp, *Families at the Crossroads: Beyond Traditional and Modern Options* (Downers Grove, IL: InterVarsity Press, 1993).

The possibilities are endless. Our congregations need to wrestle with their openness to the lonely and disabled and elderly and infirm and weak and troubled and poor. Let us create opportunities to support such people in their ministries of developing our awareness. We can help them to know they are valued and loved in the community — not as oddball specimens, but as representatives of all of us, for, indeed, we all are handicapped in our own ways. Those who most clearly experience the effects of their handicaps — often because they are visibly noticeable — can help the rest of us learn to cope with our limitations and learn the value of weakness in our faith lives.

Throughout our study of The Revelation, please keep in mind the foundations laid in these first three chapters. First, we established perspectives for working — careful attention to the historical situation in which, and the literary purposes for which, the book was written; appreciation for the book's various styles of literature; insistence on a theocentric focus. Then, we sketched these three main theological points of The Revelation: the ultimate victory of God, the opposition of the demonic powers, and the resultant struggles of the saints against evil. Third, we recognized that the best stance for this battle is an awareness of our weakness and total dependence upon God's rule in our lives. Consequently, in contrast to the world, we who are God's people value both our own sufferings and the people among us who suffer in order that the whole community might learn lessons of dependence and trust.

CHAPTER 4

A Vision to Sustain Us in Suffering:
The "Mysterious" Purposes of God

(Please refer often to Revelation 1:1-3 and 9-11
as you study this chapter.)

When I first began freelancing more than twenty years ago, when I was lonely and struggling with handicaps, the personal support of the board of Christians Equipped for Ministry kept me going. Under CEM I served as a Bible teacher and writer, and the board members held on to a vision of what CEM could become as we sought together to serve God. They believed it for me even when I couldn't believe for myself. Grasping their vision and clinging to it gave me courage to face difficulties that arose.

The Christians suffering under persecutions either by the emperor or locally in Asia Minor direly needed a disclosure of God's sovereignty to sustain them. The words of The Revelation, recording the vision of the seer John, offered them the hope they needed. The book's own introduction helps us to understand the nature of the perspective that we must hold to give us Joy in our weakness.

These days the word *apocalypse* is often used to denote terrifying visions of bizarre battles and, in the medieval phrase, hideous "ghosties and ghoulies and long-legged beasties and things that go bump in the night." The word conjures up images of variously colored horses ridden by ominous figures and battles against monsters with lots of heads and horns and crowns. Sometimes there is also a picture of a radiantly beautiful new city, but usually those who write about the apocalypse focus more extensively on the lurid scenes.

The Greek text of The Revelation begins with the word *apocalypse*, which means "revelation" or "disclosure," and it occurs without the article *the.* That suggests either that this book is merely any old revelation or that it is so precisely THE Revelation that no article is needed. Considering the subject matter of the text, translators have wisely rendered that opening phrase as THE Revelation (so I have capitalized the word *The* when naming the biblical book).

Furthermore, notice in the text of Revelation 1:1 that this is the revelation of *Jesus Christ.* From this book we will learn what Jesus is like in all the fullness of His glorified Lordship. That vision will fill us with hope. God gave Jesus this revelation to show the seer John what would happen so that God's people would be encouraged to trust His Lordship in all their struggles.

The phrase "The Revelation of Jesus Christ, which God gave Him" reminds me of a concept expressed most clearly in the letter to the Ephesians. There the first chapter's glorious doxology exults in God's plan designed before the foundation of the world, purposed *in* Jesus Christ, the Beloved One, and made manifest to humankind *through* Jesus Christ. The Greek text employs the word *oikonomia* to signify God's plan or purpose in the management of the world. How astounding it is to realize that God's best "economy" was to use the suffering and death of Christ and the weakness of His followers for the fulfillment of the divine purposes manifested in Christ!

Ephesians 1 also uses the word *mystery,* which means much more in the Bible than our English use of the word to name a puzzle to be solved. In its original sense, the Greek word *mustērion* signified a secret that has been revealed — and yet is too great to be comprehended. That word delightfully describes God's intentions — indeed, the Triune purposes are mysterious to us. Even though the Spirit has made them known to us in the Word, they are still infinitely beyond our grasp. Though we spend our lives studying the Scriptures and seeking to know God's motives and meanings, yet we can never thoroughly understand the Lord's deepest designs.

That forces upon us a truly humble attitude as we study the Scriptures. We might do the best we can to gain more faithful interpretations of The Revelation, but, ultimately, what God reveals to us will always remain mysterious. The Triune One is infinitely beyond us in eternal majesty and incomprehensibly close to us in gracious compassion.

That is why we delight in Jesus Christ. He reveals God's mysterious plans in ways accessible to human understanding. He makes things comprehensible to us because He was like us. We can relate to Him as one who lived among others and had to work at developing relationships with them. He was tired and had to sleep, hungry and had to eat, sad and had to grieve. Moreover, in relating intimately with us, He brought us into the possibility of relating intimately with His Father by the power of their Spirit. Through Him, the divine is brought down to earth in order that we might be exalted to the heavens.[1]

Indeed, the book we are studying is The Revelation of Jesus Christ — the way He both fulfills and makes known to the people of Asia Minor God's mysterious purposes, the things that were about to take place as they struggled to understand the meaning of a persecution or complacency that nearly destroyed their faith. Furthermore, we, too, can now learn about the mysterious Lordship of Christ in the things that are about to take place for us in the twenty-first century. The Jesus Christ who made God's purposes known in the first century is still the same (Heb. 13:8), and still today He reveals the hidden things of God, so that we might have hope in times of tribulations.

Notice that once again in Revelation 1:2 the contents of this book are said to be the witness of the Word of God and the testimony of Jesus Christ. The seer John places his own name as bondservant between two references each to God and to Jesus Christ in order to make quadruply sure that we keep it straight. It is not his witness, his device, his artificial construction. The things that he is about to tell us are the very things of God, made available to us through the work of Jesus Christ on our behalf.

To make sure that we understand the importance of receiving this revelation as it comes to us from God Himself, John continues by offering this guarantee: "Blessed the one reading and the ones hearing the words of the prophecy and heeding the things which are written in it." In other words, those who participated in the leading of worship by reading the seer's letter to the early Christians would find blessing in that action, and those who participated in the worship celebration and who applied the word of prophecy to their lives in practical ways would also benefit.

Because we have never been deprived of Bibles, we twenty-first-century Christians in the U.S. can too easily begin to take for granted the great blessing of reading and hearing the texts of God's Word. Orthodox Christians, especially under former tyrannies, have much to teach us in the ways

---

1. This cycle is one of the great themes of the Gospel of John — as proclaimed, for example, in such passages as John 1:11-14 and 3:13-21.

in which their worship services focus — with all the eagerness that scarcity produces — on the Word. Their liturgies date back to the earliest centuries of the Church and include numerous passages from the Bible. They use candles, incense, icons, and processions to highlight the majesty and mystery of God. Even in the days of Soviet persecution, many Orthodox continued to celebrate the *mystery* of their faith and to read and sing the Word. Some of Alexander Solzhenitsyn's short stories mention the peaceful effect that the Russian countryside once had on people because of all the churches; they also tell of the continued faithfulness of Russian peasants in ceremonies and Easter processions that focus on the Scriptures.[2] Anthony Ugolnik shows the powerfully converting effect this reading of the Word had on the atheists who watched.[3]

Notice next that the seer John identifies himself by the name of "brother" and "fellow participant in the tribulation." He does not write as one superior to his readers or distant from them. He understands their sufferings from the inside. He is participating in their anguish, too.

Moreover, John doesn't stop with the assurance that he shares their sufferings. He adds that he also shares in the kingdom and in the patience in Christ that they are all practicing.

What a Joy it is that the seer and the people to whom he writes are fellow participants in Christ's kingdom — and so are we! Let us celebrate the universal and timeless encompassing of the kingdom. Since "the kingdom" was a focus in His message and throughout the ministry of Jesus, let's consider how the word *kingdom* was used in the first century and how it relates to us in the twenty-first.

There is much scholarly debate about the meaning of the word *kingdom,* the extent to which Jesus understood His role in its coming and fulfillment, and the significance of His ethics for the meanwhile before its culmination. The book of Revelation, however, simplifies these problems with its many images of His kingdom and its unabashed portrayal of Jesus' divinity in equal partnership with the Father and Spirit.

The term *kingdom* designates, of course, the place or people over which

2. Alexander Solzhenitsyn, *Stories and Prose Poems,* trans. Michael Glenny (New York: Farrar, Straus and Giroux, 1971).

3. Anthony Ugolnik, *The Illuminating Icon* (Grand Rapids: Wm. B. Eerdmans Publishing Co., 1989). This book gives a superb introduction to many lessons that we can learn from Orthodox believers.

a king reigns, but in the Bible the word emphasizes more the way in which God's kingdom affects the lives of all who engage in it. As J. I. H. McDonald stresses, "all are invited to join in the action by responding to God's incursion into their lives at the present moment of encounter, and by allowing themselves to be reoriented to God's future, the Kingdom in its fullness."[4] Christ's kingdom, then, changes all those for whom His Lordship is supreme, who acknowledge that He is ruler over everything.

The Revelation constantly affirms that Jesus is indeed Lord over the whole universe, that we can participate in His reign, even though the usurper Satan and his minions are trying desperately to convince the world that they are its ruler. Moreover, in falsely claiming that throne for themselves, those deceivers usher in the heavenly battles that the book of Revelation describes.

When Jesus began preaching in Galilee, He announced that the kingdom of God had come (see Mark 1:14-15). The Greek perfect verb tense recording that announcement suggests that in a decisive moment the kingdom came and, consequently, it remains in effect. Such a verb form underscores the truth that in His coming Jesus indeed brought the reign of God to bear on those who were present and that in His reign Jesus changed everything forever. Similarly (though negatively), the explosion of the first atomic bombs at Hiroshima and Nagasaki permanently changed the world by plunging it into the nuclear age; now we can never totally remove the world from this age, though, thank God, the world powers are working to reduce their weapon stockpiles. Positively, the coming of Jesus changed the world radically, decisively, permanently. For those who believed in Him, the reign of God continued to hold sway even in persecution. Now under His Lordship they would choose to seek the fulfillment of His purposes in their lives.

Furthermore, when Jesus sent out the disciples to proclaim the kingdom (see, for example, Luke 9 and 10), He sent them with this message: "The kingdom of God has drawn near." Once again, the Greek perfect verb underscores the fact that the disciples were bringing the kingdom, and it would continue to exist wherever God's people go.

What exciting things can happen when we join in the action of God's

---

4. Bruce Chilton and J. I. H. McDonald, *Jesus and the Ethics of the Kingdom* (Grand Rapids: Wm. B. Eerdmans Publishing Co., 1987), p. 48. This is the best book I have found that responds to the scholarly debates on the meaning of the kingdom image in the Bible.

incursions into human history and life and become reoriented to God's future — when we recognize the precious commodity we carry with us, in us, through us, wherever we go. Have you ever stopped to think that you bring the kingdom of God to your local grocery store?

One day a woman in front of me in the grocery checkout line was weeping silently. In a very stumbling way I said to her something like, "Excuse me. I don't mean to meddle or anything, but you seem so sad. I wonder if there is anything I can do to help." She seized my offer eagerly, pouring out to me the troubles that weighed her down — and the kingdom of God was there. How often I wish for more such opportunities to bring God's reign to bear on local situations! I am sure there are many more openings than I see.

John's introduction reminds us that we are fellow participants in God's reign and bring Christ's kingdom wherever we go. Moreover, because we are fellow sharers in it, we *together* bring it wherever we go. That can be a tremendous source of strength for each of us as we pursue our various ministries. Many faithful supporters of CEM (Christians Equipped for Ministry), under which I freelance, assure me that they uphold my speaking engagements in prayer and thereby encourage me for my work in the kingdom.

Once, before spending a graduate-school break teaching in Idaho, I asked the Mennonite congregation in which I participated to pray for the various activities that were planned — especially as I tried to deal with some divisive problems in churches I would be visiting. Two days after I arrived in Idaho, a member of one congregation ended his life. Though a caring man, he had been deeply discouraged by the struggles of kidney dialysis and chose an early death in the mistaken belief that it would make things easier for those who attended him. The news overwhelmed me with sorrow. During my previous visits to that congregation he had become a special friend, but I had not yet had a chance to see him. His suicide seemed to be more than I could bear along with the week's other anxieties. But in the midst of that time of mourning, I became suddenly very aware of the supportive prayers of congregation members back in Indiana. Past experience had taught me that when they promised to pray for me, they really did. In fact, one member had sent a note just before I left to assure me that her family was indeed praying. The whole congregation truly shared with me in kingdom work far away from them.

This is a crucial part of the vision necessary to sustain us: a recognition of the community in which God's kingdom is experienced. We are not alone as we seek to bring Christ's reign to bear on the situations of our times. Just as John was there to encourage those struggling under various persecutions and temptations, so we have each other to be fellow participants in both the tribulations and the kingdom as we live today.

Finally, John's trio of what he shares with the Asian Christians includes participation in their patience, *hupomonē*. We will study this word extensively in Chapter 18, but now it is important to notice how these three terms work together to provide the context in which John shares his vision.

He calls himself brother to his readers and then exults that he is a fellow participant in their *tribulations* (which they have to undergo because they have been doing the work of the kingdom), in the *kingdom* (which makes all the suffering worthwhile), and in their *patience*, the means by which the other two elements are brought together. It is the gift of patience that enables us to keep undergoing the suffering that doing the kingdom work brings us. Just as we are encouraged by the fact that we do not ever have to suffer tribulations alone, nor do we have to work alone as we carry out our particular kingdom calling, even so we also have each other to increase our patience.

That is why I dedicate this book to Linden and to Tim. More than twenty years ago when I first envisioned this book, those two men, more than any others, shared with me their patience. Their steadfastness and profound trust in God's mysterious purposes helped me in many times of discouragement about my physical limitations. Still today the memories of past conversations help to sustain me when I get tired of struggles.

One time when I was deeply frightened by crazy insulin imbalances and the seeming impossibility of maintaining good health, I cried my terror and despair over the telephone to Tim: "These blood count swings are taking years off my life!" Hooked to his dialysis machine, he calmly replied, "I just always try to remember that Jesus is Lord over my body, too." His gentle patience increased my own.

That is why John's words to us are so refreshing. He does not write as a distant observer. He is there in the midst of the persecution, exiled to Patmos for his witness to the Word of God and the testimony of Jesus (notice again in verse 9 the repetition of this phrase from the beginning of the book). When he reports his vision, then, we can celebrate it with him more deeply because we know that he understands our pain. We are not alone in our struggle; therefore, we can join him in the hope.

To that vision of hope we will turn in the next chapter.

CHAPTER 5

Who Is Christ for Our Suffering?

(Please refer often to Revelation 1:5-8
as you study this chapter.)

"Can you really believe that old book about one man Adam at the beginning and Jonah being swallowed by a whale and all that?" "Did God really create the whole world in just seven 24-hour days?" "How can God be good when there is so much suffering in the world?"

These are the kinds of questions asked mockingly by those who like to deny the relevance of the Scriptures. They want to prove that the Bible is not believable and thereby to render the claims of Christianity not viable.

While we must readily acknowledge the skepticism of inquirers in the face of modern science, it is important to stress that such questions are not the place to *start* if we want to discuss the relative merits of various faith claims. If we want to debate the authenticity of Christianity or its relevance in the twenty-first century, then we must begin with this central question: What do you think of the Christ?

Right at the beginning of his introduction to The Revelation, the seer John proclaims to us his understanding of who the Christ is and His significance for our lives — and the Holy Spirit enlightens us to accept and believe what he writes. Before proceeding with this chapter, look carefully at the picture that Revelation 1:5-8 offers. Several elements in the description are important for our theological hope and comfort.

First, Jesus is called the faithful witness. The Greek word order of placing the adjective after the noun stresses the point emphatically for us in English; this is not just any testifier, but "the witness, the faithful one." Indeed, Jesus faithfully presents to us God's self-revelation. Everything He shows us about God is guaranteed to be true. What confidence it gives us to know that we can always trust all that Jesus has demonstrated to us in His life and teaching about God. Just as Jesus never turned anyone away who came to Him in need, so we know that His Father always hears our prayers. Just as Jesus touched the weak with kindness and sensitivity, so we know that the Holy Spirit understands us thoroughly, no matter how desperate we are.

We know deep in our beings that anything's witness to itself ought to be true — that is why it is so frustrating whenever we are deceived. When advertisements mislead us, when a friend who promises to stand beside us in a difficult time abandons us in a moment of crisis — in our reactions to such failures, we recognize how necessary it is for a witness to be faithful.

The seer John's declaration that Jesus is the faithful witness is the challenge that we can set before others who question Christianity's merits. We can demonstrate from His life, death, resurrection, ascension, and sending of the Holy Spirit that Jesus is who He claimed to be. We can sketch in the First Testament His fulfillment of God's promises for the Messiah. Jesus incarnates for us what God is like so that we can begin to grasp the infinity of Triune love.

Second, the seer calls Jesus "the firstborn of the dead" — a monumental, crucial statement in both its facticity and its implications. Though the facticity of the physical resurrection of Jesus is vigorously debated in postmodern theology, the burden of proof lies with those who deny it, and we who believe can boldly question their claims to demonstrate any other way to account for the evidence of the empty tomb, the dynamism of Christianity's spread, and the long traditions and experiences of faith. Some implications are elucidated when Paul writes, "If Christ has not been raised, your faith is worthless; you are still in your sins" (1 Cor. 15:17). Christ's resurrection from the dead positively assures us that His work of redemption has fulfilled God's purposes, and therefore we are set free from our sins. Furthermore, His resurrection comforts us with the hope that someday we, too, shall rise (1 Cor. 15:20-22). Consequently, as we struggle with the limitations of this body and life, we can look forward with Joy to the time when those limitations will be swallowed up in death and we will receive a new body and an incorruptible existence.

Third, the seer tells us that Jesus is the one ruling with power and dignity over all the kings of the earth. What a substantial security that must have given the early Christians being persecuted by Roman or local powers. Similarly, this statement has tremendous implications for us who live in an age threatened by terrorists and regional wars, social and economic chaos. Sometimes it seems that everything is out of control, but the fact that Christ rules over all human governments gives us a different basis for approaching political questions.

The amazing thing about the reign of Jesus Christ over all the kings of the earth is that it is coupled with love. When we think about the governments of the world, we would hardly think that any of its rulers love us. The idea is almost ludicrous. On the other hand, throughout the Scriptures God's reign over the world has been described most uniquely as a Lordship that combines sovereignty with infinite love.

The seer describes Christ as the one who both loves us and has released us from our sins by His blood. Not only does His love reign now in our lives, but also that love caused Him to be willing to sacrifice Himself to make possible our release from the humanly inescapable rule of sin.

Think of some of the great heroes of the world who have sacrificed themselves in order that others might be released. For example, Dietrich Bonhoeffer died in a prison camp because he attempted to confront the tyranny of Hitler. But Bonhoeffer had no power; he did not rule. Rarely in the history of the world can we find anyone who possesses a profoundly sacrificial love and also reigns.

Furthermore, this loving Christ made us a kingdom and priests together with Himself. As participants in His reign, we extend its sway over the world. Moreover, all believers serve as priests, ministering to others by means of His love and bringing the intercessions of the people to Him.

That is why the seer reminds us that all glory and power belong to Him into the ages of the ages. Once again this statement gives us a new perspective for responding to the powers of this world. If all the glory and power belong to Jesus Christ, then why do we so easily give it to other rulers?

John wrote to encourage Christians tempted to give up their faith because of the oppressive powers or selfish luxuries of the Roman state. Similarly, in our century we are constantly tempted to give undue authority to national powers and cultural idolatries. The Revelation calls us back to the priority of Christ, the only true source for our values and choices.

Indeed, the power and glory belong to Jesus "forever." The original Greek phrase, "into the aeons of the aeons," underscores not only the duration of the reign of Christ but also its depth and scope. In contrast to the aeons of this world — its systems of practices and the standards associated with mundane society — God's kingdom invites us to find Christ's Lordship in everything. Christ Himself is in charge of all aeons. His reign forever stands over and against the world's thinking and its cares (see, for example, Mark 4:19 and 1 Cor. 3:18). His glory is displayed whenever we live according to His Lordship in the midst of the world.

Next, the seer alerts us — with a strong "Behold!" — both to the promise that Jesus is coming with the clouds (a frequent biblical image for the presence of God) and to the assurance that all eyes shall see Him (including those of the present powers, who won't want to). When Jesus announces this in Luke's Gospel, He makes very clear an important part of His timing that has great relevance for our interpretation of The Revelation.

In Luke 21, Jesus sets up a pattern that repeats itself to differentiate between signs of the times and signs of the end. In connection with two ends, the destruction of Jerusalem and His coming at the end of time, Jesus declares that many things will happen, but that only one sign announces the end. First, regarding the desolation of Jerusalem, He announces that persecutions and trials before the Roman and religious governments will afflict believers, but that the end will be recognized at the time when armies lay siege to the city (Luke 21:20). In other words, they will know the end has come because it will be the end.

Similarly, there are many signs of the age, the times in which we live — such as wars and rumors of wars, earthquakes, disturbances in the heavens, and so forth. All these signs of the age remind us that it is an evil aeon, that the reign of God has not come to total fruition. On the other hand, the one and only sign of the end will be this: the great vision of Christ coming in the clouds, which will cause every knee to bow. Till that time, Jesus warns, we are not to go chasing after those who speculate about the end (Luke 17:23 and 21:8). Instead, we are to be doing the kingdom work — caring for the needy, helping others to know about God's love, bringing Christ's reign to bear on the realities of this world. We are to remain watchful, to be prepared for the end so that its coming will not take us by surprise, but we are not to chase after it, for no one can know the time of its coming, and its purposes are mysterious. No one will miss it when the time comes, however, for every eye shall see Christ coming in the clouds (that is, with the fullness of God's presence).

We must keep this context of Jesus' words in mind when we consider the meaning of The Revelation. One reason why the book causes great anxiety for many people is that so many theologies try to use it to pin down the calendar, to try to ascertain exactly when these things shall take place. *But Jesus told us specifically not to chase after such things.*

We cannot know the times or seasons for God's purposes. Jesus declared that even He didn't know. That is not the reason for the pictures and announcements of The Revelation, as Chapter 1 stressed. All that we can know about Christ's second coming from this chapter's text is that when He comes no one will miss him. That is all we need to know. And because we know that, we don't have to fear about the end but can be busy until it happens doing the work of the kingdom and being faithful to our priesthood.

One other fact that is clear about Christ's return is that those who have rejected Him will regret that choice. The text claims that those who have pierced Him will beat themselves on account of Him. The next phrase, "all the nations of the world," suggests that the passage refers not only to those who pierced Jesus on the cross, but to all those from any nation who continue to pierce Him by rejecting His reign.

Finally, the last phrase, "Even so, Amen," doubly emphasizes that God's words shall indeed come true, and then extra affirmation is added by the potent reminder in verse 8 of who this God is who declares these things, for the Lord God Himself is the Alpha and the Omega, the beginning and the end (a concept found in such places as Isaiah 41:4). The idea that God was and is and is to come is also a strong image throughout the First Testament, implied in the very name *YHWH*, the "I AM." The title *Almighty* is a favorite in Genesis and Job and is suggested in the scores of uses, especially by Isaiah and Jeremiah, of the name "Lord of hosts." In contrast, the name *Almighty* is used for God only ten times in the New Testament, but nine of those instances occur in the book of Revelation. Surely here, as nowhere else in the New Testament, the image of God as the powerful one, able to do whatever fits the divine purposes, is especially reinforced. This is the God who stands behind the announcement of the dividing of the world at the second coming of Christ. As surely as God has always been and always will be and truly now is — as surely as the Triune One is the beginning and end of everything, the Almighty, totally capable of accomplishing all that is best — so surely can we know that when Christ comes the whole world will know it, and everyone in it will be compelled to acknowledge His Lordship.

All sorts of principalities and powers do battle against that Lordship (as we will see in other parts of The Revelation), and many times the circumstances in which we find ourselves seem to indicate anything but Christ's Lordship. That is why we need the book of Revelation — to keep reminding us of this essential perspective: the Christ is the fulfillment of all God has promised; in Him the witness to God's love and power is faithfully presented; when He comes again the whole world shall recognize the truth of His claims.

CHAPTER 6

Who Is the Son of Man?

*(Please refer often to Revelation 1:12-20
as you study this chapter.)*

The grotesque painting showed a man in brilliant white garments and a golden belt; his hair was hoary white and belonged to someone ancient, and that was totally incongruous with his youthful, virile face. Furthermore, a huge sword coming out of his mouth destroyed any sense of reality or comeliness. The artist had obviously tried to produce an image of the Christ described in the introduction to the seer's vision in Revelation 1. His peculiar portrait, unbefitting of Christ, but representing the text graphically, illustrates well the error of interpreting the book of Revelation too literalistically.

We must distinguish between *literal* and *literalistic* interpretations in order to learn better skills for understanding The Revelation appropriately. The first term means to take the Scriptures seriously, to believe that what they say is indeed God's vital Word, authoritative to guide our lives in truth. To interpret the Scriptures literalistically, on the other hand, is to forget that God's Word is magnificent literature, making inspired use of symbols and metaphors and other artistic devices to underscore its meanings and mysteries. The book of Revelation offers many pictures that are not to be understood as "visual reality," but as true symbols signifying various dimensions of God's character. Thus, from the picture of Christ in Revelation 1:12-20 we learn much about who He is, but we certainly cannot draw a portrait of Him.

One of my fiercest childhood arguments with an older brother was over whether or not Jesus was handsome. To my very young mind holiness meant that He had to look perfectly elegant. When my brother insisted that Jesus probably wasn't all that spectacular, I went to bed in tears. I couldn't cope with His humanity yet.

Much later, someone taught me the passages in Isaiah 52–53 that portray a Suffering Servant so disfigured as to be beyond recognition and desirability. Certainly Jesus took upon Himself a humanity so perfectly thorough that He could suffer temptations, ugliness, deprivation, torture, and death as truly as any person.

Of course, we cannot use the Scriptures to describe anything other than the character that Jesus reveals to us. All their images are designed to usher us into His presence, but once there we realize that He is too glorious in His Lordship for us to do anything but describe Him inadequately and recognize our limitations in perceiving Him. The seer uses the best images possible to convey to human minds the impressions that he experienced in his visions, but we all know that any words are going to fall short.

This does not at all discount the fact of inspiration. Rather, it underscores the wonder that the Holy Spirit condescended to inspire the biblical writers to convey the truth of Christ's character in words that bring His presence to readers who would be unable with their human and finite abilities to comprehend His transcendence.

Thus, the seer describes Jesus with many expressions of majesty, each of which brings to mind images and attributes revealed in the Hebrew Scriptures. When the seer first sees Jesus (1:13), he uses the title "Son of Man." Occurring more than fifty times in the book of Ezekiel and at a strategic spot in the book of Daniel, the term was well known in Israelite circles, to the extent that when Jesus called Himself by that name He was greeted immediately with charges of blasphemy (see, for example, Mark 14:62-64). In Daniel 7:13-14 the Son of Man goes to the Ancient of Days and receives dominion and glory and a kingdom that shall not be destroyed. In ascribing this title to Jesus, then, the seer claims for Him the authority of deity and the fulfillment of God's promises to restore the kingdom of Israel under the messianic rule.

Furthermore, this Son of Man is found by the seer in the midst of seven golden lampstands (discussed below) and dressed in the golden belt that might be expected of one so royal. His long flowing robe reaching to His feet, however, differs from the usual short tunic worn by warriors and lords of power. His head and hair are also unusual in their brilliant whiteness — white as wool and as snow. In the context of this picture such an image does not signify premature aging; instead it perhaps suggests purity and victoriousness and, undoubtedly, the wisdom and spiritual maturity that are associated with white hair in the Hebrew Scriptures. The whiteness of wool and of snow reminds us of Isaiah 1:18 and comforts us with the assurance that this Son of Man is the one who forgives our scarlet sins and makes us clean and pure, too.

We can also understand the images of fire because they come from Daniel 7:9-10 and 10:6 and Ezekiel 1:26-27. Eyes that are flames of fire and feet that glow like bronze refined in a furnace emphasize the penetration of His vision, the strength of His power, the radiance of His majesty.

From the book of Ezekiel comes also the description of the voice like the sound of many waters. As the listeners to John's word of encouragement in The Revelation heard this phrase, they probably remembered the Hebrew context of that picture at the beginning of the prophecy about the departure of the LORD's glory from the temple and its return when the people of Israel were restored after the Babylonian captivity (see, e.g., Ezek. 43:2). In the same way, then, first-century Christians could draw hope for their eventual deliverance from the present captivity under the Roman emperor. Similarly, we Christians in the twenty-first century can look for the final restoration of God's people, though now our world is captive to the materialism and self-centered egoism of our age. The voice of the waterfalls still flows.

One element of the picture that cautions us against interpreting any of the pictures in The Revelation too literalistically is the detail of the seven stars (see below for their significance) in the Son of Man's right hand, for in the next verse He puts that same right hand upon the shoulder of the seer. A graphic representation of these verses would necessitate picturing the seer getting poked in the shoulder with stars. These comments probably seem too simplistic and self-evident, but principles for an appropriately literal interpretation should be firmly established at the beginning of our study together so that we won't fall into the temptation later to be literalistic about such things as the 1,000-year reign of Christ or the 144,000 saints who will inhabit heaven.

Perhaps we can associate the two-edged broad sword coming from the Son of Man's mouth with the sword of Hebrews 4:12 or Ephesians 6:17, even though the Greek texts use different words for "sword" (but the same word for "two-edged"). The image of the Word of God as a sword seems to have been "in the air" in the first century — that is, in the environment of the early pacifist Christians, the figure of the Scriptures as their sword was used in contrast to the various weapons used by the Roman military.

This concept of figures of speech "in the air" is very important for our historical perspective on The Revelation. Many images used in the book are not accessible to us any longer. Since they have fallen out of our Christian vocabulary, we cannot be sure to what they might refer. We can make educated guesses, but we can never know for certain whether we have correctly cracked the code. Most likely the images were clearly understood by the seer's readers, for he employed those that were utilized in the worship and conversation of early Christians so that his letter might lucidly convey the hope he intended.

Because twenty centuries have intervened, however, it is dangerous to suppose that we can know precisely to what the images refer. Our guesses must always be tentative. We certainly can't pin down various elements of these visions and assert that they are particular signs being fulfilled in our age to help us calculate the chronology of Christ's return. As emphasized in the previous chapter, the only way we will know for sure when Christ will return is when we actually see Him coming in the clouds — and, since clouds always represent in the Scriptures the presence of God (see, e.g., all the references to *YHWH* descending in a cloud in Exodus, Leviticus, and Numbers and also at the Transfiguration of Jesus in Matt. 17:5), that image, too, is a symbol rather than an actual description of how Jesus will physically come.

Once again, the Son of Man's power is underscored in the description of His face shining like the light of the sun in its strength. This image is easy for us to grasp — we know the power of the sun in its brightness, its ability to burn us if we stay out in it too long. No wonder the seer, upon seeing Him, immediately fell at His feet as though dead. Throughout the Scriptures we read of those who, confronted by the holiness and majesty of God, fall down in worship and dread. No one can face the holy God and stand, unashamed.

Imagine a whole page filled with descriptions of God — each phrase etched in a different bright color and style of calligraphy. The words are stacked together tightly, as if to pile image upon image in a brilliant engraving of the spectacle of God's appearance. Finally, at the bottom of the page, the transition, "And when I saw it," is printed in a neutral color — and suddenly, upside down, is the response, "I fell face downward on the ground."[1] The majesty of God turns us upside down, and we fall on our face in unworthiness. It throws us to our knees in adoration and utmost humility.

This great awe and trepidation are usually accompanied in the Scriptures, however, by the invitation not to fear. Similarly, here in Revelation 1 the Son of Man reaches with His right hand (which symbolizes fellowship in the Bible) and tells the seer, "Do not be afraid." Though we deserve to be slain, though we cannot bear to face the holiness that cannot tolerate our sinfulness, yet we are invited by the pure and holy One to enjoy His presence without fear. What amazing grace! What a wonder to be welcomed in this way!

When the Son of Man continues by naming Himself "the First and Last" (v. 17), His words carry tremendous import. That title has already been used in Revelation 1:8 to signify the Almighty One. At that point we didn't know who was speaking since the names of God and of Jesus Christ had both occurred with about the same frequency in the earlier verses of the book's introduction. Now, however, it is clear that the Son of Man is speaking, and in claiming to be the first and last He uses images from the Hebrew Scriptures and thereby asserts unequivocally His deity. He takes for Himself the titles of *YHWH*, the covenant God of Israel.

In keeping with our theme in the last chapter, this identification raises again the most important issue in all of life, this question that we can ask the world around us: What do you think of the Christ? Is He God — more than simply a good teacher, more than a prophet, and more than someone whom God adopted to fulfill divine purposes? Is He actually both God Himself incarnated in human flesh to dwell among us and yet also God who was and is and eternally is to come? Do we believe that this Word was always God, though now He takes a human form? The seer John and all the rest of the Scriptures answer Yes; the early Church and its persecuted believers answer Yes; we boldly answer Yes and invite the world around us to answer Yes, too.

Next, the Son of Man fills that name, First and Last, with new meaning, for He received the dominion and glory from the Ancient of Days, not by

---

1. This is Timothy Botts's wonderful calligraphic rendering of the description of God in Ezekiel 1, which undoubtedly served as one source for these verses in Revelation 1. See Timothy R. Botts, *Doorposts — Sixty Calligraphic Renderings of Bible Passages with Notes by the Artist* (Carol Stream, IL: Tyndale House, 1986).

any huge manifestation of power, but by dying and then being raised to life. Thus, we can know that He holds the key of death and of Hades, for surely He has passed through their clutches and has come out on the other side as victor over their purposes. Into the aeons of the aeons, therefore, He reigns as Lord over death and of life.

The divinity of this picture is constantly underscored by all the sets of threes. Throughout the Bible, even in the First Testament before the triune Father, Son, and Holy Spirit could be recognized, groupings of three represented divinity. The angels' song in Isaiah 6, for example, announced that the LORD of hosts is "Holy, holy, holy," and the Aaronic blessing of Numbers 6:24-26 includes three statements of *YHWH's* gifts to the covenant people. The prophet Isaiah commonly uses three names for God in a series, such as his phrase, "the LORD, your Redeemer, the Holy One of Israel" (Isa. 48:17).

Then, the New Testament records Jesus' references in various discourses to the persons of the Trinity, though no Trinitarian doctrine is overtly stated. Many of the earliest formulations of the Church are the products of long discussions in the attempt to understand more clearly the nature of the unity and distinction of the three persons in one Godhead. (Can anybody clearly understand the idea even today?) Truly it is a mystery, yet the paradox is apparent in the Scriptures, which describe the various persons and yet claim the oneness of God. Thus, the number three enters into that mystery and symbolically underscores the deity of things that are grouped in threes. It is interesting to observe all the events in the life and teachings of Jesus, for example, which the evangelist Matthew records in sets of threes.

Here in Revelation 1 the instruction is given to the seer to write (1) all the things he has seen, and (2) the things that are, and (3) the things that are about to take place after them. These three dimensions seem to correspond to the description of God who was and is and is to come by denoting the past, the present, and the future.[2]

The last verse of chapter 1 makes clear that images in The Revelation stand for practical realities of the first-century Church.[3] After the seer re-

---

2. Some translations, like Today's English Version, miss this symbolism entirely by using the verb *seen* as a summary and dividing it into two parts — the things the seer has seen about things that are and the things he has seen that will soon take place.

3. Throughout this book I will use capitalized *Church* to signify the ideal as Christ would have His Body be and lowercased *church* or *churches* to name concrete fallen (and seeking to be faithful) realities.

ceives explicit instructions to write the things he is learning, he is told overtly what the stars and the seven golden lampstands represent. Yet their definition is shrouded in mystery because we do not know what the angels of the seven churches are. Does that name refer to angelic beings who watch over the churches in these seven cities of Asia, or does the term mean "a messenger," someone who might visit the churches to bring them words of hope and encouragement from John on Patmos? Perhaps the angels of the churches represent the local pastors in each situation. That last possibility seems very likely since each of the seven letters that follow immediately after this description of the Son of Man begins with the instruction that the seer should write specific messages to the angel at each particular place. It would be tremendously comforting to the leaders of these churches to receive letters which assert that the Son of Man holds them in His right hand, the scriptural symbol for fellowship and personal relationship.

Finally, we are told that the seven golden lampstands stand for the seven churches themselves. This, too, is a vastly comforting revelation, for at the beginning of His portrait the Son of Man was depicted as standing in their midst. Various scholars recognize that these seven cities to which the letters are addressed form a rough circle in the order in which they are given, that they were also the postal hubs for the seven regions of Asia Minor, and that they were primary centers for emperor worship. For whatever reason they were chosen, the churches in these particular cities are assured that the Son of Man stands in their midst, that He is present, right there in the area of persecution, with all the power and glory that has been described.

Just as the Christians of the first century struggled to keep their heads above water in the flooding of persecutions and tribulations, so today we face numerous conflicts in being Christians in a post-Christian age and need to hear again the encouraging word that the Son of Man walks in the midst of the lampstands. While we are called to be light givers in a sin-darkened world, the Son is walking among us to trim the wicks, to stir up the flames, to make our lamps more effective in transmitting His light. Indeed, the seven letters to the churches represented by those lampstands do just that as they call the churches to repentance and to new insight. In our weakness, we need to catch a clearer vision of who the Son of Man is and how His dominion and power are available in our very midst.

CHAPTER 7

Flaws and Virtues

(Please refer often to Revelation 2 and 3
as you study this chapter.)

"You're never going to find the perfect church," I had to keep telling myself as I searched for a congregation in which to participate when I first moved to Vancouver. One congregation conveyed no sense of Christian community. Another congregation's music seemed to be stuck in a rut; one was not very biblically oriented. Some sanctuaries made no use at all of our rich heritage of Christian symbols. Most important, very few parishes indicated that they concentrated on "equipping the saints" for ministry in the world. To what congregation is God calling us that we might both offer our gifts for the sake of the church's discipleship and be strengthened for evangelism and service to our neighbors near and far? Churches need to balance reasonably well all the dialectics of Christian community life.[1]

Because so many dialectical factors must be held in tension in the Christian life, it is very important for us to overview the second and third chapters of The Revelation before we look at each particular letter. We need a larger picture of the whole in order to grasp the major thrust of these chapters.

1. For discussion of practices of the Church, especially in worship and for the sake of the world, see Marva J. Dawn and Eugene H. Peterson, *The Unnecessary Pastor: Rediscovering the Call* (Grand Rapids: Wm. B. Eerdmans Publishing Co., 1999); Marva J. Dawn, *Reaching Out without Dumbing Down: A Theology of Worship for This Urgent Time* (Grand Rapids: Wm. B. Eerdmans Publishing Co., 1995); and *A Royal "Waste" of Time: The Splendor of Worshiping God and Being Church for the World* (Grand Rapids: Wm. B. Eerdmans Publishing Co., 1999).

First, let's clarify the meaning of the term *dialectic*. When two things seem to contradict each other, yet both are necessary to keep all of a certain truth in between them, they form a dialectical tension. A prime example is the paradox that Jesus is both true God and true man. If we overemphasize His divinity, we lose sight of the model that He provides for us of God's design for our true humanity (before it was spoiled by the Fall). As a truly human person He is able to understand us in our temptations and discouragements. Also, in His true humanity He could really — and not just theoretically — suffer and die for us.

On the other hand, if we overemphasize the humanity of Jesus, then we deny His eternal membership in the Godhead, that He existed before the creation of the world and became incarnated (not merely adopted later into a previously existing human person) at the conception and birth of Jesus of Nazareth. Indeed, Jesus is both God and man, and, although those two facts seem to contradict each other, we must keep them both in tension in order to have the whole truth about who He is.

Similarly, when considered as a whole, in relation to one another, the seven letters to the churches in Revelation 2 and 3 show us several dialectical tensions, such as the joining of truth and love. These must be kept in balance in order for our congregations to become the kind of churches that Christ wants them to be — lovingly truthful and truthfully loving.

Furthermore, the letters follow the same basic pattern. The repetition of this pattern seven times suggests to us the cyclical and cumulative nature of the entire book of Revelation (which we will see frequently). That cyclical orientation is underscored by the geographical locations of the seven churches, which roughly form a circle in the order in which they are given in chapters 2 and 3. Moreover, five of the churches were in cities that lay on an important imperial trade route (Pergamum, Thyatira, Sardis, Philadelphia, and Laodicea), so they seem to serve as the focus for the whole region of Asia Minor. It seems that the seer intended his vision to be spread throughout the territory by means of these churches at the center of the communications network.

In order to practice skills of careful text reading and to overview for yourself the patterns and dialectical tensions in the letters, sketch out for yourself on a separate piece of paper the chart on the following page. For each text, list the name of the church that is addressed, the description of the Christ who speaks to that particular church, and the praise, rebuke, challenge, and promise that He offers each one. In the following seven

Text	Church	Description of Christ	Praise	Rebuke	Challenge	Promise
2:1-7						
2:8-11						
2:12-17						
2:18-29						
3:1-6						
3:7-13						
3:14-22						

chapters, we will consider more carefully the interrelationships of these elements within each letter, but for now it will be valuable, before we summarize them, for you to discover the contrasts and comparisons between the letters as a whole.

As you filled in this chart, you certainly noticed many connections between the way Christ is described in a particular letter and how that church is challenged or rebuked or praised. Almost all of the descriptions of Christ in this section are taken from the composite portrait at the end of chapter 1, and now the references to the various parts of that description show us how intimately these words to the churches are tied to the nature of Christ and His care for the churches.

Even though most of the letters contain stern rebukes, they are intimately tied to the person of Christ, who holds their leaders in His hand and walks among them to comfort, to admonish, to praise. That would indeed be a great source of consolation for the struggling Christians of the first century. In the same way, we can find it vastly comforting that Christ is present in all His grace and glory even when we deserve His rebuke.

In our times of physical weakness, in our handicaps and limitations, in our discouragements and various emotional hardships, we need the comfort of these seven letters in The Revelation, for, though the churches were weak and failing, Jesus walked among the lampstands. In our doubts, or lack of trust, or attempts to know today all the answers for tomorrow, Jesus is with us — as the First and Last, as the One who holds the seven stars in His hand, as the One who says, "Do not be afraid."

Repentance is a prominent theme in the seven letters to the churches. Five of the seven letters contain a call to repentance — for immorality, for false teaching, and for losing the first love. In all these instances we recognize ourselves. When we glibly rely upon ourselves — our own wisdom to figure out doctrine and life, our false pride as we gauge our morality, our own enthusiasm to be the focus of our love — then we need to repent.

The good news is that our failure to be the people that God would have us be does not remove us from the sphere of Christ's care. His call to repentance is a sign of His continuing grace and the constant opportunity to be restored in relationship with Him. Furthermore, all the calls to repentance in these letters are followed by this summons: "Let the one having an ear listen to what the Spirit is saying to the churches." The Spirit keeps talking with us and inviting us to hear Christ. Repentance cleans out our ears!

While filling in the chart, you probably also noticed that some churches have the opposite problem of others. The church of Ephesus has lost its first love, although it won't tolerate wicked doctrine. Thyatira, on the other hand, is commended for its love and service but rebuked for tolerating false teaching and immorality. The promises given to these churches with opposite problems are suitably appropriate — those without love are promised the tree of life (for, indeed, the return of true love will bring new life), while those with false doctrine are promised authority over the nations (which cannot be exercised when the teaching is wrong).

The combination of differences and similarities in these letters tells us something else about being churches in the twenty-first century. All of the churches are given a challenge, and all of them receive a promise, even those most strongly rebuked — and even Laodicea, which receives no praise at all. No matter how desperate we think a situation might be in a particular congregation, God still gives promises to that church. Grace is always present for any group of Christians, no matter how much they might be struggling.

Furthermore, even those churches which are not rebuked — notice carefully the letters to both Smyrna and Philadelphia — are still given a challenge. We dare never think that our Christian community has reached perfection. There are always certain ways in which we still must grow. We will always need to be motivated by these letters in The Revelation to stimulate our fellowship, to search for aspects of our community life and witness that are not in keeping with God's intentions for us.

The fact that each church receives a challenge and a word of promise is especially relevant for our purposes here in learning the meaning of Joy in our suffering and the importance of the weak in our Christian communities. Each church of the seven has something to offer the other churches and things to learn from the others. The churches are addressed in a circle, with the same pattern for each letter — thus, the literary form itself underscores the invitation to each to pay attention to the message for all.

No Christian community can stand alone, nor can any individual within the community think that he or she does not have to be in relationship with the rest of the body. The dialectical tensions between the letters challenge us to keep the diverse personalities of the various churches in balance. The pattern similarities keep us mindful of our unity. The references to specific parts of the picture of Christ in chapter 1 remind us that His character is what holds us all — different churches and unique individuals — together.

Finally, consider the phrase that is exactly repeated in every letter: "Let the one having an ear listen to what the Spirit is saying to the churches." We all are challenged to use our spiritual ears to pay attention to these letters and apply them to ourselves.

God's Word to the churches applies in any age. These letters do not project different dispensations that set up a calendar for history to unfold until the last ushers in the final age of Christ's return. Rather, the letters are part of the whole biblical narrative that nurtures the character of God's people. Each letter gives important warnings, and at specific times our particular churches might need them directly. At other times, to hear what the Spirit is saying helps us to know how weighty each matter is — that we regain our first love as well as maintain pure doctrine, that we persevere as well as repent.

What a shame that the book of Revelation is so often ignored or so often used for bizarre purposes. It must be understood as a book of prophecy, but to prophesy is to speak the Word of God to a particular situation (with or without implications for the future). This book of prophecy applies God's truth to each of us and to all of us together.

"Let the one having an ear listen to what the Spirit is saying to the churches." In the following chapters we'll be listening to what the Spirit has to say to each of the seven churches — and to us.

CHAPTER 8

Ephesus: Losing Our First Love

*(Please refer often to Revelation 2:1-7
as you study this chapter.)*

S ometimes putting up with physical handicaps gets so hard that suffering individuals start becoming terribly inward-turned. We have to focus so intently on trying to take care of ourselves, and it is such a time-
consuming chore, that it throttles any desire to help others. We lose our
sense of grace and the Joy of worship. I experienced that as I worked on
an earlier draft of this book; sores on my shattered foot, which increased
the likelihood of amputation, required extra days with orthopedic specialists for multiple cast changes and adjustments. It is hard to live in loving response to God's grace when we can't understand why we have to
suffer unreasonable pain and anxious distress.

This seems to have been the problem with the Christians at Ephesus.
They are commended for their deeds, their work, and their patience —
their ability to remain faithful in tough situations of persecution. They
were even able, in the midst of it all, to stay strong against the false teachers, who are described as "evil ones" — those who claimed to be apostles
and yet were not. They could not tolerate these false teachers. They also are
commended for hating the false teaching of the Nicolaitans (to be discussed in the following chapter). Nevertheless, they had lost their first love.

How is this possible? How can they still be patiently enduring the
struggles of faith, standing firm against false teachers, and involved in
works of faith, and yet have lost their first love?

The lesson is especially essential for us because our personal and corporate faith lives can so easily fall into the same trap. Too often, particu-

larly if we have been believers for quite a while, there is great danger that we will perform acts of faith without any love underneath. Marriages run into the same trouble when the outward form remains, but the inward quality of caring love is missing. We can understand this problem better if we more thoroughly define the word *love* and look at reasons why we are likely to lose it.

First, what might have been the problem afflicting the church at Ephesus? Were they tired of putting up with the chore of being Christians against all the cultural temptations? Were they weary of the struggle? Or did they regret their strong stand against false doctrine? It seems primarily that in their works of faith they had lost track of the motivation. The work was not to be loved for itself, but as a means to a greater end — as an expression of their commitment and devotion to the One who holds the seven stars.

We all run into this danger when we use our spiritual gifts. At first, in response to God's grace, we love doing what our gifts enable us to do. We know great Joy in fulfilling what we were created to do, in celebrating who we truly are, in freely serving the Lord according to God's master design. We might grow physically weary in our service, but, when love inspires us, we derive new energy and enthusiasm in the midst of the tasks.

The hazard, however, is that we might start loving our ministries for the wrong reason, envisioning the tasks as the end rather than the means. We might choose to do them because they bring us human happiness and affirmation, rather than because they are ways to respond to the God who designed them for us to do and us to do them (see Eph. 2:8-10). Then our service becomes self-centered instead of God-centered, people- rather than God-pleasing.

We cannot do eternal work if we do not work for the sake of the eternal One. We mistake the journey for its end and love the road instead of the One who called us to walk on it.

This is an especially great danger because then our service points to the wrong focus. We do not direct others to God, but to our work, our ideas, our deeds, ourselves. The Ephesians' ability to have patience in hard times was a powerful strength, but if its end result was merely patting themselves on the back for their own courage, then God was not glorified.

Prime specimens of losing our first love might be studying Sunday school lessons only for what we will teach the children or preparing sermons for how they will affect others, without first allowing the Scripture texts to confront us with their truth. We have no right to proclaim to others the transcendent power of God and how the divine Word changes people, unless that Word is constantly changing our lives.

The hazard is especially great for professional church workers. Once, while working intensely to prepare retreat Bible studies appealing enough to counteract high school students' penchant for entertainment, I could not figure out why my plans just would not come together. The more I studied, the more restless I got — until finally I realized that I had been studying the text for the kids without first letting it speak to me. How ironic that I was working with John 15 and Jesus' declaration that we are pruned by His Word! I needed immensely to repent and be pruned before my thoughts could return to the youth.

May our Christian communities turn to those who have retained their first love well to teach all of us the secrets of their staying power. One aspect of their faithfulness is the awareness of how precious a treasure God's love is. In the trials of life, we learn that we cannot keep ourselves, that God's love must keep us. Consequently, those whose lives have been tested have often been purged of the dross, the superficial affections of lackadaisical Christians.

If those with fragile lives have allowed sufferings to point them to God, they usually have a deep sense of life's preciousness and giftedness. For example, our blind piano tuner also tuned my Celtic harp this year and commented on how much he enjoyed playing it. When I offered to lend it to him for awhile, he responded, "Oh, how good the Lord is to me! I've had two offers from people to let me play their harps." Do we who see take such gifts for granted?

Another aspect of the secret of retaining love is the discipline of nurturing it. Sometimes senior citizens or handicapped people or others who struggle with various obstacles retain their love well because the disciplines necessary to overcome their limitations also deepen their commitment.

One 92-year-old, frail, but twinkling-eyed woman at a senior citizens retreat told of the trials of her life and how God had safely led her through them all. Her love for her Lord radiates from her face and in all her behavior because she has intentionally focused on His goodness to her.

We know from the analogy of human marriage relationships or friendships that love can remain strong only if it is continually nurtured. As life gets busier and busier with my work responsibilities, my husband's teaching career, the daily hours of health disciplines that keep me alive, and the typical tasks of maintaining a home and eating nutritiously, Myron and I know that it is essential that we do deliberate things to nourish the affection that supports a loving will. Candles at every dinner, bike rides to see the neighborhood flowers and walks among Myron's, sipping tea and conversing in the back yard at twilight — unless we deliberately take the time for such expressions of affection, our love can get swallowed by bustling activity. Do we find ourselves, in our marriage or friendships, not taking the time for such nourishing?

One day while writing the first draft of this book, in my prayer before the noon meal, I was overwhelmed by all the blessings of the day — the home where I was staying to write, the loan of a typewriter, the friendship with my hosts that had lasted for fourteen years and over great distances, God's gifts of food, time, flowers, good work to do. To recount blessings increases our sense of gratitude and deepens our love for the Creator and Giver of every perfect gift.

The desire to retain our first love invites us to have a daily devotional period for reading the Scriptures, meditating on them, and spending time in prayer. Do we participate in such disciplines daily in order to focus our attention on who Christ is and how He loves us, how the Holy Spirit has gifted us, and how the Father's grace sustains us? As we ponder those blessings, truly our love will be quickened and nourished and sustained.

The Ephesian Christians were extraordinary in many ways. Their continued patience in afflictions, their faithful performance of good works, and their battles against the opposition of evil persons and false doctrines tell us that they were tremendously devout people. The fact that they nevertheless needed to be reprimanded helps us see the grave relevance of this letter. No matter how active our Christian faith, we do not serve God's best purposes if love does not motivate what we do.

The seriousness of this problem is also demonstrated by the threat to the church at Ephesus that their lampstand will be moved out of its place if they do not repent. This threat is being fulfilled in many churches today that have fallen away from their first love. As they are less and less motivated by adoring commitment to their Lord, the focus of the congregation's strength begins to shift. Then folks start moving away to other churches where the love of God prevails, where Joy inspires commitment and adoration. This is one of the many reasons why some mainline Protestant denominations are losing members to more on-fire churches that radiate God's love and the response of deeper discipleship.

On the positive side, the message to the Ephesians stresses that if they repent of this loss of love they will experience an open possibility to eat of the tree of life, which is clearly defined as the place of blessedness (the paradise) of God. If they repent and recognize their need to nurture their love for God, they will be enabled to make use of all the divine nurturing gifts.

Christ so wants us to be in love with His Father that He makes it possible for us to be nurtured in that love through His gift of the Holy Spirit. The Spirit makes Christ's presence always available to us as the High Priest who guides us to focus on His Father in adoration and praise.

The practices that deepen our love require discipline — not at all a favorite word in our postmodern society, which would rather do only the things that feel good. The original Greek verb (which is stronger than our English translations) criticized the Ephesians because they had *abandoned* their first love. Their desertion reminds me of the bumper sticker, "If you're not feeling close to God, guess who moved."

If we are not passionately in love with the Trinity, it is not because God has stopped blessing us. We might be going through difficult times at the moment, but God is still the same at work in our circumstances to gift us in other ways and eventually to bring the best for us. The letter to the Ephesians invites us, when we have moved away, to repent of that movement and to receive again God's immense love for us.

Love grows when it is fed — such a simple principle, but so easily forgotten. Love dies from malnourishment — so major a problem that the letter warning of its danger comes first in the set of seven. This is where we must start in learning the meaning of The Revelation: with an honest assessment of our lack of love and an open confession of our failure to accept God's grace and forgiveness. Let us clearly recognize that the Lord will produce in us the love for Him that must be the foundation of our faith lives if we let Him have the time to create it in us.

In our busy world, we rarely give Him the time. Thus, one of my goals in this book is that our study together of the lessons of The Revelation might usher us into Christ's presence, so that our love for Him might be nurtured.

CHAPTER 9

Smyrna: Limitations of Suffering

(Please refer often to Revelation 2:8-11
as you study this chapter.)

I love to sing an older translation of the great Reformation hymn, "A Mighty Fortress Is Our God." Its lines reverberate with the triumph of God over "the cruel oppressor," "the old satanic foe," and all the "craft and dreadful might" of the powers of evil that "threaten to devour us." What glorious assurance it is that "God's Word forever shall abide," that "God Himself fights by our side with weapons of the Spirit," and that "the Kingdom's ours forever." How comforting it is to know that we don't have to be the ones who overcome by our own efforts. Instead, our hearts soar with the realization of the tremendous hope we have in God. The Lamb who was slain for us has already overcome all evil and weakness (see Chapters 30–31 below) — and someday all believers will fully participate in His victory.

It is crucial that we deliberately note here that a theology of weakness does not preclude eventual triumph. The assurance of ultimate victory and an understanding of weakness work together to give us courage for facing the meanwhile time (see the following chapter). Our desire to learn biblical patience is founded on the assurance of our eventual participation in the triumph of the slain Lamb.

The letter to Smyrna, this chapter's subject, is the only one of the seven that does not have any warning or negative criticism of the church. Because of their sufferings the Spirit has only words of encouragement for this community's members. The letter does not invite us to read these words blithely and apply the totally positive report to our own churches, but seven phrases of the message to Smyrna give us hope and comfort today.

The first is that in our tribulations and poverty we are actually rich. The letter does not specify in what that richness lies, but in context with the rest of The Revelation and all the Scriptures we can easily suggest good possibilities. We are rich, obviously, in our relationship with Christ and in the gifts He showers upon us. We are rich, furthermore, in our relationship with the community of His people and in the support for our tribulations that the community provides. Moreover, our wealth is founded on the assurance that these tribulations are not God's last word to us; rather, the promises of this letter can carry us through them.

Secondly, the Spirit assures the Smyrnans that God knows about the slander they are receiving from those who claim to be Jews, but actually are "a synagogue of Satan." We don't know specifically to what situation these words refer, but we can make educated conjectures from earlier troubles with the so-called Judaizers and with others who rejected the claim that Jesus was the Messiah.

When the earliest Christians proclaimed Jesus as the fulfillment of the Hebrew prophecies, they encountered opposition both from Jews and Romans who did not become Christians and from Judaizers who acknowledged Jesus as the Christ but demanded that Jewish ritual obligations be imposed upon new Gentile converts. Indeed, the latter's demand denied Jesus' message — that salvation comes by means of the grace of God and not by fulfilling religious obligations. (See Paul's diatribes against this heresy in Galatians 1:6–3:29.) This work of Satan continues in our time whenever the message of grace is lost in efforts and works. The Spirit comforts the Smyrna church by declaring that God knows the blasphemy against them.

We must put such a text carefully into its historical context to prevent it from being mistakenly perceived as anti-Semitic. Revelation 2:9 is not slander against a people or against their ethnic heritage — indeed, it was written by a Jew for Gentiles *and* Jews. Rather, the verse reproves those who claim to be God's people, but in reality deny God's purposes. We must pay attention to the warning because we can easily appear on the surface to be Christians and yet, by our legalism and failure to forgive, reject Christ's grace.

Next, the people at Smyrna are urged not to fear what they are about to suffer. This comment becomes especially valuable when we consider their situation of intense suffering in persecutions — whether local or of the Roman empire. Certainly we would all greatly fear what might have to be undergone in the future. However, the Spirit's words remind us that fear about what we might experience does not really help us endure the suffering. Rather, our fear usually does the reverse — it makes the suffering more difficult to bear.

Fear increases both physical pain and psychosomatic agony. Most of the things we spend time dreading turn out to be harder because of our panic.

At first when I shattered my foot, alarm about the probability of amputation prevented me from thinking of ways to cope with the daily difficulties. Only after ten days of traveling and teaching did I begin to trust that other people and ingenuity would help me get around all right and that Christ could use me for His work anyway. When I panic about the unknowns of the future, I need to remember those lessons in trust.

However, the invitation in verse 10 not to be afraid involves more than simply a recognition that fear does not really help us deal with our life's sufferings. Even more important is the underlying basis for trust that is given by all the reasons for hope in the rest of the letter to Smyrna.

Several dimensions of verse 10 itself underscore the truth that for no reason do we have to fear. The sentence begins with a word that accentuates the meaning of *nothing*. It says intensely, "In no way." Then the imperative *to fear* is in the present tense to stress continuation. Thus, the phrase literally declares, "Under no circumstances do we need to be fearing" that which we are suffering (also a present continuing infinitive). This combination of verb forms underscores the present action — we are about to be suffering many things, but, in the process of it all, for no reason do we need to be fearing.

The first reason not to fear is that the suffering is limited to ten days. The number ten in the Scriptures symbolizes completion. The ten basic commandments cover all the important dimensions of life. Tens of tens of tens (a thousand) suggests a complete number of years — that Christ will reign for a thousand years promises that His reign will be divinely fulfilled. The promise of only ten days, then, limits the suffering and confines it within God's sovereignty. Satan might throw us into prison, and in the process we will certainly be tested, but we will not be tested beyond what we can bear, until the tribulation is completed.

When I was in graduate school, a visiting Jewish philosopher, Emil Fackenheim, lectured on God's testing of Abraham. He recounted a midrash (interpretive story) told by Jewish rabbis to explain the odd situation in Genesis 22 of God asking Abraham to sacrifice his only son Isaac. According to the midrash,

> Abraham said to God: "Why did I have to undergo this experience? Did *you* need a test to determine my faithfulness?"
>
> And God answered, "No, I didn't need a test."
>
> Then Abraham said, "Did *I* need a test to prove my own faithfulness?"
>
> Once again God answered, "No."
>
> "Then why did I have to go through this experience?" Abraham asked.
>
> God replied, "As a witness to the nations."

This answer offers tremendous comfort when we are plagued by the endless "Why?" questions. We don't know why God allowed Satan to throw the people of Smyrna into prison, nor why we might have to suffer in various ways. Ten years ago I went through a seven-month period of near-blindness because of retinal hemorrhaging and of needing crutches and wheelchairs because of wounded feet. Searching for meaning in that incapacity (which started just two weeks after receiving my Ph.D. when I was eager to be moving in new directions), I was prodded to faithfulness by this hope that God uses even our times of trial "as a witness to the nations." The Smyrnans' faithfulness recorded in The Revelation still stands as a proof to the world of God's love and care, as a witness to the nations that Jesus is Lord.

This is a substantial hope for our times of trials. Those around us who wonder about God might observe our response to suffering and then judge accordingly. Our attitudes in suffering can be powerful vehicles for evangelism.

Long ago when I taught "Literature of the Bible" in a university English department, a few colleagues in the department enjoyed making fun of my faith and giving me hassles. One of my students came to see me right after I had been particularly harassed. I had been crying from the frustration of it all, and yet the Spirit had given a great sense of peace that God would bring something good out of that situation. Later that same student told me that my reaction in that difficulty was one of several factors leading him to recognize the gifts of Christianity. We can, indeed, be encouraged not to fear in the midst of times of tribulation, not only because we know that the struggles are limited to ten days, but also because we know that they can be vehicles of proof to those questioning the reality of Christ and the truth of the gospel.

The next reason why we need not be fearful in times of suffering is that we have this promise: if we continue to be faithful unto death, the Lord will graciously crown us with life. God does not *have to* give us the crown of life as a reward for our faithfulness. Even though we might go through many trials and remain thoroughly faithful in them all, we still couldn't deserve heavenly life. That gift to us in spite of our inadequacy is utterly the product of divine grace. Knowing, then, that the gift is ours — not by virtue of *our* success in remaining faithful, but because of *God's* — gives us the assurance to keep carrying on. We are released from the pressure that if we fail we will lose everything. Rather, we know that we have everything to gain, and therefore we can have courage to keep trying to be faithful in all our tribulations.

A two-mile community run illustrates that motivation well. Because all the participants of a retreat I was leading were entering, I joined them in the Columbia River Run almost twenty years ago. Though my leg was not yet crippled, still metabolism problems slowed me down, so I knew before I even started that I would come in last of the whole retreat group — and, sure enough, I did. However, what makes such an event fun is that no matter what our running time is, people cheer us as we finish simply because we *are* finishing. Now when I wear the T-shirt from that event, no one knows that I came in last. I did, indeed, come in!

In God's kingdom what is important is that we stay in the running, that we don't give up on the truths or tasks of discipleship. If we reject the kingdom's truths as not worth receiving and living, God won't cram the crown of life down our throats. But when we participate in Christ's life, as long as we faithfully remain in the running, then we are assured of the crown, no matter how poorly we finish.

This doctrine must be distinguished from heresies on both sides. It does not proclaim a once-saved-always-saved theology that allows us to slough off with a "I like to sin, God likes to forgive, isn't that a nice arrangement" attitude. Nor, on the other side, do we perpetually have to worry whether or not the crown of life can be ours and if we have been good enough to earn it.

The necessary balance is found in the contrast of "Be faithful . . ." and "I will give. . . ." On the one hand, we are called to continual participation in God's kingdom. On the other hand, we keep in dialectical tension the fact that we cannot achieve the crown of life at all. It is purely a gift of God's grace, never to be deserved or earned or repaid, as is our very faithfulness.

Finally, after the recurring invitation to hear what the Spirit says to the churches, the believers at Smyrna receive another promise: the ones who overcome in this time of tribulation shall never be injured by the second death. Have you seen the button that proclaims, "Born once, die twice. Born twice, die once"? This assurance gives us the ability not to fear in times of tribulation: if we are born both physically and spiritually, we do not have to fear the second, or spiritual, death. Physical death won't be a source of worry for us because we already possess eternal life.

Undoubtedly, this passage means so much to me because I have come close to death a few times. Even as my life becomes more and more fragile, I realize that physical death is merely a door through the last barrier between us and God. Throughout our lives we confront various barriers that separate us from God, which we go around or cross over or smash down. Finally, when we come to the point of death, only one obstacle remains — the confinements of this earthly, mortal body. When we pass through that last door, we are set free from all the limitations that kept us from seeing Christ face to face.

I originally wrote this chapter just after leading Bible studies on The Revelation for a senior citizens retreat. I remember vividly the glow on the faces of those folk — a few of them in their 90s — as we studied passages describing heaven's splendor. Their radiance bespoke their eagerness for the last door. They were more than ready to conquer that last barrier and to enter into a life of total, perfect relationship with God. For this reason they could describe with great courage various physical afflictions through which they were passing.

Their descriptions and hopes greatly encouraged the young staff people at camp. Perhaps our congregations could invite such radiant senior citizens to speak to our youth groups or Sunday school classes about their hope for the crown of life. Perhaps in worship services or in visits to those who are ill or hospitalized they could share with others in the community how they have learned, through many years of faithfulness, to look at death without fear and to wait for the crown of life with Joy.

CHAPTER 10

Pergamum: The Importance of the Word

(Please refer often to Revelation 2:12-17
as you study this chapter.)

I had given my college roommate a secret name. Only she knew it, and I used it for her only in certain circumstances. One day we were chatting with our choir director in his office, and she was complaining that life was just too much of a struggle. I simply said her special name, and her entire countenance changed. In the midst of her despair she knew that she was loved.

The letter to Pergamum ends with the promise of a new name, known only by the one to whom it is given. Seer John writes to the angel of the church that when the believers there have repented and overcome their temptations, they will receive this special signification of their new relationship with God. The vital key is heightened recognition of the importance of the Word.

No matter how frustrated I might be by physical struggles, as soon as I truly enter into personal devotional study or start teaching a Bible study, I forget the pain, the inconvenience, and the exasperation in the Joy of hearing God's Word. The Word of the LORD overcomes the pains of life.

God's Word was precisely what the members of the Christian community at Pergamum needed. It is exactly what contemporary society needs, though few would acknowledge that.[1]

This letter describes Christ as the one who has a sharp, two-edged sword.

---

1. In contrast, see William H. Lazareth, ed., *Reading the Bible in Faith: Theological Voices from the Pastorate* (Grand Rapids: Wm. B. Eerdmans Publishing Co., 2001).

We have previously discussed the notion that this image for God's Word was probably "in the air" — language floating around in the early Christian environment. Both Hebrews 4:12 and Ephesians 6:17 characterize the Word of God as a sword. Moreover, the early Christians certainly understood Christ as both proclaiming the Word and being God's Word to them. The image is a favorite for the Gospel writer John, for his account of Christ's life begins with the wonderful poem about the *logos,* the Greek noun for *word.* That thoroughly cosmopolitan poem brings together the Greek philosophical connotations of the *logos* with the Hebrew faith understanding that God's Word bears within itself the power to bring about its own fulfillment.

As previously noted, the description of Christ that begins each of the letters to the seven churches is integrally connected with the specific message that a particular church receives. Here the connection is quite obvious. God's people can keep living righteously right where Satan has his throne only by continual participation in the Word.

The letter praises the saints at Pergamum because they have remained true and have not denied their faith in Christ, even though they have been threatened by the death of one of their greatest witnesses. We do not know specifically who Antipas was, but his martyrdom could have caused much fear and consequent backsliding — and to the praise of the Pergamumians, it did not. He was killed right among them; therefore the letter repeats that, indeed, this is the place where Satan lives. As we ponder this repetition, we will also find profound encouragement for us in whatever struggles we might be encountering.

Where does Satan live? What gives him a throne? Craig Koester points out that the city of Pergamum, a cultural and administrative center in Asia Minor, was on a high hill and featured an acropolis with a massive altar to Zeus. It was also the site of an acclaimed library, a temple to the emperor Augustus, and a shrine of Asclepius, the god of healing, as well as the judgment hall for hearings before the Roman proconsul.[2] Any of these forces could have led to the epithet "Satan's throne," for many cultural, political, economic, and religious powers can threaten believers.[3]

---

2. Craig R. Koester, *Revelation and the End of All Things* (Grand Rapids: Wm. B. Eerdmans Publishing Co., 2001), p. 59. See also M. Robert Mulholland, Jr., *Invitation to a Journey: A Road Map for Spiritual Formation* (Downers Grove, IL: InterVarsity Press, 1993), p. 163.

3. My doctoral dissertation on "The Principalities and Powers" explored some of

One misunderstanding in faith these days, highlighted by the novels of Frank Peretti, is an overly simplistic notion that evil is caused by some sort of little demons (even if we don't picture them with red suits and horns and flying around with pitchforks and spitting sulfur!). On the other hand, we must not over-intellectualize the whole matter of evil and define Satan merely as the evil deeds of human beings.

The biblical picture takes a position between these two extremes and recognizes that there are myriads of forms and causes of evil and that there is a significant supernatural element. There are definitely powers of evil external to ourselves, but usually they make use of our own humanly sinful inclinations. No one can rightly say, "The devil made me do it." The powers of evil certainly are constantly tempting us, but we ourselves and our failures of will are to blame if we give in to their temptations.

However, in distinct situations demonic influences more easily take control, and we must walk very carefully if we are called to go into them. I highly respect former Senator Mark Hatfield, whose book, *Between a Rock and a Hard Place,* very openly described the easy temptations of power in high governmental positions. Certainly our nation immensely needs Christians in politics, but anyone who chooses to enter the higher echelons of power will probably discover there Satan's throne.

And what about you? Perhaps you work in an office situation where everybody curses or cheats or is involved in sexual immorality. Or maybe the demonic influence is much more subtle — perhaps in the power plays office colleagues use constantly to manipulate each other. It is difficult to maintain one's Christian integrity and witness in such an atmosphere.

Similarly, those challenged physically or mentally often encounter difficulty as they try to keep clinging to Christ in the constant discouragement of worsening handicaps. Illness and disability are certainly not God's intention for human life, so we might also say that in our afflictions we can also recognize Satan's dominion.

Yet the people of Pergamum are praised. They have remained true in their circumstances. They have clung to the name of Christ, by whose

---

the ways in which the demonic forces function today — through money, power, accusations, divisions, deceptions, destructions. Their influence manifests itself in many aspects of our culture, such as politics, economics, personal and international relationships, the media, institutions (even churches), and technological developments that control us.

power Satan's thrones have already been cast down and exposed (see Col. 2:14-15). Their faithfulness provides a model of the ability to continue in contexts largely overwhelmed by evil powers. The name of Christ enables His people to be true.

However, the seer has to criticize some of the Pergamumians for their failure to stay true to *all* of Christ. He calls their backsliding a turning to the teachings of Balaam and the Nicolaitans. Both names give us important information, though we will reserve discussion of the second for the following chapter.

Balaam is best remembered for his unsuccessful attempt, under contract with Balak, king of Moab, to curse the Israelites (Num. 22–24). Since in the first story about him he wound up blessing God's people, we might wonder why he became a symbol of false teaching here in Revelation 2 and in Jude 11. (The reference to him in 2 Peter 2:15-16 accords with the story in Numbers 22–24.) The seeming contradiction is resolved by Numbers 31:16 and Revelation 2:14, which indicate that Balaam kept teaching women and Balak to entice the Israelites to unfaithfulness through eating food sacrificed to idols and by committing sexual immorality. We know from Israel's history that the Moabites were a continual source of conflict and consequent pressure to turn from *YHWH* to idolatrous practices. Their story thus offers extremely important lessons for us in the twenty-first century.

The powers of evil know that they cannot conquer us through direct confrontation — even as Balaam could not curse the Israelites, but blessed them instead. Therefore, evil powers come to us more subtly and lead us astray by small increments. In the first century, the question of eating foods sacrificed to idols was a touchy issue (see Paul's comments in 1 Cor. 8) since oftentimes the only meat available in Roman cities came from various temples through their festivals and feasts and, indirectly, through the markets. Moreover, in the society of the empire, sexual immorality was an accepted part of the life of Roman officials.

Very obviously, this second sin is as rampant in the twenty-first century as in the first and needs to be more thoroughly addressed by the Church. But how does the problem of food sacrificed to idols impinge on our lives today?

Many aspects of our culture involve the same material entanglement in idolatrous practices. For example, many youth buy CDs and videos from rock groups with obviously violent or sexually immoral themes and thereby support their practices and influence. Contrarily, God's people must often choose carefully how to avoid bolstering various idolatries of power and wealth. For example, some Christians have boycotted certain pineapple companies that bulldozed the farms of poor peasants in Latin America and made them merely seasonal laborers in order to raise pineapple for the rich in the U.S. and elsewhere. Meanwhile, the peasants' children are malnourished because the families can no longer grow subsistence crops on the land now added to the fields of the wealthy. Similarly, Christians have organized boycotts of major corporations that construct weapons systems and consequently lead the lobbying for escalating use of tax money for military purposes.

All kinds of economic and political questions are involved in the practical application of this warning to Pergamum. Where do we invest our money? Are the agencies using those funds to finance the construction of weapons of annihilation? Perhaps we might want to invest in alternative agencies, such as money markets that were established to provide funds for programs that build economic stability in poorer countries. Or we can choose to deposit our savings with such Christian agencies as Dwelling House Savings and Loan, which finances loans for the (primarily black) poor of Pittsburgh and follows up with counseling and support, or Jubilee Housing, Inc., which was begun by members of the Church of the Saviour in Washington, D.C., to renovate apartment buildings for the poor.[4]

Living intentionally requires study as well as deliberation so that we can carefully choose actions, investments, and purchases to avoid contributing to various "thrones of Satan" occupied by holders of power and wealth in our culture. Of course, we can't always be successful since so many aspects of life are out of our control. However, my main goal here is simply to challenge our thinking, to invite us to live with more deliberation, to question ways in which our eating of meat (any economic aspect of life) might be related to idols (of any political or religious sort). Nation-

---

4. These two agencies are decisively Christian in their approach: Dwelling House Savings and Loan, 501 Herron Ave., Pittsburgh, PA 15219-4696, phone: (412) 683-5116; and Jubilee Housing, Inc., 2482 Ontario Road N.W., Washington, D.C. 20009, e-mail: Jubileehousing@yahoo.com. Some examples of alternative money markets are Pax World Funds, P.O. Box 8930, Wilmington, DE 19899-8930, web site: www.paxfunds .com, and Working Assets, P.O. Box 5420, Indianapolis, IN 46255-5420, web site: www.workingforchange.com. Information about boycotts as described in the previous paragraphs can be obtained from INFACT, 256 Hanover Street, 3rd floor, Boston, MA 02113, web site: www.infact.org.

alism, militarism, other ideologies, accumulation of possessions, intellectualism, even simplicity for its own sake can all become idolatrous.

The name of Balaam is also linked to leading the children of Israel into sexual immorality, and that seems to be the case also with the Nicolaitans. Since that is such a large topic, appearing also in the fourth letter, we will reserve discussion of it until the next chapter.

We must note essentially at this point that the people at Pergamum are called to repent for these sins. Our society explains them instead. We can rationalize most of our sins — they are due to bad environment, a failure in upbringing, inadequate love in the home, social pressures. The Word of God simply says to repent. This is an urgent message for our times, too, that few want to hear.

God's command leads again to the theme underlying this book. A great gift that those who suffer can bring to the Christian community out of their weakness is a deeper sense of repentance. If we struggle to survive or if we spend long hours lying on a bed of pain, usually we are brought more in touch with our sin and the need for repentance than when we are strong and think we can figure everything out and accomplish it all by ourselves.

One reason why meetings of Alcoholics Anonymous have been so successful is that those involved repent publicly. Each individual declares to the rest that she or he is an alcoholic, wanting to change, but an alcoholic nonetheless. In frankly admitting our failures we begin the process of change.

In a world swarming with various idolatries, we need this simple call: Repent! In times of greatest weakness, God invariably wakes me up to my inherent sinfulness — not to destroy me, but to begin to heal other parts of me besides my body. Moreover, we all know the intimate connection of spirit, soul, and body. Often repentance clears the way for restoration of the body.

The community at Pergamum is warned that if they don't repent Christ will fight against them with the sword of His mouth. His Word will slay them in their sinfulness.

This does not at all mean that Christ will destroy sinners, for immediately after the threat of His warring against them with the sword of His mouth come the warning to listen to what the Spirit says to the churches and then a particular promise for Pergamum's saints. Christ never gives up on us, even if we are thoroughly saturated by sin. He visits us with His

Word in order to call us to repentance, to cut sin from us, to enable us to listen to what the Spirit is saying.

The promise given to this community is singularly appropriate. If they will give up eating the food of idols, they will be given the hidden manna. Again we see close connections with the Gospel of John and with the Hebrew Scriptures. In John 6, after the incident of the feeding of the 5000, Jesus challenges the Jews not to work for food that perishes (v. 27, reminiscent of Isa. 55:2) and calls Himself the bread of life who comes down from heaven (vv. 48-51). He invites people to eat of Himself (John's Gospel's subtle reference to the institution of the Eucharist), but some are offended and draw back at that point. Here in The Revelation, the people of Pergamum are offered the true food, which is the Word of God, even as Deuteronomy 8:3 reminded the people that they could not live by bread alone, but by the words that proceed from the mouth of God (see also Matt. 4:4 and Luke 4:4).

The triple connections between the First Testament, the Gospels, and other parts of the New Testament are important. These themes weave throughout the Scriptures: we dare not get too caught up in material things of this world and lose sight of the need for our spirits and souls to be nourished by the food of the Word.

Yet what a promise is given to Pergamum! In our repentance, we will receive that which is truly nourishing. We are reminded of Isaiah 55:2, where the LORD challenges the Israelites in this way:

> Why do you spend money for what is not bread,
>   And your wages for what does not satisfy?
> Listen carefully to Me, and eat what is good,
>   And delight yourself in abundance.

This is the best food around!

Why do we seek so intently for what does not satisfy? Why do we chase after the world's idols? I don't write such questions to nag you, for certainly I am just as guilty — thinking my life will finally be complete if only. . . .

God wants to satisfy us with the only true manna, Christ the Word. Divine grace has made Him readily available for us.

The other promise given to the people at Pergamum is indeed intriguing. To the one overcoming his or her sin (by means of repentance) Christ promises a white stone with a new name written on it, a secret name known only by the one who receives it.

Is the white stone equivalent to a modern ticket, a token for gaining admittance to a pagan temple where idol food would be consumed, so that the new stone and name given by Christ would indicate the new character and way of life of believers, as Edwin Walhout suggests?[5] Is it simply an image for impermeability, or purity, for strength and sacredness as a covenant? Whatever its original intent, we can assume that the image denotes a special gift, even as the name itself signals a new and graced relationship with God made possible by repentance.

The call is issued to us today. We cannot leave this letter without asking ourselves these searching questions: Of what idolatries do I need to repent? In what areas of my life do I need the cleansing/pruning of the Word of God? The hidden manna of the Word will enable us to remain true to His name and to live by our new name.

---

5. Edwin Walhout, *Revelation Down to Earth: Making Sense of the Apocalypse of John* (Grand Rapids: Wm. B. Eerdmans Publishing Co., 2000), p. 44.

CHAPTER 11

Thyatira: True Authority

*(Please refer often to Revelation 2:18-29
as you study this chapter.)*

Numbers 24:17 prophesies that a star shall rise out of Jacob and a scepter out of Israel — a prophecy which, in hindsight, we see fulfilled in the coming of Jesus, the Christ. Most interestingly, the image comes from the mouth of Balaam, to whom the seer John referred in the previous letter of The Revelation.

Later, in Revelation 22:16, Jesus names himself "the Root and the Offspring of David, and the bright Morning Star." Consequently, when the Christian community at Thyatira is promised that Christ will give the overcomers there the morning star, we understand that to mean that He will give them the gift of Himself, His very own presence in their lives.

This name for Jesus is especially beautiful. Since my metabolism deficiencies make mornings difficult, I rarely arise before the sun, but when I have to fly east for speaking engagements I sometimes notice the morning star. At those times its sparkling beauty overcomes the bleakness of early-morning flights.

Some who suffer sleepless nights because of pain often say that they, too, rejoice greatly at the morning star. It promises that soon the day will appear and the night of anguish will be over.

Jesus is the bright Morning Star. Only this letter to Thyatira offers to a church such a particular promise of the presence of Christ. However, only this letter also adds a particular word of caution to the phrase included in all seven letters, "To the one overcoming. . . ." The additional words here, "and does my will to the end," seem to suggest that the presence of Jesus is integrally connected with the doing of His will.

This connection does *not* turn faith into an effort of works to create our own righteousness — an unbiblical notion we adamantly reject. We are not warned by this letter to earn the presence of Jesus by being good.

Rather, the combination reminds us again that we miss Christ's constant presence if our faith does not change the practical dimensions of life. We do not know His Spirit at work in us if we reject His way of life. We fail to appreciate His loving presence if we are controlled by other gods.

On the other hand, when we continue doing God's will, we experience the intimate connection that is possible with Jesus. We sense His presence in our thoughts and actions. We live *in Christ.*

One Christmas a former student of mine and his wife wrote that they were newly learning what it means to be "in Christ." That small phrase carries immense power for us if we can more thoroughly realize how Christ really wants us to dwell in Him in every single aspect of daily life. What an incredibly transformative promise!

We miss it, however, if we insist on our own immoral and idolatrous choices. Every time we trust in other gods, we diminish His encompassing presence. Every deed we commit contrary to His will widens our alienation.

The very gravity of what we often consider "dabbling" in pleasures is underscored by the unsettling, quick move away from the strong praise for the people at Thyatira and the stern image of Christ at the beginning of their letter. Here alone He is specifically called the "Son of God" to emphasize His divinity, and His power to command their repentance is stressed with the picture of His eyes like blazing fire and His feet of burnished bronze.

The members of the Thyatiran church are commended for their deeds, their love and faith, their service and perseverance, and for the fact that they are now doing more than they did at first. What a noteworthy list! But those extraordinary accomplishments do not matter if the grand successes are marred by the idolatry and immorality to which the Son of God immediately turns.

That contrast should be more often noted in the twenty-first century. Instead, we excuse "little" sins if a person "faithfully" attends worship. We succumb to various idolatries and excuse them because we are "pretty decent Christians," doing nice things and being loving toward our neighbors. We don't take seriously enough how much any sin mars the whole.

Certainly we have no grounds for self-righteousness. Indeed, all of us fail in at least one point. Being human, we indubitably fail at several points.

No one can be perfect. That is why we need grace.

On the other hand, we dare not misinterpret judgment. This letter's strong warning does not mean that the Thyatirans are a lost cause. Similar to the previous letter, this one is intended to draw its recipients back to grace — to call them to repentance and forgiveness.

The problems of the Thyatirans are the same as those of the folks at Pergamum — idolatry and immorality — but here there is a greater emphasis on the latter, so that will be this chapter's focus. This time the warning is more urgent. The blazing eyes, the name "Son of God," the warrior feet, the searching of minds and hearts and giving to all as their works deserve — these images together portray more wrath because in this case "Jezebel" was given time to repent already, but she refuses.

The letter declares that the people who commit adultery with her will be cast into great distress. We dare not falsely universalize these statements. They do not mean, of course, that everyone who suffers has committed "adultery." One of the worst griefs that we who are handicapped endure is the frequent "witness" of others that we must be suffering because of unconfessed sins.

The images in verses 22-23a are profoundly appropriate: those who violate God's designs for human sexuality in bed will also find suffering there, for the children of sin are stillborn pleasures. Wantonness never satisfies; pleasures of indulgence never last. We also see a terribly tangible fulfillment of this text in the twenty-first century, for a high proportion of the babies conceived in fornication are aborted.

Churches in our day have neglected biblical warnings against sexual sin and have often been afraid to call a spade a spade. We join the culture in euphemizing sexual sins as "sleeping together" or "playing around" instead of truly naming them adultery or fornication. The designation "single parent families" fails to acknowledge that the children were born out of wedlock or have suffered the trauma of divorce. So many situations specifically violate God's design for the committed, permanent, covenantal relationship in which loving sexual union is to take place and by which children are most soundly raised.

Single people frequently tell me, however, that remaining celibate in this world is too terribly hard, and for many years I struggled, too, with my own sexual needs as a single person. Certainly it is extremely difficult — but it is not impossible.

Faithful Christians with disabilities can teach us two very powerful lessons about godly sexuality. All the young people in our church communities need to hear lessons about discipline and wholesome chastity.

Those who must struggle constantly for life and movement know better than most people in our society how to discipline their bodies and wills. In an age when most people go by the philosophy, "if it feels good, do it," the disabled much more wisely know how empty that cliché is. They understand that immediate good feelings often bring lasting negative consequences. They know the importance of maintaining sturdy disciplines in the care of one's body.

Of course, I'm not saying that physically challenged people are more sexually pure than their healthy peers, but I am stressing our world's desperate need for lessons of discipline, for self-controlling acts of the will over emotions. Those whose very lives depend on medical procedures strictly followed (in spite of feelings) are the best teachers of careful discipline.

Elizabeth O'Connor's *Cry Pain, Cry Hope* suggests that the concern of someone who is ill with his or her own illness is not as self-centered as that might seem, for, in a time of sickness, the illness IS one's work.[1] That insight is extremely encouraging to me as I struggle daily with difficulties of exercising, with multiple blood tests and insulin injections, with extra dietary precautions because of kidney weakness, with procedures against various deteriorations and failures of intestines, feet, jaws, and eyes. All the disciplines my health problems require are part of my work, and they teach me vital insights about the superiority of will over feelings. Those who are tempted to immorality must counteract their sexual urges with decisive acts of will that supersede emotions.

Linden, my friend who is quadriplegic, taught me a crucial lesson about wholesome sexuality. Before his marriage, he once lamented to me that he was thoroughly sick of being treated as if he were a-sexual just because he could not demonstrate his masculinity genitally. I had never thought about that before; I had always loved him as a dear *male* friend, sensitive and very strong, even though seated in a chair. He awoke me to a

---

1. Elizabeth O'Connor, "Learning from an Illness," *Cry Pain, Cry Hope: Thresholds to Purpose* (Waco, TX: Word Books, 1987), pp. 114-29, especially p. 114.

large dimension of the suffering of the disabled — the opinions of others concerning their sexuality.

As Linden explored that topic with me, he enunciated many ways in which he expressed his masculinity, his social sexuality. His descriptions articulated the profound character of his manhood, and his lessons helped me learn more about expressing my own femininity in social, not genital, ways.

If our churches would more thoroughly support youth in expressing their social sexuality (by being family, friends, and colleagues to them), we could spare many of them the ravages of a genital sexuality that is unprotected because it is outside the bonds of a covenant, permanent relationship. How desperately our youth need some encouragement for sexual purity in this age of "free" licentiousness. Why is it that our Christian communities so tragically fail to provide for their youth better education and support for positive, godly sexuality?[2]

The One with eyes like a flame of fire declares that all the churches will know that He is the one who searches minds and hearts. In the Bible the word *heart* never refers merely to feelings. Rather, the word conveys the idea of deliberate will, of careful intentions. God does not accept the excuse that our feelings were too strong so we couldn't resist sexual temptation. Instead, Christ searches for the will that would project itself over feelings and act on the basis of what the mind knows about God's commands against committing adultery.

Though Christ warns those who refuse to repent, He has a precise word of encouragement for those steadfastly trying to remain pure. He urges them simply to keep holding on to what they have — their faith and love, their perseverance, their good deeds and service, their deliberate will and mind to stay away from the idolatry and immorality of their brothers and sisters.

Hang on till I come, Jesus says. Perhaps many times you and I have hung on till someone came to relieve us on a work shift, or to help us cope with the leaking sink and screaming kids, or to assist us in walking up stairs when that task was proving impossible. These experiences teach us that a strong way to resist temptation is to keep reminding ourselves that Jesus is coming.

---

2. Audio and video teaching tapes on "Godly Sexuality" for teenagers and also for parents are available from Christians Equipped for Ministry, Dottie Davis, tape ministry coordinator, 10918 NE 152nd Ave., Vancouver, WA 98682; telephone (360) 892-3618.

He is coming someday to end temptation and evil forever. We certainly want to be faithful to Him when He comes.

Furthermore, He is coming now to aid us with His power in the fight against temptation. Perhaps He is coming in the person of a friend who will stand by us with strength for resistance. Perhaps He is coming in music or beauty to uplift us and sustain us. He came to me just now in the phone call from a fellow member of my church who said that he would take me to the doctor today in the emergency of a new wound inside the brace on my leg.

How does He come to you? How remarkable it is that He comes to each of us in ways appropriate to our particular loves! One day I was immensely cheered and strengthened just by seeing something pink (though I don't even recall what it was), because that liturgical color for Joy always makes me glad.

Our Christian lives are a matter of holding on till He comes. If we persist in abiding in His will, then He will give us authority over the nations.

This promise is especially important as our world becomes smaller and smaller — more and more linked by telecommunications and by economic and ecological necessities. However, contrary to some voices on the political right, the United States does not presently demonstrate such a Christian life that abides in God's will and, consequently, reaches out to the rest of the world with godly authority. Especially after the fall of communism, many claimed a moral superiority for the U.S., but we Christians should seriously recognize that the U.S. is not respected by most other nations. We have little moral credibility.

The U.S. has often been imperialistic instead of fostering the well-being of nations. We have robbed the Two-Thirds world instead of promoting its economic health. Participating in a college-choir mission tour around the world, I was shocked by the hostile attitudes toward the U.S. in many places because our tourists act boorish, thinking that the whole world must cater to their whims. Meanwhile, seeing the contrast between our wealth and the poverty of the global community changed my life forever.

We mistakenly think that the Lord is on our side! How can God be when we are not in the center of the divine will to feed the hungry and clothe the naked and care for those who are homeless? How can we think we are God's people when sexual immorality is so rampant in our society?

Revelation 2:26-27 quotes Psalm 2:8-9 (and also Isaiah 30:14 and Jeremiah 19:11), part of a messianic passage proclaiming God's ultimate sovereignty over all the kings of the earth. We dare not think that our nation can have such sovereignty when we do not have the authority of moral uprightness. The authority that Jesus gives is that which He received from the Father, and He received it because He did the Father's will — constantly, obediently, faithfully. Only those who "do His will to the end" will have a similar authority. And they also receive the morning star.

Christ wants to be present in us and to impart His authority to us — our church communities, our country, our peoplehood. He calls us away from sexual immorality and sacrifices to other gods and empowers us instead to live in the center of His will. Are we hearing what the Spirit is saying to our churches?

CHAPTER 12

Sardis: The Call to Renewal

*(Please refer often to Revelation 3:1-6
as you study this chapter.)*

At one point in a long medical struggle, a doctor tried a new medication to cut down swelling in my leg. It was supposed to stimulate nerves to signal blood vessels to constrict. However, it also made me terribly sleepy and not a little nauseous. I was eager to work on this book and prepare for speaking engagements, and I desperately wanted to sleep. Which did I want more?

It was possible to shake off drowsiness and force myself to work because the enjoyment of work helps me forget illness, but it took a deliberate effort. I had to make a conscious choice and back up that choice with straining exertion.

The difficulty of that situation parallels a problem in my spiritual life. In many aspects of it, I'd rather just sleep. It takes a deliberate effort to choose, and engage in, certain spiritual disciplines beyond weekly corporate worship — to take time for Advent devotions with my husband, to set aside the Sabbath every week, to reserve morning time for Scripture meditation, prayer, and hymn singing. Periodically I need new motivation; regularly I need spiritual renewal. I suppose you do, too.

Consequently, the letter to the Christian community at Sardis is an excellent resource for us. That church's problem of seeming to be vital when they actually weren't is repeated in the life of God's people throughout history, for all kinds of forces draw us consistently away from a Christ-like way of being.

Immediately the image of the Christ-life is brought to our attention, for the beginning of this letter describes Christ as the one having the seven spirits and the seven stars. This portrayal of Christ is integrally connected to the problem for which the church at Sardis is rebuked.

Readers of this letter would perhaps instantly associate the seven spirits with the messianic prophecy of Isaiah 11:1-2, which declares that the Spirit of the LORD (the Almighty *YHWH*, the covenant "I Am") would be upon the shoot from the stump of Jesse. This first element resting upon the branch from Jesse's roots we see fulfilled in the Gospels: Jesus, anointed with God's Spirit, was perfectly attuned to doing the Father's will and lived in complete reliance upon God. Other aspects of the sevenfold spirit itemized in Isaiah 11 and demonstrated by Jesus are the Spirit of wisdom, understanding, counsel, strength, knowledge, and the fear of the LORD.

All these aspects of the Christ-life point to the indispensability of being aware of our weakness. We cannot be filled with God's wisdom or understanding when we rely on our own (insufficient) intellect and insights. We don't remain in God's counsel when we employ the world's strategies for doing things. We consistently grasp for power if we deny our utter dependency upon God. In our culture's emphasis on information and computer access to it, we think we can learn everything we need to know, but only by God's grace and as we live in a personal and community relationship with God can we discover the meaning and truth of the Word and of life. Only Triune grace can create a healthy balance of both knowing that we deserve God's wrath for our sinfulness and believing the assurance that we are loved anyway.

The letter to Sardis also pictures Christ as having the seven stars. Not only does He model for us, and call us personally to, His own dependent way of life, made possible when the whole Spirit of God indwells every aspect of our being, but also He remains intimately connected to, and challenges, the entire Church.

Revelation 1:20 told us that these seven stars are the angels of the seven churches — in other words, the representatives of representatives. The angels might perhaps be the human leaders of the churches or the spirit that characterizes them; in addition, as noted in Chapter 7 above, the churches were in prominent cities that seemed to serve as the focus for the whole region of Asia Minor. Consequently, when Christ is depicted as holding them in His hand, it reemphasizes this glorious truth of grace: that Christ always continues to embrace His people in His care, no matter how desperately they need renewal. All of God's people everywhere need to listen to this letter challenging churches to new reliance upon, and empowerment by, the Spirit.

Right away, the Christ so characterized berates the people of Sardis for their false front; though they appear to the rest of the world to be alive, He knows that they are really spiritually dead. He criticizes them, not for any particular sin, but simply for the fact that their deeds are not complete — and the only thing to do about that is to wake up!

The letter is like an alarm clock that rings every few minutes: Wake up! Strengthen the things that remain which were about to die! Remember what you have received and heard! Obey! Repent!

The heaping of these phrases intensifies the prodding. We cannot strengthen what remains by ourselves. That which we have received and heard — the gospel! — revitalizes us. Our deeds, like those of the people of Sardis, are not complete in God's sight, but the Spirit constantly calls us with the gospel to new life, new hope, new response. This letter wakes us up to hear Christ's call.

We have all missed opportunities, failed to use our spiritual gifts as fully as we could, or been spiritually dead in other ways. When I first wrote this book, I deeply regretted not having used well a recent seven-month period of near blindness to learn lessons of listening to God. My constant "Why?" questions had kept me from hearing God's answers to "what" the Spirit would strengthen instead.

But grace offers another path. When we would flounder in regrets or confusions, God's forgiveness enables us instead to strengthen what remains. Christ's grace empowers us for the disciplines that strengthen us; we respond to His immense love by spiritual exercise.

For the people of Sardis the situation was critical — the things that remained were about to die. Our spiritual lives, too, shrink and get flabby without training. When we neglect the means the Spirit has provided for us to receive grace — God's Word and prayer, the sacraments and forgiveness, Christ's love incarnated in the Christian community — our spiritual lives get weak. Those gifts are given to strengthen what remains.

Two of my friends, out of their weakness, have taught me vital lessons about the urgency and the gift of strengthening what remains. Linden, quadriplegic, illustrates by his physical discipline the importance of spiritual exercise. Though deprived of most upper-body functioning, he chose for several years not to have an electric wheelchair so that he had to push himself wherever he went. This strengthening of the one functioning muscle in each of his arms now continues to give him amazing control of them so that he can cook, do photography, and even develop his own pictures. Similarly, when we receive Christ's grace through spiritual exercises of Word and worship, the Spirit empowers us to serve the Father in many ways.

Another friend, Connie, who is blind, demonstrated long ago the important lesson of rejoicing in what remains. She admitted to me that for a while she had been envious that at that time I had escaped diabetic complications with my eyes. As she was praying about her attitude, she heard God's comfort to her so powerfully that it seemed almost audible. The voice assured her, "That's OK, Connie. For what I've called Marva to do, she needs her vision. For what I've called you to do, you don't necessarily need your eyes." Connie was program director for Vision Northwest and helped thirty-four support groups and over five hundred people in Oregon cope with the difficulties of living with visual impairment in a seeing world!

Connie's words rang in my ears the next day when an orthopedic specialist informed me that I faced possible amputation of my foot. "It's OK," God says. "Connie needs her feet to visit support groups, but you don't really need your feet for what I've called you to do." Connie's insight motivates me to write books as well as I can as long as eyes and brain and typing skills still remain. By myself I can't accept crippling and diminished eyesight, but coping with losses is made easier by the challenge to focus instead on God's gifts to strengthen what still remains.

The Christians at Sardis are commanded to remember — a common scriptural theme — what they have received and heard. Constantly the Word urges us to remember what Christ has taught, how the LORD has intervened in history, what we have learned from the traditions of faith. The gospel in our memories, then, leads to these results: obedience and repentance. As we hear again the Spirit's exhortations, we want to respond with eager acceptance of God's commands and desires and will, and we are sorry for the many times we have failed to respond positively. Our repentance (the Greek *metanoia*) is a genuine turning around of both thought and behavior.

All the warnings of the letter to Sardis summarize excellently the elements needed for true renewal. Growing spirituality requires a steady repetition of the truths of faith, which will lead to repentance for our failures, a turning around of mind and deed, a desire to strengthen what remains, and an eagerness to obey in the future. Moreover, we need often a summons to new spiritual alertness.

Christ says that there are a few in the church at Sardis who have not soiled their clothes. In context with all the rest of the Scriptures, this certainly cannot mean that these people are without sin. Rather, their lives are already constantly being renewed. Since only Christ's grace makes us worthy to walk with Him, they are undoubtedly folk who are constantly aware of their need for His forgiveness and guidance and, therefore, are people who have not soiled their clothes by wandering away from Him or by becoming proud of their own purity.

They are given as examples. If any others in the church can overcome their failures by repentance and the Spirit's renewal, they, too, can become like these models. All who overcome will know the same purity. They are promised that they will all be dressed in white. Their renewal in faith will keep their names in the book of life, and they will, therefore, be acknowledged by Christ in heaven.

Now in the twenty-first century you and I also have some models and these same promises. We know people who are constantly seeking renewal in their faith and, as a result, live with faithfulness and purity. Those who recognize their own weakness and trust God's empowerment provide excellent models. I think, for example, of Joni Eareckson Tada, whose faith has radiated from her wheelchair and touched thousands of lives through her books, art, and ministry to the handicapped. This past weekend she and I were on the same airplane, so I could observe the great love of God with which she greeted all whom she encountered. Another who trusted God to strengthen what remained was Toni Carson, who did not let painful cancer prevent her from organizing prayer groups for her children's schools. Similarly, Audrey Kershner, a senior citizen I met through my childhood paper route, continued throughout the rest of her life to pray for my work and to inspire me through her beautifully Christ-like life. On a larger scale, Christians in Mexico and Poland and Madagascar taught me out of their poverty what it means to share.

Certainly in your Christian community you know some saints who model for the rest of us what the faith life means. Their spiritual example invites us to wake up, to remember, to repent, to obey afresh, to strengthen what remains so that we can serve God to the best of our ability for the rest of our days.

CHAPTER 13

Philadelphia: An Open Door

(Please refer often to Revelation 3:7-13
as you study this chapter.)

How inspiring it is that God is able to use us powerfully when we are weak! My friend Toni, while battling breast cancer metastasized to the lungs and brain, strengthened the faith of many people with her incredible tenacity of trust in God's wisdom and care. She experienced God's healing grace in a remarkable extension of life, but she also courageously faced the ravages of her illness with the true hope that only weakness can bring.

What a glorious promise we receive when Christ declares in the letter to the saints at Philadelphia that the ones with little strength will become pillars. They have kept Christ's Word and have not denied His name. They have endured patiently and so will be spared the hour of trial that will test the whole world.

As usual, the description of Christ for these saints at Philadelphia is singularly appropriate. Their letter begins with a picture of Him as the holy and true One who holds the key of David, the One whose opening and shutting no one can oppose.

It is amazing that in His holiness Christ can look at our weakness and commend it. How different the values of Christ are from those of the world, which praises those who are beautiful, successful, rich, ambitious, skillful, or powerful. We praise such attributes, too, because we are not holy, and in our lack of perfection we fumble for the "best," which seems to be epitomized by those who have it all.

In contrast, the holy/set apart One sets apart those who know they are not at the top of the ladder. He who is true praises those who know the truth about their inadequacies and do not claim any false superiorities.

Christ holds the power to open and close all that pertains to the true Israel, for He holds the key of David. Therefore, He can open a door before these humble Philadelphians who have no power. He knows them truly — that they do not falsely pretend to be greater than they are — and so He gives them unrestricted entrance. The sky isn't even the limit to what they can do in His name.

Christ's gift of an open door for those with little strength is being closed these days by churches that accept our society's contradictory emphasis on success. The need to climb the ladder of power and fame shuts out the weak and hinders them from offering their gifts to the community.

Truly, however, the door cannot ultimately be shut, for no one can shut what Christ has opened. The weak who depend on Him will serve Him and become what He has in store for them with or without churches' approval and care — but in the process we lose the gifts they could bring to the Body.

Three times this section of the letters uses the Greek word translated "Behold!" to rouse our attention toward what we are failing to notice. First, God wants us to grasp that the open door is set before those who have little strength — in whatever form that might take in history. The mentally deficient are often very sure about God's love and dearly capable of loving others. Those whose handicaps make them utterly reliant upon God's strength are often profoundly taught by their situation to forego the world's methods of power. If we are caught up in our own capabilities, we won't notice such things now, but we will some day.

The second "Behold!" demands that we ask ourselves if we are numbered among those who are of "the synagogue of Satan." When The Revelation was written, as noted in Chapter 9, that phrase may have designated the group that history calls the Judaizers — those who tried to force legalistic Jewish practices on Gentile believers. In so doing, they negated both the grace of true Judaism and the gospel of freedom and grace in Christ.

Similarly, in the twenty-first century, many who claim to participate in Christianity negate its tenets of total dependence upon God's grace. Certainly any time we block God's purposes by our own petty prejudices we are serving the synagogue of Satan rather than the temple of God. When we pretend to be God's people or deny that others are, we negate the grace that sets us all free.

This letter challenges each of us to look at our attitudes and actions toward the weak. With the third "Behold!" Christ says that He will make all those who lie to come and fall down at the feet of the weak and acknowledge that He has loved them. In postmodern society we often falsify God's love for the weak by our own refusal truly to welcome them into our fellowships. Maybe we misrepresent God's mercy for them by not helping to care for their physical needs. Sometimes our lies are more subtle — animosities disguised as compassion, repressed impatience that we don't vent.

Three uses of "Behold!" call us to the truth of who Christ's people are before whom He sets an open door. Then He promises that those who have kept His Word of patient endurance will be kept from the hour of trial that is coming to test all the people of the world.

We must be very careful when we discuss the tribulation from which the Philadelphians will be spared. It grieves me that Revelation 3:10 is often taken out of context, slapped together with Luke 17:34-35 and 1 Thessalonians 4:17 (which speak of entirely different truths in their original contexts), and made into evidence for "the rapture." This procedure constructs a major doctrine on the basis of an illegitimate reading of texts.

Instead, an essential rule for reading the Scriptures faithfully is that each verse must be read in its own context. In the setting of Christ's words in Luke 17 and 21 the verses about "one taken and the other left" do not mean that God's people will suddenly be raptured while unbelievers are left wondering, but instead stress that when Christ comes suddenly we won't know who is part of His kingdom.

Chapter 4 of 1 Thessalonians was originally intended to comfort people who had lost loved ones before Christ's expected return. The apostle Paul offers this hope to them: they will all be together when Jesus comes. He uses the image of Christ gathering everyone in the clouds (the symbol throughout the Bible of God's presence) to assure his mourning readers that in the future they will be together both with God and with those who had already died.

These verses in Revelation 3 about being spared the tribulation cannot be disassociated from the words to the people in Smyrna that they would suffer in the coming peril. Not all Christians will be spared the suffering.

Such differing contexts in Luke, 1 Thessalonians, and Revelation prohibit an indiscriminate conjoining of these three isolated texts. Each passage must first be studied for its intended meaning for the original readers;

then immersion in the warnings and comforts of these texts will form us to respond to our times with similar character.

Furthermore, some groups who read these verses out of their historical and literary context also spend much of their time debating various aspects of the rapture that they have created — even though Jesus specifically told His followers in several texts (such as Luke 17:23 and 21:8) that they should not chase after the people who claim to know about the time of the end. Since we do not know how the world will end, how Christ will come or when, how we will be taken from this world to be with Him, and so forth, we would do much better not to speculate about such things and instead to concentrate on these messages that Christ gave us for the meanwhile: repent, watch, tell others, do justice and mercy, walk humbly with God. Perhaps one aspect of weakness I have not stressed enough yet is the weakness of not knowing, of accepting that certain dimensions of God's kingdom are beyond our ken.

In Revelation 3, Christ declares that He is coming soon. How can we reconcile this promise of quick fulfillment with its delay of almost 2000 years?

The fact is that Christ IS coming soon, though not necessarily to bring the history of the earth to an end. His promise to come is not falsified by history, but by our lack of receptive weakness to receive Him.

When I began to use insulin at the age of 16 because the measles virus had killed my pancreas, my lifespan as a brittle diabetic was forecast to be limited, and various doctors since then have suggested gently that perhaps I might be in my last decade. These forecasts have been very valuable — not to scare me, but instead to make me know a healthy sense of urgency that I often wish others had. Most of my life has been undergirded with a deep, abiding recognition that I must use time well.[1] This sense of the nearness of Christ's coming to take me home with Him usually frees me to care more deliberately about others, to be concerned for their reconciliation with God, to choose more intentionally what I do with my time.

Christ commands those with little strength in Philadelphia to hold fast to what they have so that no one will seize their crown. Perhaps they have

---

1. That doesn't mean not having fun, for using time well also means enjoying God's gifts, including God's design for Sabbath rest. See Marva J. Dawn, *Keeping the Sabbath Wholly: Ceasing, Resting, Embracing, Feasting* (Grand Rapids: Wm. B. Eerdmans Publishing Co., 1989).

been persecuted for so long that they wonder if they can hold out any more. The very gift of God's crown of life enables them to continue persevering. Even so, the anticipation of Christ's coming soon, the experience of His gracious coming now into our lives, and the process of holding fast to faith meanwhile enable us to enjoy that crown to some extent even now. We have already been crowned with the Joy promised in the messianic age (Isa. 35:10), which makes us look forward all the more to the perfection of Joy we will experience someday when all the present tears and pain, the sorrow and sighing, will flee away.

The promises to the Philadelphians with little strength are delightful. Not only will they not ever have to leave God's temple, but they will be pillars there. Those who the world thought were weak will be revealed as those with the strength to support God's dwelling. Christ's kingdom is carried, not by domination according to the world's ideas, but by the weakness that lets His grace shine through.[2] Those who suffer or grow faint already wear the crowns that cannot be taken if they hold fast. Their mettle will someday be proved, to the astonishment of those who served Satan's purposes by buying into the world's stratagems for power and success. Those who scorned the weak will discover that faithful people with little strength are the beloved of God.

The other promises of the letter to Philadelphia are equally encouraging. The ones overcoming by holding on in their weakness and consequent humility will be inscribed with several names. Remember that the idea of *name* in the Scriptures always refers to the character of the one named. That is why, for example, we can know that our prayers will be answered if we pray in Christ's name, for, holding His character in our consciousness, we would only pray for what accords with God's will.

Thus, to receive God's name suggests that someday those who lack strength now will become totally fashioned after God's likeness. Furthermore, they will receive the name of God's city, the New Jerusalem — which will be described later in The Revelation. Then in John's vision we shall observe all the glory and splendor and purity that will be manifested at the end of time through those who depended on God.

Finally, Christ promises that He will even write on them His new name. Throughout the Scriptures we read that at the end of time, having finished

---

2. See Marva J. Dawn, *Powers, Weakness, and the Tabernacling of God* (Grand Rapids, MI: Wm. B. Eerdmans Publishing Co., 2001).

all the work that the Father gave Him to do, Christ will be magnified above all. In that supreme exaltation, He will share His character with those who trusted Him in spite of their weakness. The Scriptures never give such a promise to those who trust their own capabilities. Only by profound humility does one truly enter into the grace of Christ, which makes possible participation in His greatest glory.

Of all the letters to the churches in Revelation 2 and 3, this one most thoroughly underscores my plea to value our own weakness and to encourage others with little strength in our Christian communities. Only as we all become totally dependent upon Christ and His grace will we find ourselves part of this great company that will receive the very name of God at the end of time.

CHAPTER 14

Laodicea: Whatever Our Limitations We Don't Have to Be Tepid

(Please refer often to Revelation 3:14-22 as you study this chapter.)

The waiter looked at me in surprise. I had asked him to take the teapot back to the kitchen and bring me one with BOILING water. I didn't mean to be obnoxious, but the best flavor is not drawn from teabags unless the water is really scalding. What a treasure is a *steaming* pot of herbal tea!

The letter to the Laodiceans in Revelation 3 is often misunderstood because we don't interpret historically the image of water that is hot, cold, or lukewarm. Some people who teach this text use the cold side of the dichotomy to emphasize that often those who are the most violently opposed to God's kingdom are the closest to entering it. Certainly this is an observable phenomenon: atheists or agnostics sometimes move suddenly from a coldly vicious opposition to the gospel to a surprising and very warm acceptance of it.

However, it could hardly be the case that the Lord of the Church is here advocating such coldness, nor that He would think it desirable for persons to be violently opposed to the gospel — even though it might suddenly become real to them. Though they might become quite hot in their appreciation of His truth later, we can hardly imagine Him saying at their initial rejection, "I'm *glad* that you are cold, that you are spurning my grace and love."

Rather, let us discern that the letter to the Laodicean church fits in very well with the actual geographical circumstances of that city. Its message poignantly rebukes the Christians there because its various images are true to their experience and thereby underscore the point more forcibly.[1]

Laodicea was an extremely difficult city to defend because it lacked its own water supply. Aqueducts brought drinking water from the springs near Denizli six miles to the south. Colossae, the site ten miles away of a sister church to the one in Laodicea, was known for its cold, pure waters. What a contrast these waters were to the tepid waters of Laodicea, which were not very refreshing. Meanwhile, six miles to the north of Laodicea were the hot mineral springs of Hierapolis. However, these healing and restorative waters flowed across a wide plateau and over a broad escarpment opposite Laodicea and then fell about 300 feet in a mile-wide cascade. It was a spectacular phenomenon, but the water was lukewarm and filled with sickly minerals — not very soothing.

Thus, Christ's message to the church at Laodicea is very clear: don't be like your water — lukewarm from the journey, neither invigorating nor healing, but merely to be spewed out. (The Spanish translation says "vomitar.") The message projects a clarion call to decisive commitment, as well as the recognition that our commitment functions in different ways according to the needs we confront.

At certain times our dedication will be manifested in soothing, healing warmth — comforting words, gentle caressing of weary spiritual muscles. Sometimes we serve as a jacuzzi in our ministry to others. On the other hand, at times we must be more like an ice-cold drink or shower, to refresh, motivate, resuscitate. We attend as prophets, stirring people up and alerting them to the dangers of sloth or greed.

Just as first-century people chose the waters of Hierapolis or Colossae according to their health concern, so in the twenty-first century we must become more discerning and learn whether to minister to others with a cold plunge or a hot sauna. Paul instructs the church at Thessalonica to "admonish the unruly, encourage the fainthearted, support the weak, and be patient with all" (1 Thess. 5:14). Our care for one another must match the need.

---

1. The following information about the city of Laodicea — its waters, banks, medical school, and sheep for black wool — was taken from Robert H. Mounce's commentary on *The Book of Revelation*, rev. ed., The New International Commentary on the New Testament, gen. ed. Gordon D. Fee (Grand Rapids: Wm. B. Eerdmans Publishing Co., 1998), pp. 105-15.

In that discernment, however, let's not forget our theology of weakness. Our ability to minister as either hot or cold springs does not come from our own efforts to produce a certain temperature of water. The middle portion of the letter to Laodicea (Rev. 3:16-18) warns us against such presumption.

The problem with the believers in Laodicea was that they had too many things going for them. Because the city was so prosperous, they weren't aware of their desperate need for grace. They did not know the weakness and dependence that are essential for true ministry in Christ. First-century Laodicea was famous for many things, and the members of the church there might have participated in the well-being of the city. In contrast to the church at Smyrna, this congregation was probably more comfortably self-sufficient.

The city of Laodicea was renowned for its financial institutions. Supposedly even the philosopher Cicero banked his money there. Consequently, it makes sense that Christ's words should remind the believers there not to trust in human gold. Instead, the members of the Laodicean community are to buy from the Lord of the Church His gold, which has truly been purified by means of fire. Then they will have genuine riches.

Though financial resources are usually helpful, human wealth does not in and of itself accomplish God's purposes. This truth is urgently needed today, when so many churches in the U.S. seem to think that prosperity is essential to serve God.

There are enough harangues against ostentatious riches in the Church to make it unnecessary for me to add another. Moreover, no doubt all of us have a basic concern for the poor that causes us to want to keep our own use of wealth in balance. However, reliance on human gold often creeps in when we are unaware.

Jacques Ellul's insightful book *Money and Power*[2] points out the subtle ways in which the false god Mammon so easily deceives us and commands our allegiance. We worry about not having enough money; or we have too much and hoard it; or we use it carefully and in our "responsible stewardship" lose the generosity of grace; or we become too proud of our refusal to accumulate it.

We need immense vigilance to fight the enculturation to which we are

---

2. Jacques Ellul, *Money and Power*, LaVonne Neff, trans. (Downers Grove, IL: InterVarsity Press, 1964).

so susceptible. Once we start to let thoughts of human wealth control us, the god Mammon takes over more and more.

A radical example (by which I mean "getting to the root of the issue") might underscore my point. When I first began writing, I decided that all royalty monies would be given to charitable organizations — not only because I didn't earn enough as a freelancer to be able to give away very much, but also to free me from writing to please the market. Book royalties provide the means to act on my convictions concerning sharing with the poor, until the time when my declining health might necessitate using them for medical care.

Once when a royalty check arrived (in the days before I had arranged with publishers to send them directly to specific ministries), I was tempted to question my previous decision about such monies. I was in graduate school in the Midwest and yearned to visit my friends on the West Coast. Perhaps I could keep for myself just enough to buy one plane ticket.

However, it became apparent immediately how hard it would be to draw the line! If I kept some to buy a plane ticket to the West, then why not more? In fact, why not keep all of it, and then I could afford several trips over the next years to visit friends? When I realized what was happening, I knew it had to be all or nothing. Keeping any of the money for this one trip would too easily lead to hoarding it all for myself.

A few days later a friend suggested that I should instead just keep out enough money for a few long distance phone calls. It certainly wouldn't be selfish to give myself a few pleasures, I rationalized — the delight of talking with distant friends would certainly be a boost to my studies. And then, of course, a little could be set aside for celebrations — just enough to go out for dessert or to enjoy a concert with friends.

Once again, the amount I would "need" began to multiply. How easily my selfishness spread, and I got more and more covetous of treats, events, experiences, and conversations until once again all the money was in my mental possession.

The use of one very small royalty check might seem a petty issue, but it presented to me a major ethical decision. The situation forced me to confront my own tendency to multiply my "needs," in contrast to an earlier careful determination to follow Jesus' command to divide my wealth so that others less fortunate than myself might also have opportunities for well-being and education.

My graduate assistantships were certainly adequate for all my needs, and there was plenty left over for celebrations if I lived carefully. Only selfish greed prompted the sudden yearning to keep royalty money for myself. This small issue forced me to face my own human craving to accumulate and to realize how easily we are tempted away from our desire to live as Christ would have us live in simple, more extensive sharing with others.

So easily our churches and our personal Christian lives become enculturated! We think we *need* all the things that make for a pleasant life. As our income increases, our requirements and requests grow to match it. Unless we choose deliberately to live more simply and to care more intentionally for others, we can easily spend all that we have.

Tragically, the First World has been doing that for centuries. The rich have gotten richer and the poor have gotten poorer, because we have not taken the first steps to follow Jesus in how we use our money.[3]

This idea is intriguing (compelling?): what would happen if we took seriously Christ's command to sell what we have and give to the poor, if we cut short our growing propensity to accumulate and said, "Thus far will my budget go and no farther"?

The other two images in the letter to the Laodiceans make the same point. The city was well known for its medical facilities and, particularly, for a special salve prepared there for the treatment of eye problems. Also, Laodicea produced illustrious garments made out of a beautiful black wool taken from sheep who grazed in the area. Consequently, Christ cautions the church to recognize their need to be clothed in white garments (always the symbol of restoration and purity in the Scriptures) and to be treated with an eye salve that would enable them to see spiritually. Any reliance on human resources to see, to be clothed, or to possess wealth should be recognized for what it truly is — a dependence on that which cannot meet their deepest needs, with the result that they were "afflicted, miserable, begging poor, blind and naked." Material resources are bound to fail for spiritual purposes.

Christians are called to a different response. Christ, the "faithful and true witness" (3:14), reminds us that He reproves and disciplines us out of His love for us (3:19). Therefore, we are aroused to respond with zeal and repentance. Christ Himself is at the door, and He is knocking. If anyone hears His voice and opens the door, He will enter in to that person and will eat with her and she with Him.

3. See Marva J. Dawn, *Unfettered Hope: A Call to Faithful Living in an Affluent Society* (Louisville: Westminster John Knox, forthcoming 2003).

This is plain and simple: Jesus summons us to repentance. Let us each consider in what ways we have turned to false gods and mistaken human goods for God's purposes and how desperately and thoroughly we need the Lord's discipline and instruction.

Besides that challenge, this text also gives great comfort for many reasons. First of all, the ones whom the Lord reproves are the ones He loves. The original Greek word emphasizes "bringing to light" in the sense of revealing or correcting, but because that reproof comes from love it is not an exposure that destroys us.

Correlatively, "to discipline" includes educating, bringing up with training. That act, too, offers comfort. My parents trained me in all sorts of things — not only in the basics of my Christian faith, but also in skills of pitching and hitting baseballs, in arts of cooking and cleaning, in appreciation of great music. Out of their love, my parents brought me up to know how to do many things — not only for useful purposes, but also for enjoyment.

In the same way, the Spirit instructs us not only in what we might do in God's service, but also in truths that give our lives value, purpose, and meaning. Therefore, knowing that Christ's reproof and discipline are designed to develop our Christian character, we respond zealously and repent for whatever keeps us from loving Him in all aspects of our life. We know that we need to change our mind about many things to have the mind of Christ.

Revelation 3:20 is misread when Christian circles use it in evangelism programs to describe the relationship of Jesus to people who do not yet believe in Him. I have heard many Christians tell nonbelievers, "If you just recognize that Jesus is standing at the door of your heart and knocking to get in and if you will just open the door, then He will come in and He will remain with you and have fellowship with you." To use this verse in such a way is to put the passage in the wrong environment — and to make ourselves (because *we* open the door) the agents of God's redeeming grace.

One major rule for reading Scriptures is to keep them appropriately in their context. This verse is not addressing non-Christians who need to repent in order to come to faith. Instead, it rebukes Christians who have failed to trust God for their life-giving water, wealth, health, and covering. Believers are to repent and recognize that Christ waits at their door and desires to come into their lives more thoroughly.

We shut Him out when we succumb to the temptation to trust other sources for life — money, possessions, and human remedies for our happiness. In our failure to repent we miss His grace in our lives. That grace frees us to become zealous to choose God's ways more intentionally, and then we experience the presence of Christ more profoundly. The promise of eating with Him implies the deepest fellowship that Christians can enjoy in God's company.

Experiencing Christ's presence in this way was the outcome of the situation described above in which I was tempted to hoard royalty money for myself. After the money was safely sent away and no longer a temptation, several subsequent events showed me how richly God continues to provide for all my needs and even my enjoyments without my having to be selfish. The situation also made very clear the necessity for repentance for my false trust in human gods.

Awareness of our failures and of the limits of our human weaknesses and appreciation for the riches of God's resources cause us to be more zealous to repent and to find Triune grace sufficient for all our needs. Truly Christ will give us gold refined in the fire, garments that are white and pure, eye salve that will enable us to see spiritually, and His very own presence to sustain us. Then we can live out the commitment to which the first part of this passage calls us: to be not like the lukewarm water that has traveled a great distance over plateaus or through aqueducts, but like the healing hot springs or the invigorating cold springs themselves — comforting or stimulating one another as we seek to serve the Lord with full commitment.

CHAPTER 15

The First Reason for Praise: The Gift of Life

*(Please refer often to Revelation 4:1-11
as you study this chapter.)*

B efore he moved after his marriage, Tim's dialysis room was gaily deco-
rated with bright red and blue festoons, ropes of brilliant plastic loop-
ing from one corner to the other. Several other cords hung like crepe paper
garlands across each other and down the walls so that the room hardly
seemed like a place for serious medical treatment. It couldn't be austere
with such colorfully merry ribbons.

The impression those bands made on Tim's visitors, however, changed
drastically when they learned that the celebrative festoons were made of
the ends of the artificial kidneys used on his dialysis machine. Each red or
blue inch-long loop of plastic represented more than eight hours on the
machine, so those long, draping cords pictured years of added life, the gift
of modern technology, the grace of a machine to cleanse Tim's blood and
stave off death.

Each year I celebrate the anniversary of his first dialysis run (the date is
written in my birthday book) because those treatments make possible the
gift of his friendship. I met Tim a few years after his kidneys failed, so I was
always conscious when I visited that room that the treasures of his love and
all the lessons learned from him are especially gracious presents.

Similarly, in periods when various health issues go crazy, when I have
felt the fragility of life gone totally out of control, I am reminded afresh
that God's design for the human body with all its profound interrelations
is a precious gift. How amazing it is that all the parts of our systems continue to function and support each other with incredible regularity and

precision — just the right amount of hormones, the proper beating of heart and pulsing of lungs and blood, the right exchanges of carbon dioxide and oxygen, the appropriate rate of metabolism. How can anyone look seriously at the gift of life and not acknowledge a Creator?

How wonder-full it is that a normal person's pancreas automatically introduces into the lifeblood exactly the amount of insulin needed to keep blood glucose levels precisely where they should be. Diabetics constantly have to judge how much insulin to inject. My extreme brittleness causes severe insulin reactions if I work too hard or don't eat enough. On the other hand, the difficulties of controlling glucose levels lead to the kinds of complications I am experiencing after almost forty years on insulin — deadened nerves, fragile and cracking skin, hemorrhaging in the eyes, failing kidneys and malfunctioning of the intestines, inability to heal after injuries, susceptibility to gangrene, deficient metabolism and resultant slowness and pain. How I long for a body that functions properly so that I wouldn't have to be adjusting all the time to new troubles, including my unrelated crippled leg, deafness, arthritis, and cancer!

However, I must honestly confess my gratitude for these snags because they remind me that life is a treasure to be stewarded and celebrated. I constantly need their reminder not to take all God's stupendous gifts for granted.

Revelation 4 points to the gift of life as one reason for praise. The progression leading to that conclusion, however, also suggests an important process for us to undergo so that we will value praise more deeply and enter into it with greater Joy.

The story begins with the seer John being invited into a new vision of that which lies on the other side of the door of heaven,[1] where he will be able to see the things that must necessarily happen "after this." There is no direct antecedent to this second use of the phrase "after this," whereas the first use of the phrase simply designates the timing of this vision after the dictating of the seven letters. Since the subsequent vision takes the seer to

---

1. Craig Koester points out that Revelation 3 ended with Christ knocking at the door and that the cycle of the seals begins with John being shown a door already standing open (4:1). As Koester remarks, "The contrast is provocative: as Christ asks the community to open their door to him, he opens heaven's door to them through John's prose" (*Revelation and the End of All Things* [Grand Rapids: Wm. B. Eerdmans Publishing Co., 2001], p. 71).

the heavens, we might assume that *this* refers to the time of trials, since the book is specifically addressed, as we have seen, to those who are suffering the tribulations of governmental persecution and societal alienation. After the time of testing, after the pain of this world, then all will be restored as we go through the door into the Joy of a perfect life in relationship with God.

Next the seer reports that, being immediately ushered in spirit into the heavens, he became aware of God's throne. How vital it is for us to catch visions of that throne to restore our perspectives in life on this side of the door.

We cannot properly learn to praise unless we begin at the throne, for praise is the recognition that God is there, worthy of our adoration, the ruler of our lives and all that is. True praise prevents us from focusing on ourselves. It is wonderfully theocentric.

John's description of the throne and its occupant is breathtaking — and yet terribly inadequate. No matter how splendiforously we might picture it, we could never capture the overwhelming magnificence of God's throne and the glory of divine presence in human, finite words — that's why I sometimes have to make them up! But the richness of the seer's inspired description here begins to capture for us (until we actually experience it in glory) the transcendence that we must discern to view the throne now with praise.

That the seer is using the best possible, yet inadequate, words to describe his vision is indicated by his reference to the aura around the throne as that of a rainbow like an emerald. Of course the rainbow was not just green, even as the One on the throne, pictured like jasper and carnelian, wasn't stony. These gems were the finest available images in the first century to describe indirectly the tremendous beauty and radiating brilliance of God.

The picture of a rainbow's shimmer around the LORD comes from Ezekiel 1:28 and reminds us of the entire context of the description there and its significance for the Jews in the Babylonian captivity. Here the seer has added the luster of the emerald to heighten our focus on God. Surely he was overwhelmed by the lushness of the vision that he had been privileged to see on the other side of the door.

Next he displays the population of that heavenly scene — twenty-four elders dressed in white garments and golden wreaths. The white garments are used throughout The Revelation to indicate perfection and purity (see

3:5 and 18; 6:11; 7:9 and 13; 19:14), and the golden wreaths remind us of royal splendor and victory. The vision of the elders with the ruler gloriously fulfills the promises in Revelation 2:10 (crowns), 3:5 (white robes), and 3:21 (to be at Christ's throne) and Isaiah 24:23 (the LORD's manifestation before the elders, but the number of elders is not given in that Hebrew text).

The number twelve is used frequently in The Revelation, especially in chapter 7, where it is multiplied by itself and used in connection with the names of Jacob's sons. The number always represents the people of God. Even as there were twelve tribes of Israel and Jesus had chosen twelve apostles, most likely to represent the continuation of the people of God, now the doubling of the number seems to indicate that these elders represent all of God's people, from both the first covenant (Israel) and the second (the Church).

The seer interrupts his description of the occupants of the throne room to comment again on its radiance and majesty, and that element of this chapter's style hints at the awe with which it was written because a vision of **GOD** is its subject. The literary montage reminds me of a child, full of great things to tell his mother, running into the house and crying out, "and then I saw this . . . and looked at that . . . and oh, yes, they were so big . . . , but wow, that was so wonderful!" The seer can hardly keep pace with his impressions as he jumps from the magnificence of the stones, to the rainbow radiance, to the golden-wreathed elders, to the lightning and thunder, to the strange-looking creatures. The vision stuns, with spiraling collages of divine splendor that human words can hardly begin to describe.

It is important to insert a note here about the nature of the biblical writings. So much contemporary theology accentuates the humanity of the Scriptures and raises great doubts about God's inspiration. The two components — human and divine — must be kept in dialectical tension. Certainly the Holy Spirit thoroughly inspired the apostles and prophets as they wrote, and the resultant books of the Bible are definitely God's Word to all people and authoritative for their lives.

On the other hand, the writers were not mechanical robots as they recorded the Lord's Word to us. Each writer's personality is evident; his style is unique. They wrote under the limitation of human words and invite us into their wonder at the infinity of God's majesty and grace. We jump into their awe and are astonished and speechless; we know the limits of human words to articulate our Joy and terror and delight.

The vision of the heavenly throne room in Revelation 4 makes us quake as Dorothy did in her first encounter with the Wizard of Oz, when she saw the lightning and heard the voices and thunder — but here there is no deceptive man behind the curtain pulling the levers. Instead there are seven torches blazing, representing the seven spirits of God (perhaps a reference to Isaiah 11). With its lightning and peals of thunder, the scene reminds us of the terrifying appearances of God on Mt. Sinai (see, e.g., Exod. 19:18), so it carries implications of *YHWH's* covenant relationship with the people of Israel. Finally, before the throne there is a sea of glass, which looks like rock crystal — an image from Ezekiel 1:22.

That reference from the First Testament gives us a hint at its reason, for the expanse is described there as "sparkling like ice and awesome." I remember seeing the bright vision of the Mendenhall glacier in Juneau, Alaska, on a sunny day, with all its glintings and gleamings of sparkling ice. Refracting and dancing all around my head, the myriad beams of light sent shafts of blazing glory through my whole body and filled me with wonder. Imagine the reflection of the heavenly throne's (that is, **GOD's**) brilliance from such an expanse of icy glass!

Next, the seer describes the four living creatures (again in images taken from Ezekiel 1) with faces like those of a lion, an ox, a man, and an eagle. This bizarre picture of four-faced creatures from Ezekiel is then combined with the drama of Isaiah 6, where the seraphim (literally, fiery beings) have six wings, are full of eyes, and sing throughout the day and night in resounding antiphony these words of praise: "Holy, holy, holy, LORD God the Almighty."

However, instead of declaring next that "the whole earth is full of his glory," as the song does in Isaiah 6, the song in The Revelation continues with a reminder that the Lord is the One who was and the One who is and the One who is to come — also an image from Isaiah, but from other sections of the prophecy. This song, therefore, reminds us again of the uniquely unchanging and incomprehensible nature of the eternal God whom we are worshiping. The fact that the four living creatures never cease to sing it suggests that we can't ever sufficiently praise God for all the fullness of Trinity, nor can we ever comprehend the meaning of divine infinity.

As the drama in Isaiah 6 continues, the prophet cannot cope with his experience of seeing the holy God. He responds, "Woe is me, for I am *annihilated* [Luther's emphasis], for I have seen the LORD." That is not the creatures' response here, for they don't have such a sense of shame and trepidation. Rather, the Revelation text shows their glad response of worship, giving the One upon the throne all the glory and honor and thanks. For our purposes now, we observe how much all the terms in this entire scene put into the center the One sitting upon the throne. God is celebrated as living into the aeons of the aeons and thereby perpetually receiving all the glory and honor and thanks that are due the exalted "I AM."

At this point all the elders are overwhelmed — they fall on their faces before the One upon the throne and offer their total reverence. They throw their wreaths before the throne because they know that truly the Lord God Almighty is the victor who deserves their crowns. Once again the text reminds us that this One upon the throne lives forever and ever — the Lord's eternity has been summarized three times already in as many verses.

This piling up of images is intended to create an atmosphere of great awesomeness, to immerse us in a profound sense of wonder at the privilege of our relationship with such a One, at the splendor of knowing the Lord who controls and surpasses time, even as we are limited by it now. We rejoice to be swept up into the song that fills the heavens and closes the scene in its exultation of the worthiness of the Lord our God.

All these images, stirring in us a heightened sense of mystery and magnificence, now culminate in the declaration of an outstanding reason why God is worthy of such praise. Surely all the accoutrements of the scene have prepared us for this splendor, but now the declaration is explicit. God is indeed worthy of our adoration because by His will all things were created. The idea of His creation here at the end of the Bible reminds us of the pictures of His ordering work at the beginning. This God who could bring existence out of the chaotic mass without form and full of nothingness (or vanity) is certainly worthy of our praising recognition of His power. Furthermore, the song declares that, having once given order and form, the Lord does not leave the creation to its own devices, but remains the means by which that creation has its being. By His will He sustains all life; by His grace He allows it to continue. The combination of a Greek aorist (once-for-all) declaration of creation with an imperfect (continuing) state of being reminds us that everything, from beginning to end and everywhere in between, is totally under the Lord God Almighty's perfect control.

Just as Tim's festoons of kidney valves gloriously display the wonder of a precious life kept alive by modern technology (which also serves God), so we each need this picture of the One on the throne, by whose will we are sustained, in order to put the gift of life into its proper perspective. One of the reasons why I value the feeble and the infirm and the elderly in my life is that they continually remind me of the fragility of our existence and our total dependence upon the Creator and Sustainer of life. Let none of us take these gifts for granted.

The One who sits upon the throne, the Holy One who was and is and always shall be, the One whose glorious magnificence heightens His claim upon our adoration, has by His most gracious will designed, brought into being, and sustained all creation. That is the first reason why we are invited by the seer to learn better to praise God. Our next chapter will give us an even more important reason.

CHAPTER 16

The Second Reason for Praise:
The Lamb Who Saves by Suffering

*(Please refer often to Revelation 5:1-14
as you study this chapter.)*

The inscrutable mystery baffled everyone. Only the redoubtable
Sherlock Holmes would be able to solve it, and then only with inten-
sive efforts and brilliant probing. He alone had the brain power to find the
murderer of the heiress.

The fifth chapter of The Revelation poses a much more difficult case
that requires an unparalleled kind of power. Near the throne, so magnifi-
cently described in the previous chapter, is a book sealed with the perfect
number (7) of seals. The book has been written on both inside and outside, so that it is full of sacred decrees, but no one is able to unlock its mysteries. No one has the authority to set open its contents.

Such a book was previously imaged in Ezekiel 2, where the prophet
was given a scroll written on both inside and out with words of lamenta-
tion and mourning and woe (2:9-10), and in Isaiah 29:11-12, where that
prophet speaks of a scroll that is sealed so that no one is able to read it.
The picture here in The Revelation might also hint at the end of the book
of Daniel, where the prophet is told to seal up the words of prophecy because they concern the distant future, which should not yet be known,
and at Psalm 139:16, which praises God for the fact that all the days of the
poet's life had been ordained before he was born and written in the
Lord's book.

Now in the seer's vision the call has gone out by the voice of a "strong
angel" for someone to open the scroll, but even the angel is not able to
break the seals. In all of heaven, all of the earth, and all of the underworld

there is no Sherlock Holmes able to undertake the task, the kind of work that is necessary to unlock the mystery.

One poignant aspect to note is the seer's reaction to this state of affairs. He is absolutely devastated by it. What a great tragedy it is that no one is able to unlock the secrets of the great scroll! The original Greek sentence emphasizes that the seer was crying vehemently because there was no one worthy. Remember that even the strength of the mighty angel who had called out was not sufficient. Creatures' power cannot unlock the secrets of the mysteries of the Creator. The task requires divine worthiness.

One of the twenty-four elders offers a comforting word. Indeed, there is One great enough to open the scroll, and that individual is described in terms of power and strength. He is named the victor (obviously One with power great enough to overcome all opposition) and the lion of the tribe of Judah. The lion is always associated with devastation of its prey and here fulfills Jacob's death-bed prediction (see Gen. 49:8-9) that Judah will have his hand upon the neck of his enemies because he is a lion's cub and, like a lion, crouches and lies down. Finally, the One who is able to open the scroll and its seals is called the root of David, which brings to mind all the promises that David's house would always rule over the nation of Israel, for his reign was the epitome of her history in terms of military strength and victory.

All these titles and the contexts from which they come in the First Testament prepare us for an image of great strength and daring and devastation of the enemy. We are not at all ready for the appearance of the One who is called worthy . . .

For He comes as a Lamb, and not only as such a gentle creature, but also as a Lamb that has been slain. Furthermore, the original Greek verb form underscores the thoroughness of that slaying; because the Lamb was once slaughtered, the benefits of that slaying remain for us. Thus, the Lamb's worthiness lies in what His suffering conveys. This Lamb, standing as One having been slaughtered, has seven horns (the perfect number of symbols of power) and seven eyes (having perfect insight and understanding), which are the seven spirits of God (a reference perhaps to the messianic expectation in Isaiah 11:1 that the LORD's shoot from the stump of Jesse will be endowed with the sevenfold spirit of God). With such divine endowment and sacrificial accomplishment, this One is able to take the scroll.

Because of the glaring contrast between the names "victor," "lion," and "root of Jesse" and their actual fulfillment in a Lamb who was slain, we are forced to recognize this major theme of the New Testament in its entirety and particularly in The Revelation: victory comes through sacrifice.

This theme is critically important in the twenty-first century, which primarily emphasizes victory through domination. We have certainly seen the demonic effects of demagogical power in the rise of Nazi tyranny, despotic communism, and some multinational corporations that dominate the global economy. Surely our society ought to be more afraid of power than it is. However, it seems that all who aspire to power think that it will not corrupt them, that they will be able to remain pure and in control.

Our society's history negates such an assumption. We have seen time and again that power corrupts, that it is virtually impossible to control by power alone without becoming controlled by it.[1] Yet at various points in history churches themselves have fallen into the great error of trying to find their place in the world through demonstrations of dominance. Consequently, we have seen the proliferation of wars fought in the name of Christ, the entrapment in power mongering of churches that were called by Jesus to be servants in the world. A critical contemporary issue with which Christians wrestle in lands formerly controlled by the communists is the question of how to deal with church leaders who allied themselves with the secret police in order to secure power.

As a contrast to the world's lust for power and control, this book pays special tribute to Linden and Tim. They have taught me the meaning of Christianity more deeply than brilliant theologians, for their sufferings teach what true victory is. In their courage and perseverance they exhibit more strength than those men caught up in their own machismo.

Think what would happen if we would get this straight in our churches: victory is won through sacrifice. Could we aspire to have, not the most conspicuous church building in the city, but one that also provides shelter for the homeless and meals for the hungry? How could our church communities invest ourselves more deeply in the lives of the poor and the dispossessed to teach them skills, to help them find health care and jobs? How could Christians secure land and the potential for self-sufficiency for

---

1. Perhaps all Christians should read J. R. R. Tolkien's *Lord of the Rings* trilogy to understand, from its potent descriptions, power's corruptions. See J. R. R. Tolkien, *The Fellowship of the Ring* (Boston: Houghton Mifflin, 1955); *The Two Towers* (Boston: Houghton Mifflin, 1955); and *The Return of the King* (Boston: Houghton Mifflin, 1955).

the disenfranchised? What would happen if God's people could truly enter into the situations of our neighbors in order to bring God's kingdom to slums, tenement houses, ghettos, the emptiness of riches, the struggles of the physically or mentally disabled?

A pastor friend of mine, who was unemployed for a while and is now ministering to street people, has known poverty from the inside. He has taught me a little of what it means to go hungry, though I recognize the deficiency of being only an observer. We need the dispossessed, the strugglers, the failures, the lonely, the alienated to teach us what it means that the Lamb was slain.

This became much clearer when a graduate school professor struggling with physical limitations grieved with me that no one in the academic ivory tower except a blind professor was able to listen to her pain. It often takes another disabled person truly to stand beside a handicapped person. The "victory, wealth, healing, and power" heresy that invades churches and the emphasis on academic self-sufficiency cause those who suffer to feel that they cannot match up to the requirements. Instead, the gift of weakness and trials is that they help us perceive the true meaning of faith in the Suffering Servant.

In Revelation 5 the fact that the Lamb has been slain calls forth profound adoration on the part of the elders and living creatures. Holding harps and golden bowls of the prayers of the saints (see Chapter 20 below), they burst out with a new song proclaiming the worthiness of this slain Lamb to receive the book and to open its seals. He is worthy because in His submission to the slaying He has brought back to God — by virtue of His sacrifice and death — people from every corner of the earth. The song uses a symbolic four to declare that persons from every tribe and tongue and people and nation are brought back to God by means of the Lamb's sacrifice.

Gathering the laundry provides an image for understanding the scriptural use of symbolic fours to indicate universality. I collect all the clothes and towels by piling them on top of the bedsheet. Then it is easy to grab all four corners, pull them toward the center, and make a sack out of the sheet to hold everything. In the same way, the ancient use of a symbolic four imagined picking up the whole world by its corners so that nothing earthly was missed. Thus, the description in Revelation 5:9 emphasizes that persons from every part of the world were purchased for God by the blood of the slain Lamb.

Once again let us pause before this expression of praise to take stock of the situation in contemporary churches. Could it be that U.S. churches are not bringing in people from every nation because we have lost the essential focus on the One who was slain? Furthermore, is our evangelism weak because we are not willing to submit our lives to the slaying and sacrifice that make true witness possible? To be followers of Jesus means that we are willing to suffer for others as He did.

The elders and living creatures fall before the mystery of it all. In grateful reverence they acknowledge that this sacrifice is what has enabled the people of God to be a kingdom and priests who will rule upon the earth (see also comments about Rev. 1:6; 3:21; and 20:4). We must take special note of this: our ruling is made possible by the Lamb's suffering. The Church is not to seek control by means of earthly power, but to rule by virtue of Christ's sacrifice for others and our devotion to the Lamb that was slain.

The rest of Revelation 5 records the tremendous crescendo of praise that comes in response to this worthiness. The many angels around the throne who join in this paean of praise number in the thousands upon thousands, the myriads upon myriads. Undoubtedly, these multiples of ten carry symbolic weight, for ten indicates totality/completion. Thus, the suggestion of totalities times totalities impresses us with the uncountable grandiosity of the angelic choir.

I formerly used the word *skillions* to describe it, but then a mathematician friend taught me about googols (10 with 100 zeros behind it) and googolplexes (10^{googol}), numbers which still can't come close to the reality of heavenly praise! All the creatures of all time and all space resound with a great voice that the slain Lamb is worthy to receive their adoration. All power, wealth, wisdom, strength, honor, glory, and blessing (notice the perfect seven!) belong to Him.

This song is especially poignant for me whenever I read it because Lutheran liturgies include magnificent settings of these words as the hymn of praise, "This Is the Feast of Victory for Our God." One setting in particular uses a constantly running base line on the organ pedals and a majestically marching melody to heighten the awe and splendor of the scene. When I sing this part of the liturgy I wish my voice were as great as myriads of trumpets or that I could play a 95-rank organ and hit all the right pedals — but even then my feeble praises would be grossly inadequate.

In verse 13 the praise crescendos once again, as now all the living creatures from the universal four places — the heavens, the earth, under the earth, and the sea — are added to the swelling choir. Once again they sing a new song, this time with a refrain of these four (universal) elements of attribution: blessing, honor, glory, and dominion belong to Him forever and ever (literally, "into the aeons of the aeons"). It will take us all eternity to praise the Lamb for His worthiness, and even then we will have just begun.

Those who think heaven will be boring if all we do is sit around playing harps and praising God have never experienced the exquisite pleasure of playing a harp. A friend built for me a lovely 39-string Celtic harp, which delightfully offers endless variations of new things to play. I can hardly imagine that an eternity of praising God could ever be boring, for when we know God face to face we will never run out of new attributes to praise. (Perhaps I can learn to play the French horn, the cello, and the flute then — and, of course, all the other instruments that we haven't even seen yet!)

After this second song of praise in chapter 5 the living creatures cry out, "AMEN!" — surely it shall be so! — and fall down once again in reverence and worship. At first this verse might seem redundant, but commentaries note that this is the first time the "Amen" is added. Now *every creature* has joined in the praise. When we imagine the scene and think about the colossal privilege of praising Christ for His victory through sacrifice, how could we not be filled again and again with wonder and adoration?

The truth of the scene was profoundly brought home to me once during a time when I had greatly failed in human relationships. During a horrendously busy time in graduate school, I virtually stopped communicating with my friends far away on the West Coast. I was curt with them and perhaps even nasty sometimes on the phone, and yet those friends (including the one who is now my husband) continued to love me. What incredible grace! When I now remember that dreadful month, I am amazed anew. What an unfathomable gift of love — I shall never quite be able to understand its breadth and height. When I multiply that awareness by the googolplexes, I realize that I've just begun to imagine the extent of the love manifested in the sacrifice of the Lamb who was slain, and I know that I shall never get tired of learning new songs to praise Him. Truly we will say "Amen, Amen!" a skillion times and still know that we have barely begun to appreciate how the slain Lamb really has accomplished such a redemption, how He has made us into a kingdom and priests. Will we ever really know what that means? Will we ever get tired of praising Him for it? Perhaps we'd better begin now. My face touches the ground in worship.

CHAPTER 17

Don't Forget the First Horse of the Apocalypse!

(Please refer often to Revelation 6:1–7:8 and 19:11-21
as you study this chapter.)

At the height of the Cold War between the U.S. and the U.S.S.R., there was enough nuclear stuff in our world to blow it up entirely at least thirty-five times. (It seems to me that once is more than enough!) When I first wrote this chapter, leaders of the world were gathering in a conference concerning chemical weapons. It was really scary to think of what could happen if some of them got out of control. Wars raged in many parts of the earth — civil war in Mozambique, Israeli oppression and the first Palestinian *intifada,* conflict in Northern Ireland, the Khmer Rouge devastation of Cambodian peasants, the intervention of Contras against Sandinistas in Nicaragua, and civil war in El Salvador — to name just a few that were taking place when this book was first written. (Grimly, some of those same conflicts still persist twenty years later.) The devastation is enormous; the cost in human lives, outrageous.

Meanwhile, wars contribute to economic chaos. The U.S., with its massive national debt, has become the largest debtor nation in the world. Many Two-Thirds World countries pay more in interest on their loans than they can afford, so they go more and more deeply into arrears. The former Soviet Union is in economic shambles, with little hope for recovery, because of the devastating cost to the peoples there of maintaining the arms race. With poorly maintained infrastructures, the communist experiment did not provide adequate means for transporting and preserving harvests, so the people suffer extensively from hunger. Meanwhile, the amount spent throughout the world on military equipment and personnel in one day is equal to the cost of feeding, clothing, and housing the entire world for a year. New weapons continue to be constructed to destroy, while 40,000 people die each day of malnutrition and related diseases.

And then there is the plague of AIDS. As I write, no cure has yet been found for this inevitably terminal illness. When I first wrote this chapter, AIDS was the leading cause of death for women between the ages of 25 and 34 in New York City; now, in 2002, 17 million in Africa have already died of AIDS and another 25 million are HIV positive. In some countries, more than one in every four adults is infected, and 12 million children have lost their parents to AIDS. AIDS has touched us all. The world epidemic is scary. We wonder if we will be infected, perhaps while receiving a blood transfusion or while caring for an AIDS patient.

How can we face this world's situation — with wars, economic chaos, and epidemics facing us on every side? What does it mean to be a Christian in all this mess?

It seems that everybody has heard of the four horses of the Apocalypse, but few have paid enough attention to the white horse and its rider. The original readers of The Revelation faced the same three terrifying enemies that we do — wars, economic disasters, and epidemics/deaths — and the seer wrote to comfort them in the face of all these terrors with the assurance that these three forces alone do not control the development of history.

Do not forget that there are four horses in Revelation 6 and that the white one reappears in chapter 19. Do not forget that the central message of the whole book is that Jesus is Lord — over the entire cosmos!

We see here for the first time the interlocking patterns of The Revelation (see further exposition in Chapters 20 and 22). The seven seals begin with the four horses and end with an awesome silence throughout the heavens. It is important to grasp a larger view of this series than can be gained by focusing simply on the horses themselves. They are part of a greater picture that also includes the sealing of the saints and profound worship by all who observe. These other aspects of the seals remind us that the three horses of war, economics, and plagues do not have the last word in history. Their machinations and manipulations do not threaten God's sovereignty.

It is also significant that the white horse appears first. In most cultures and languages the places of emphasis are at the beginning and at the end. We don't put the most important things in the middle where they might get lost. In the sequence of the seven seals, the white horse comes first, and the adoration of all of heaven comes last. These symbols of God's sovereignty frame the other elements of the series.

Most scholars are convinced that the meaning of the white horse is the same as that of the other three horses, that its purposes are those of the demonic powers. Since The Revelation never clearly identifies the rider of the first horse, and since the first four trumpets seem to be a restatement of the same themes as the first four seals, sometimes I start to agree that this first rider is a force for evil along with the other three.[1]

However, several elements of the description convince me that the first rider is the Christ (even though it is the Lamb Who opens the seal). First, the four horses are all introduced by one of the creatures saying, "Come!" but only the creature who announces the white horse has a voice like thunder — singular and plural Greek forms of which are used in other key descriptions in The Revelation. This list helps us to see its thrust:

The word *thunder* (singular in Greek) is used in 14:2, where it describes the voice from heaven, while the seer looked at the Lamb that was slain and the 144,000 He had sealed, and also here in 6:1. In chapter 14 the first angel that appears announces an eternal gospel, and the second angel announces Babylon's fall. So here the first seal presents the horse of Christ, while the next three horses are destructive.

The word *thunders* (plural in Greek) appears in 4:5, 8:5, 11:19, and 19:6, which relate to the throne of God, the actions of God, the temple of God, and the people of God, respectively. The word is also used in 10:3 and 4, related to God's messages spoken by an angel (which the seer was not permitted to record), and 16:18, where thunders occur just after the voice from the throne says "It is done!" and God vents wrath on Babylon.

---

1. Craig Koester is the most persuasive, because he links the first horse with the Parthian threats in 53 B.C., 36 B.C., and A.D. 62, which brought Roman expansion to a halt (*Revelation and the End of All Things* [Grand Rapids: Wm. B. Eerdmans Publishing Co., 2001], pp. 83-84 and 175-78). He calls the threat of this horseman "conquest by a foreign power." However, I do not see too much difference between that sort of warring (with a bow) and "the violence that can erupt within one's own society," symbolized by the sword of the second horseman. Arguments for picturing Christ as the first rider seem equally strong in matching the details in the actual text and the seer John's purposes of comforting.

The final occurrence at the seventh bowl (16:17) seems to match the thunder at the first horseman and give us another example of the Alpha and Omega. This is a strong argument for that rider being Christ, for the Word was in the beginning (in The Revelation with the first seal in that first set of three sevens), and in 16:18 the thunders accompany the statement, "It is done!" (as the last of the bowls in that last set of three sevens). The conquest introduced in 6:2 is complete with the Fall of Babylon in 16:17-21.

Also, the language of "conquering" is usually used in The Revelation in connection with Christ and His followers. At the beginning of the Apocalypse, every one of the seven letters to the churches ends with a promise to those who conquer in following Christ (2:7, 11, 17, 28; 3:5, 12, 21). Revelation 5:5-6 emphasizes that the Lion is able to open the seven seals because the Lamb "conquered" by being slaughtered.

Furthermore, the description of the white horse is significantly abbreviated in comparison with that of the other horsemen since the kind of conquest he does is not displayed at all. In contrast, the second horseman is "permitted" to take peace from the earth, and the third's effect on economic conditions is announced. Then the fourth, Death, is "given authority" along with Hades over a fourth of the earth to kill by the sword (the work of the second horseman), by famine (the work of the third), and by pestilence (his own work). In this final summary again the work of the first horseman is not mentioned — I think because it will be elaborated in chapter 19.

Finally, *only* the white horse and its rider reappear in chapter 19, and there all of the details refer specifically to the rider as Christ. We will discuss that portrait more thoroughly at the end of this chapter, but here we must note this crowning title rendered Him in chapter 19: King of kings and Lord of lords. Applying that title to the same rider in chapter 6 reminds us that, though other forces in the world seem to be in control, still Christ is Lord over all; He is never absent and is still conquering, even while the powers of evil seem to reign. All these other forces cannot get out of the hand of God's sovereignty.

The other forces are awful indeed. Certainly the fiery red horse of war has dominated history. Jesus warned us of that when He said that there would be wars and rumors of wars until the end of the age (Matt. 24:6-8; Mark 13:7-8). These are not the signs of the end; they are the signs of the times. Throughout the history of fallen humankind there have been all sorts of conflicts and wars. They keep reminding us that this is not God's will for the world, that human beings have violated divine designs and continue to destroy God's creation. Greatly contrary to those who think that a nuclear war might usher in the end of time, this text suggests that the fiery horse of war must be kept distinct from the plan of God. Human beings slay each other. God certainly never intended the well-created world to be at war!

The black horse of economic disorder comes next. (Though not its intention in The Revelation, the horse's color painfully reminds me that minority peoples in the U.S. suffer disproportionately from the economic injustice of our society.[2]) The voice among the living creatures tells us how bad it is — one can get only a small amount of wheat or barley for a full day's wages. This is certainly true in many poverty-stricken lands today. The final command not to damage the oil and wine suggests that only God's sovereignty prevents the world from being entirely overwhelmed by economic disaster.

The fourth seal discloses the pale sickly horse of Death with Hades following. These forces have caused destruction (it is important to note here that they are limited to a fourth of the earth) by means of sword, famine, plague, and the wild beasts of the earth. If we modernized the first three of those four destructive elements (symbolizing universal causes of death), we might list racial riots and ethnic cleansings as examples of war, welfare cutbacks and Two-Thirds World debt as examples of economic disaster, and AIDS as an example of a plague. I wonder what we might call the "wild beasts" of our times — maybe killer ants and bees or cancer cells out of control?

The fifth seal (6:9-11) is such an important interruption of this scene of the four horses that we will save a fuller explication for the following chapter and only mention briefly here its significance as a reminder that believers will always participate along with the rest of the world in the sufferings inflicted by the three evil horsemen. In addition, they suffer for their testimony concerning the first horseman. They ask for God to judge and avenge their blood, and that plea introduces the results of the sixth seal.

The sixth seal, indeed, gives a strong description of the terrors that will appear when God comes. Biblical depictions of a theophany (i.e., the coming of God) are used — images from Sinai and Egypt — but our focus is immediately drawn to the people who flee from God's appearing.

2. See David P. Gushee, "Race," in *Christian Ethics as Following Jesus*, ed. Glen M. Stassen and David P. Gushee (Downers Grove, IL: InterVarsity Press, forthcoming).

The sketch includes all of the earth's powerful — the kings, the great men, the commanders, the rich, the strong, the free men — with only one word signifying the humble, the slave. Certainly the list illustrates that people from all walks of life will flee from God's wrath, but the proportion of words might also indicate that the power and wealth of the mighty make them more susceptible to trusting themselves rather than turning to God.

Immediately after the record of their fleeing and seeking shelter (the description of which again utilizes many passages from the First Testament, which you could find in commentaries or cross-reference Bibles), chapter 7 moves to the sealing of God's people, the 144,000. The first three verses of the chapter emphasize that the angels are prevented from bringing totally annihilating wrath upon the earth (or the sea and trees) until the Lord's people are made secure.

Consequently, there is a dramatic switch from seals of destruction to a sealing that gives hope. This is another reason why I think the first horseman is Christ. God's sovereign care undergirds all the processes of history, even though powers of evil wreak their devastating havoc.

The list of those sealed given in 7:5-8 is certainly intended to be symbolic. First, it begins with Judah, who was not the oldest son of Jacob (and therefore is never named first in the Hebrew lists), but who was the forefather of the tribe from which the Savior came, thus implying a notion of grace. Secondly, the list does not contain Dan, most likely to emphasize that that tribe's horrendous sins were utterly contrary to God's purposes.

However, there must be twelve tribes of twelve thousand each to emphasize that all of God's people are there — since twelve brings to mind both Israel and the disciples, and 1,000 is a number of multiplied completeness. Consequently, the number of tribes named is kept intact by including in the list both Joseph (v. 8) and Manasseh (v. 6), Joseph's son.

The list emphasizes that it is not by birthright (since the list doesn't follow the ordering in the Hebrew Scriptures of the twelve sons of Israel) nor by accomplishment (since they are sealed by God) that anyone is preserved from the destruction of God's wrath. Only by grace are we part of the elect, the number of which is certainly not limited to 144,000, as we shall see in the following chapter.

Now we can return to the four horses, for the first one mentioned briefly in chapter 6 must have more of a role than only riding out as a conqueror bent on conquest. In chapter 19 we meet this horse and rider conquering.

There the rider is described with all sorts of images used earlier in The Revelation and with names that enable us to know with certainty that the rider is Christ. He is called the Word of God (an appellation that links us to the portrait at the beginning of the Gospel of John), the Faithful (used in 1:5) and True (all names that remind us of His character and draw us into deeper trust), and the King of kings and Lord of lords (titles that speak of the power and authority that He is about to demonstrate).

What is most important for us to note about the final war in Revelation 19 is that it isn't a war. In contrast to all the interpretations of The Revelation that specialize in painting lurid scenes of the end of the world, the text says simply that all the kings of the earth who had assembled to make war against Christ were killed with the sword that came out of His mouth — that is, the Word. The beast and the false prophet, who have deceived all the people into worshiping the demonic powers, are thrown into the lake of fire, and the dragon himself, the Devil or Satan, is thrown into the abyss (20:1-3). When he is released after the thousand years for a short time, he will try again to deceive the nations and gather them together for war, but once again they will be easily dispensed with (and by no human effort). Fire from heaven will devour all the nations, and the Devil will be thrown into the lake of fire along with the beast and false prophet (vv. 7-10).

In other words, the final end of evil will be easily accomplished — because, as is recorded in other places (such as Col. 2:13-15) as well as in The Revelation, Christ has already conquered the principalities and powers at the cross and empty tomb. He is already King of kings and Lord of lords.

This is underscored by the fact that in Revelation 6 Christ rides out with the other three horses as influences upon history, but, in the end, He is the only one still riding. Other forces of history — other rulers and authorities — might think they are having a great influence, but their truly feeble power is dismissed with one or two verses. The rider of the white horse, on the other hand, comes again to conquer ultimately and to save eternally.

How we can live in the light of this fact is the subject of the next chapter. If Christ is King of kings and Lord of lords already, what does that mean for our suffering now?

CHAPTER 18

Endurance: The Meaning of Biblical Patience

*(Please refer often to Revelation 6:9-11 and 7:9, 13-15
as you study this chapter.)*

Advertisements for pain remedies promise faster relief than that of their competitors. All the problems on television situation comedies are solved in only half an hour. Surely we live in an age of instant fixes and gratifications. Tragically, as Christians become more and more enculturated, they begin to demand instant spiritual gratification, too.

That is why I have chosen these two texts from consecutive chapters of The Revelation to illustrate the biblical concept of patience, though that word is not used in these passages. The people of the church at Ephesus were commended for their perseverance, as were the folks from Thyatira (see 2:2-3 and 19). In those places the Greek word *hupomonē* is used. Understanding this word properly is essential for a biblical theology of weakness.

The original Greek word is composed of the preposition *hupo*, which means "under," and *monē*, which comes from the verb meaning "to remain." The biblical concept of *hupomonē* carries this connotation of being able to remain under or continuing to bear up under difficult circumstances — not just a patience until things change, but a remaining-under perseverance made possible by the knowledge that the Lord is there with us!

When I pray in the midst of the frustrations of chronic illness, I cannot pray only to have patience until God changes my body and makes everything easy. If that is what I expect, then I would have run out of patience long ago. Rather, biblical patience means to bear up, even if the situation never changes, even if it becomes worse, because Christ is there in the midst of the anguish to comfort and to guide and to continue His work of healing.

How precious this concept is when we minister to those with physical challenges or struggle with them ourselves! I do believe, and have even experienced, that at times God grants miraculous healing — and that we do not ask often enough for such interventions. However, in many situations we are left with the "thorn in the flesh," and how then can we understand the Lord's sovereignty? If God is all powerful and good, why aren't we healed?

Theologians have wrestled with that question ever since Job, and it won't contribute much for our purposes here to hash through all the answers. Instead, it is critically important for us to note the lesson that these sections from The Revelation can teach us about biblical patience — about patience especially when we don't have any answers.

Notice that when the fifth seal is broken (6:9-10) the ones having been slaughtered and waiting beneath the altar cry out to ask how long — but they are not given the answer that deliverance will come soon. Rather, they are told that they must wait while others also are martyred. Their fellow servants, their brothers and sisters, too, are going to be killed.

As we skip ahead now to the next chapter of The Revelation, we see these same persons from the other side — after the time of persecution is complete. In 7:9 they are the ones who gather before the throne of the Lamb dressed in white robes and carrying palms of victory in their hands.

The symbolism of this picture is probably familiar to all of us — white robes, signifying purity and victory, and palm branches, used even as they were on Palm Sunday to welcome the king with royal splendor. Furthermore, the text uses the symbolic number four to describe the groups out of which these saints came — from every ethnic group and nation and people and language.

Remember the illustration of the symbolic four and gathering the laundry. Here, then, the description of ethnic groups, nations, peoples, and languages emphasizes that persons from every part of the earth are included in the multitude of the saints who have washed their robes and made them white. Such groupings of fours are often used throughout the Scriptures, but especially in The Revelation, to emphasize universality, to remind us that the whole world or every earthly possibility is represented in the collection.

In Revelation 7:10 the saints rightfully acknowledge that salvation belongs to God. The passage underscores the point once again that they are not being honored for their expertise in being faithful, but that God is faithful to give them the gift of the crown of life.

After another song with seven elements (but in a different set from the song in Rev. 5:12) and the customary refrains ("forever and ever, Amen"), we find next a typical element in prophetic literature. The elder asks the seer the question, "Who are the ones clothed in white robes, and from where do they come?" Such a device is used to heighten interest in the answer to the question. The seer reports his ignorance by asserting instead that the angel who asked the question knows.

The angel's answer to his own question is accentuated by a difference in verb forms that highlights the hope we have in our suffering. When the text says that they have washed their robes and made them white, the verbs are decisive, once-for-all verbs. The action of becoming dressed with the garments of salvation is a decisive, once-for-all event.

Coming through the tribulation, on the other hand, is a process in which the seer John himself was participating. The use of a present-tense verb for "saints who come" gives us confidence that someday we, too, will join those saints who have arrived at the other side. We have, indeed, already washed our robes and become dressed in the garments of salvation in our baptism, but that does not mean that our problems are automatically ended. The Lamb justifies us and creates our relationship with Him in the washing of the robes, and the hope of eventually coming through the tribulation gives us courage for living in it.

The text says that these coming out of the great tribulation — which perhaps meant originally their suffering at the hands of a persecutor — are right now serving the Lord day and night in His temple. Moreover, someday the One who dwells on the throne will tabernacle upon them. This passage underscores the already-but-not-yet-ness of the Trinity's promises. Already to some extent God's kingdom has come to our world, but not yet has God fully tabernacled upon us. The promise of thorough tabernacling — God's total reign — is still to be fulfilled.

A very compelling biblical concept is introduced by the Greek word for *tabernacle* (translated "tent" in the NIV and "shelter" in the NRSV) in Revelation 7:15. Many years ago my M.Div. thesis work led me to discover that this word reveals a vitally illuminating aspect of a theology of weakness.[1]

To understand biblical weakness more completely, let us think about

---

1. This biblical/theological discovery is explicated thoroughly in chapter 2 of Marva J. Dawn, *Powers, Weakness, and the Tabernacling of God* (Grand Rapids: Wm. B. Eerdmans Publishing Co., 2001).

God's tabernacling (or the way in which the Lord "pitches tent") in three different verb tenses — past, present, and future. Three important passages guide our consideration of these terms. In the *past*, "the Word became flesh and tabernacled among us" (a literal translation of John 1:14). At a particular point in history, this most amazing thing occurred: God Himself became one of us as Christ pitched His tent in our midst. The text goes on to say that when the divine Word so entered into our situation, we humans were able for the first time to behold God's glory, full of grace and truth. We saw it in the person of Jesus, as He "pitched His tent" and lived a fully human (yet thoroughly divine) existence among us.

Now here in Revelation 7 we read that someday God will tent among us again. The verb is a *future*-tense verb — the Lord hasn't yet tabernacled totally among us as this world still remains and saints still come through persecutions. Rather, it is a promise for the early Christians — and us — to anticipate trustfully. Someday the Trinity will manifestly dwell in our midst.

The verb's *present*-tense use is especially significant for our purposes here, for how God can tabernacle upon us in the present is a truth full of surprises. We read about it in Paul's second letter to the Corinthians.

In 2 Corinthians 12, Paul describes his situation of suffering from a thorn in the flesh. In three periods of asking the Lord to remove that thorn he received the answer that God's grace was sufficient for all his needs. A thorough exegetical study reveals that the next phrase should perhaps not be translated with the usual English rendition of God's answer as "my power is made perfect in weakness." The Greek verb translated "made perfect" is the verb *teleō*, which is interpreted to mean some sort of ending or being "brought to the finish" in every other place it occurs in the New Testament. The verb that would be translated "made perfect" is the slightly expanded verb *teleioō*. Significantly, the simpler verb is used in this place. Furthermore, there is no pronoun *my* in the original Greek text. Therefore, the phrase could instead be translated, "for power is brought to its end in weakness." Then Paul's next sentence would logically follow: "All the more gladly, accordingly, will I glory rather in my weakness, in order that the power of Christ [instead of my own feeble power, which has ended] will tabernacle in me!"

This translation, "power is brought to its end in weakness," underscores more clearly why grace is sufficient for us in thorny times. When we give up our own feeble power and let it be finished in weakness, then God's grace can work more thoroughly on us, and in us, and through us. As long as we are capable of doing things on our own, we never thoroughly realize the power of God at work in us. But when weakness makes us incapable of doing what we would like to do, then we no longer struggle out of our feeble power. Then Christ can conform us to His Father's will. Then we are a submitted vessel in the Spirit's hands.

All of this leads up to the point of this chapter on the biblical concept of patience, for next (2 Cor. 12:9b) Paul says that he will all the more gladly boast about his weakness because then the power of Christ tabernacles upon him. In this instance, the verb that Paul chooses is the verb "to tabernacle," but with the preposition *epi* added to the front of it. *Epi* usually signifies some sort of "approaching toward or upon" something, so the verb here seems to limit God's tabernacling in us now. We miss Christ's tabernacling presence and power if we obstruct Him with our own efforts. We are never quite weak and dependent enough — our sinful natures want to accomplish our salvation and sanctity by our own efforts. But when we can acknowledge and live from our weakness, God tabernacles upon us!

Thus, just as Jesus once came and tabernacled among us in the human form of His incarnation (John 1:14), and just as God will someday perfectly tabernacle among us at the last day (Rev. 7:15), even so Christ tabernacles upon us now in our weakness! When our power is brought to its finish, we will learn the sufficiency of the Triune God's grace and the powerful presence of the Holy Spirit's dwelling in us.

This biblical truth totally throws overboard the whole contemporary emphases on winning, being number one, self-sufficiency, or having the most power. Greatly to our surprise, it is not in our competency or capability that God can tabernacle among us. It is in our weakness. In our limitations, in the times when we are suffering or coming through great tribulations, we can best experience Christ's presence.

The implications of this truth are enormous. Whereas our society tends to be impressed with extraordinary buildings, refined DVD and Web productions, dazzling special effects, and lots of pizzazz, the promise of God's tabernacling invites us to enter instead into homeless shelters, refugee camps, convalescent centers, ghettos, soup kitchens, prisons, and homes for the insane and retarded. By participating in the suffering of those who are weak, we learn the sufficiency of God's grace.

For example, I think often of Clifford, a man who suffered from muscular dystrophy and yet who served all the people around him in the convalescent center that was his home. Whenever I came with my guitar to sing for patients, he would direct me to the rooms of specific people who needed special attention — and he knew in each case which hymns were their favorites!

Or I think of my swimming friend, Perry. One day in the pool, I was on the verge of tears from the pain and from trying to face how much my body has deteriorated since the days when I was a competitive swimmer. I asked Perry how he could keep going on, and he answered with his customary gentle kindness, encouraging me not to give up altogether. And Perry has only one arm!

Similarly, my friends Linden and Tim often usher me into the presence of God. Sometimes I even imagine how God's tabernacle sits around their wheelchair and dialysis machine.

In a technological society that emphasizes strength and efficiency and, therefore, has little patience, the Christian community has great gifts to offer in our recognition of the sufficiency of grace in weakness and in our care for those who suffer. By pointing to the tabernacling of God in weakness we can encourage and honor those in our midst who are enduring various kinds of tribulation. By inviting them to teach classes or to give witness in a worship service, we could make better use of the gifts and awarenesses of those who have known God's presence most deeply in their limitations. All of us need to understand more thoroughly a patience that does not wait for things to change but instead recognizes that "remaining under" is the way to find the presence of God in new ways.

When I was first struggling with the permanent (but not eternal!) crippling of my left leg, many well-intentioned people kept asking if my foot was better, even though I had already deliberately told them that the bones had healed crookedly. Their frequent questions made me feel not acceptable because I was not making progress. The situation made me aware that many who already suffer from chronic illness or worsening handicaps suffer even more from the comments of those who want an instant fix. Instead, let us find ways in our Christian communities to encourage those with physical challenges to discover in their limitations extra opportunities for learning about the sufficiency of God's grace and the power of Christ's tabernacling.

When we remember in our Christian communities the biblical concept of patience, we are better able to care for those with various kinds of struggles, debilitating handicaps, mental or emotional disabilities, and chronic diseases. We will more effectively support them if, as they endure circumstances that might not change, we can point to our God who still tabernacles. As we participate together in sufferings and face the challenges of weaknesses, we will all learn what it truly means to be patient because God dwells with us.

CHAPTER 19

The Third Reason for Praise: Hope for the Future

(Please refer often to Revelation 7:9-17
as you study this chapter.)

Why is the world so grossly unfair? The rich keep getting richer, the poor keep getting poorer, and the gap between the two keeps escalating exponentially. How can it be that tyrannical governments, the policies of some multinational corporations, ethnic rivalries, and wars and the catastrophes they precipitate cause such immense destructions of human life and well-being? Meanwhile, as this book has primarily noted, many people suffer inordinately with handicaps, chronic illnesses, and tragedies. How can God let these things happen? God sometimes seems so cruel to allow such evil and suffering to exist in the world.

There are no easy answers. We know some things, but theologians and philosophers never thoroughly solve the mystery. Obviously, we live in a world marred by sin and ignorance, greed and cruelty. God's purposes for the whole creation are thwarted time and again. Sometimes Christians must even be willing to *choose* to suffer to be faithful to biblical principles. It all seems unfair; the global tragedies and personal pain at times threaten to drown us.

I regularly receive many telephone calls and letters from people pouring out their struggles and sorrow and pain. I can't understand why God allows such grief. In the words of the poet, definitely "the world is too much with us."

In the midst of the world's despair, the seventh chapter of The Revelation offers the only genuine hope. Not only does it picture the eventual triumph of biblical saints who experienced terrible sufferings and yet came through the tribulation, but also this chapter gives us the third major reason for praise (besides the gifts of life and the Lamb): that someday all the world's tears, too, will end, and suffering will be gone forever. Certainly we all look forward to that day with eager anticipation. Surely we are all too tired of all the pain in this world. So many people have sufferings beyond their ability to cope. Everything seems so out of control.

Because of the immensity of all the world's pain, we must beware of the ready danger of oversimplifying the text before us, of merely saying that we can endure the troubles we have now because someday God will take us away from this vale of tears to a place where there is only Joy. To look *only* to the future without acknowledging the pain of the present is to dump an empty gospel on those who suffer. Such a line is easily misused by those who do not want to participate in God's work to bring healing to the world.

Personally, I hate that kind of canned comfort, which merely pats us on the back and says, "Wait till heaven and then it will all be better." Such a response doesn't begin to touch the depth of trauma in people's suffering. It is cruel to ignore or trivialize someone's present anguish by simply saying that when we get to heaven it will be better. "Pie in the sky by and by when we die" does not truly help us cope with the endless round of struggles and woes in this life.

So how can this page from The Revelation help? The secret lies in comprehending with the patience of the previous chapter that the eternal has already begun in God's sealing assurance. Eternal hope isn't merely pie in the sky. Rather, God lets us taste it here in the gift of the Holy Spirit's seal and Christ's presence.

The eternal hope was made possible, we continue to remember, by the Lamb who entered into the world's suffering and was Himself slain. By and in this mercy, the sorrow of the world and the powers of evil that cause it are overcome, and the beloved of God are sealed in His grace to be His own and to be brought to eternal life in His presence.

In the beginning of Revelation 7, the seer is told the number of those who have the seal of God on their foreheads — 12,000 from each of the twelve tribes. The repetition of the number 12,000 twelve times reminds us forcefully that all the people of God will be sealed since 12 stands for God's covenant people and 1,000 is the number of completion (10) multiplied by itself a divine (3) number of times. Certainly such divinely complete chosenness emphasizes powerfully that not one of God's people will be missed in this effective seal!

The fact that we are sealed is recorded in the Greek perfect tense, which accentuates how, once God's people are decisively sealed, this guarantee remains in effect. Moreover, the deliberate listing of the names of each of the tribes and their numbers underscores how well God specifically knows His people — Jesus told us that He knows them each by name — but it is a symbolic number and list to emphasize that the crowd is greater than can really be imagined.

A seal in biblical times (as well as ours) indicated the security of any official document — the authenticity, ownership, and protection of the one who imprints his seal. This mark of assurance is what can give us comfort in the meanwhile as we await the fulfillment of God's promise to take away all our tears.

As we wrestle with various problems in our lives, we realize again and again that our deepest needs are satisfied by the present sealing of God. We long for the authenticating support of a Savior who values us, who urges us in His Word to do what we are capable of doing but sometimes doubt, who will stand beside us in the hard times. We ardently desire the commitment of a Lord who owns us, not in the nasty sense of fate or coercion, but in the loving sense of providing for all our needs and making it possible for us to become all that He designed us to be. We yearn for the security of being protected — especially if we face continued struggle with physical or emotional ailments. All these things are hinted at by the seal of God.

At various points in life, we agonize over such trials as loneliness, the limitations of handicaps, the frustrations and failures of community and vocation and family life. If we keep things on the surface, ignore the reality of present suffering, and instead comfort each other merely with glib statements that someday it will all be better, we fail to offer the very resource that should be most helpful in our sufferings. In fact, sometimes the comfort that Christians unthinkingly offer each other is frighteningly destructive.

The fact that the end of Revelation 7 asserts that someday the saints will not hunger or thirst any more or that the sun will not beat down upon them indicates that now they might be suffering from hunger or thirst or heat exhaustion (especially if persecution rendered them impoverished). Our solace to others must acknowledge in a healthy tension both sides of this dialectical reality: the *future* freedom from the *present* struggles. Contrary to our expectations that life should be easier, the fact is that we will most likely continue to suffer in this present world, especially *because* of our faith and testimony.

The theology of weakness that dominates The Revelation provides a way to keep both sides of the dialectic in balance. As one who himself suffered, the seer John offered visions of hope to those in tribulation. Our experience of struggles teaches us what kind of comfort really ministers to those newly entering into pain or overwhelmed by its constant proliferation.

The best way we can help each other in the suffering is to acknowledge its existence as an indelible part of our being in a world that has been marred by sin and human destructiveness — to lament with the Psalms over the seeming absence of God. We are much more able to fight the effects of sin if we are able to acknowledge its bitter reality more thoroughly. Then we are not so surprised and thwarted by the failure of our efforts to change things. We are able to keep on being faithful because the failures don't daunt us. We know that they occur in an evil world where pain is inevitable.

Nevertheless, this requires a very careful tension. We can easily fall off the other side of the tightrope into the pit of despair. If pain and suffering are always going to be the case, then why work so hard to change them?

This chapter's text provides us with the balance necessary to avoid slipping into despair. Those who have passed through the tribulation assure us that indeed someday the pain will be no more. Someday the tears will be wiped away forever. Meanwhile, as we wait for that day, we can taste of that possibility in the various fleeting moments of victory that we experience now. Learning to delight in those fleeting moments while continuing to participate in God's work of restoration, we know that they merely whet our appetite for the ultimate victory.

Thus, another factor in our remaining hopeful is a constant recognition that we are but strangers and sojourners here. This is not the real life for which we are destined. Someday, things are going to be different, according to God's perfect plan. Though we know very little about the future heaven or what happens after death, the point is that God's promise is not just an illusion. Someday things *will* be different; evil *will* be destroyed. The vision of the saints participating in that future strengthens our hope for it now.

I celebrated a moment of that present future at my grandmother's funeral. She was 94 when she died and had suffered pain and weakness and loss of physical and mental capacities for many years. Yet she had always been able to pray with me in German, and I enjoyed reading Scripture lessons and devotions to her in her native tongue. My uncle reported that her home-going was luminous. After singing and reciting German hymns and prayers for a long time, perhaps hours, and in a clear, firm voice (though earlier in the day she'd only mumbled), suddenly she said in English, "And that's all I know" — and then she died! What more does one need to know besides hymns of praise and prayers of trust?

After the funeral home visitation, the pastor read Revelation 7 to the family members. Since I had been immersed in that text for this book, its imagery made my hope tangible. My heart soared as I pictured Grand-mother, wearing her white robe, free to praise God as He is worthy to be praised (in German, of course!) and no longer suffering any pain or limita-tions. The ecstasy of that vision lifted me from the pain of my newly shat-tered foot. I cried with Joy as I exulted, "No more tears for you, liebe Grossmutter — and someday for me, too!"

This is always the emphasis of biblical eschatology (the consideration of the end-times). The Scriptures hold in tension the already and the not-yet. We already experience Triune grace, but it is only a foretaste of God's perfect presence, which is not yet realized. Someday the tears will be gone, and the assurance of the fulfillment of that promise enables us to cry less now.

We know that someday the Lamb will thoroughly shepherd us because to some extent we experience His tenderness now. Every time we have felt that we absolutely could not go on, somehow a moment of Christ's grace has slipped in to assure us of His loving care. The Christian life is com-posed of looking to those moments as foretastes of God's complete resto-ration, a recognition that already the tending has begun, even though we don't experience it fully now.

Certainly we are not able to maintain this dialectical balance of the present and future without doubts here and there. Indeed, perhaps many of the tears that God will someday wipe away forever are tears of despair from the times when we just cannot believe the Spirit's promises to us and tears of anger against God from the times when life seems so unfair and out of control.

Meanwhile, in the moments when there are no answers, perhaps we will come closer to being able to live with the questions themselves. For ex-ample, since my marriage just twelve years ago I have been constantly overwhelmed by the goodness of God that gave me such a gentle husband in Myron, whose tender care makes the questions of my physical limitations so much easier to bear. In our moments of wrestling with pain and human confusion, we will surely see the grace of God in new ways — as today, when the vision of new spring flowers lifted for a while my apprehension as I wait for biopsy of newly found tumors. Sometimes a mere glimpse of grace will dry our tears for the day.

I believe this even when I can't feel it. I experience it if I focus on serving God instead of on myself. And that takes us back to the necessity for theocentrism with which we began this book. As long as we focus on our own misery and our own questions about why God allows things to be as awful as they sometimes are, our perspectives get jaundiced and inward-turned. Then we wind up miserable in our groping.

On the other hand, when we let our perspective be theocentric, God-centered, when we declare with the living creatures of The Revelation that God is worthy to receive the blessing and the glory and the wisdom and the thanksgiving and the honor and the power and the might into the aeons of the aeons, then we can be content to believe that we don't have all the information yet. We can't come to any reasoned conclusions when all the data is not yet in our hands. We don't know how the Father will take care of us in the future, what the Spirit will show us about our troubled existence, how Christ will enable us to cope with whatever has to be, how the Trinity will use us in God's work to free others from oppression and deprivation. We just don't know enough yet *not* to trust God!

I wrote that last line with great deliberation, because it seems that our problem lies in trying to work everything out the other way around. We won't trust God unless He proves Himself, and in the course of our demanding that He prove himself we probably miss most of the data that would convince us. If, on the other hand, we could be more open to how God will work through our situations for His very best purposes, we might be more able to wait for His revelation and timing and control.

I write this with great trembling, for many times I cannot believe it. In the moments when I do, however, I am sure that the Christian community needs to be enfolding itself in this message of finding God's presence in our weakness. As Tim once said to me, "I don't even want to be well if that is not God's best for me." I pray that I will grow to be more able to trust the seal with which I am marked, too. I don't know enough yet *not* to trust God!

CHAPTER 20

Skills to Read The Revelation:
Silence and Trust in God's Vindication

(Please refer often to Revelation 8:1-6
as you study this chapter.)

O ne especially rich aspect of worship using historic liturgies is an oc-
casional pause for silent meditation within the structure of the service — but in my frequent travels to teach I have rarely participated in any
congregations who really observed the silence. That is disappointing, for
moments of reflection provide fruitful opportunities for God's surprises.

Why do we have such a difficult time being silent? Our culture does not
teach us how to enjoy periods of silence. Both psychologists and sociolo-
gists have commented on the "noise" of this present culture, the need to
have the CD player or television set always on — and they usually link that
need to an inability to live with our own thoughts, to be reflective or creative. The noise and busyness of our entertainment culture contradict the
biblical call to meditation, to stillness before God.

Sometimes what we fear in the silence is the pain of a confrontation
with ourselves. What sorts of regrets might come to us and force us to face
up to mistakes and failures? In the silence of despair we might hear the ac-
cusing voice of the Slanderer making us feel guilty about things that have
been forgiven. Perhaps in the silence we find it difficult to distinguish between God's voice showing us faults and failures that we need to acknowledge and confess and Satan's voice harassing us and trying to stymie our
ministries.

One evening during this book's first drafting, something my hostess
and I had discussed earlier touched off a barrage of painful memories of
congregational conflicts and personal betrayals that hindered my working.

I couldn't settle back into serious thinking until things were sorted through. But even as I went to sleep that night after prayers, there was some wrestling to do to reaffirm forgiveness. How can our silences be productive and good?

Because of that question I am intrigued by the half hour of silence that begins the eighth chapter of The Revelation. What a fascinating interlude! What did the seer John experience in that time? What would happen in our worship services if we stopped for half an hour to meditate without any sound?

This phenomenal quiet in the seer's vision is not explained. Were the heavens mute because no one was quite ready to cope with the immensity of the vision's events? Was the silence generated by great gratitude for the previous promise that the Lamb will someday wipe away all tears from every eye and lead all the saints to fountains of living water? Or was the quiet a hushed anticipation of the things to come — either negative as in the eye of a hurricane or positive as in the breathless expectation before a symphonic concert begins? What is the connection of this silence with the next event, the channeling of the saints' prayers to God — or with the following event, the angels' preparation to sound their trumpets and initiate the plagues of hail and fire to consume part of the earth?

We cannot know for sure with what the silence should be connected, but perhaps it should be related to everything preceding and following in the heavenly visions, for silence is an important element of praise, thanksgiving, awe, fear, reverence, dread, repentance, anticipation, and prayer. In our busy lives, silence can quietly deepen our intimacy with God.

Besides offering the heavenly model of silence for our lives and worship, the very lack of information about the silence in this text also invites us to learn skills for reading the Bible carefully and meditatively. Obviously, this book is not a commentary. I haven't offered rigid identifications of symbols nor much specific factual information about the context of The Revelation. I have written very little in this volume that you could not have figured out for yourself, given enough time and meditation. My point is that what we need most to do to deepen our biblical literacy is to learn to read the Scriptures slowly and pensively both by ourselves and in discussion groups.

We depend too much upon scholars or the Internet to give us all the answers, to tell us what we should know about the Scriptures. Certainly the clergy are specially trained to help lay persons grow in skills and to give them information that they wouldn't have the time or expertise to dig out for themselves. But they are not necessarily any better at listening to God than someone who hasn't gone to seminary.

In fact, sometimes those of us who are theologically trained are less able to hear what God is saying because we throw up all sorts of intellectualizing barriers to the Spirit's movement. One of the things I fear most about graduate theological education is that too much learning can take people away from the major lesson of this book: that in weakness — when we don't depend upon our own wisdom and answers — come the best dependence upon God and ultimately the victory of faith as Christ's Spirit works through us.

Those who have theological education have acquired it in order that they might be more faithful to their call to be "equipping the saints" (Eph. 4:12). But that is no more important a station in life than that of the saint who receives such equipping and continues to minister to others while working in a store or office. All of us are ministers together, sharing in our communities the work of the kingdom. We each contribute our part to the building up of the whole. My work is to learn as much as I can in my studies so that I can be as helpful as possible to other saints through Bible lectures and books, but I am painfully aware that I certainly don't know God as well as those who live and walk with Him in gentle simplicity.

This sidetrack is intended to emphasize that The Revelation is not a book for specialists. In fact, the specialists sometimes miss its point. If they try to pin everything down and to have all the answers for what each item in the text represents, they might miss the whole thrust of the book — to teach us the meaning and hope of Christ's Lordship for our times of tribulation and sufferings.

That is especially manifested by this text about silence. No one can pin down specifics of why this particular silence for this length of time and in this context at this point in the heavenly visions. But all of us can meditate on this text and recognize in it a heavenly model that could fittingly be applied to our earthly worship and daily life.

Long ago when I first participated in a silent retreat, I panicked at the beginning because it seemed that the long silence would be too painful for me. Too many previous nights had overflowed with tears because of past experiences of abandonment, so I was not sure that I could handle all the retreat's hours of silence.

To my great surprise, as soon as I left the retreat house for a long walk up the hill and through the fields, my spirit soared with exquisite Joy. I found myself dancing all over the hillside, singing songs with my hands, and grinning from ear to ear. What an amazing morning — such an amazing grace!

When we came in for lunch, what should be playing as background music but Pachelbel's "Canon in D," which is for me a consummate picture of God's steadfast grace! The same eight notes in the bass line repeat over and over without any variation or change (just like the Trinity's love) while the texture above in the violins, violas, and cellos keeps changing intricately. No matter what music our lives weave above, the *cantus firmus* of God's protective and enveloping grace remains constant and faithful! That music epitomized what I had been experiencing all morning in the silence. God did not leave me alone to weep during those hours. The Spirit came to me in the sunshine and field flowers, in the spring breezes and birdsongs, in the music and smiles of my retreat partners, and, most of all, in the Word, to fill me with an abundance of Joy that can't be adequately described.

Silent moments give opportunities for reflection upon the Scriptures to give way to the Spirit's teaching and inspiration. We are enabled to understand the Bible much more deeply when there is plenty of time for God's work in our minds, for the renewal that is the Holy Spirit's gift. Also, silence helps us to give the Trinity due reverence. As Habakkuk urges, "The Lord is in His holy temple; let all the earth be silent before Him!" (Hab. 2:20, NRSV). In our busyness we do not experience the awesomeness of God's holiness; in the silence we breathe in the sublimity that cannot be uttered.

Silence also gives us opportunity to observe, to listen, to be made more aware of all that surrounds us — the ways in which God acts in our environment and intervenes in our history, as well as the methods of evil in our world. We need to think more deeply about the principalities and powers that we must fight and how to combat them.

If we try to fight evil without adequate reflection and preparation, our actions are often ill-founded or unsuitable to the actual situation. If we give ourselves meditative space and time to understand, we can more accurately apply the truths of God to the circumstances we encounter. Our most important model is Jesus, who frequently retreated to the hills to pray and commune with His Father — especially before such major decisions as choosing the twelve apostles (Luke 6:12-16).

For all these reasons, the silence observed in the seer's heavenly vision seems to be not only a response to the Joy of chapter 7 but also very closely related to both of the following events in chapter 8. One special element of style underscores these connections.

The text mentions immediately after the silence that seven angels were given trumpets, so certainly the silence is meant to prepare us for the agony when those trumpets sound and usher in momentous destructions. However, their work does not begin until after the account of the saints' prayers. This literary construction of interruption and framing, which is also used frequently for emphasis by the Gospel writers, here highlights the connection between the silence and the prayers.

The symbolic number seven occurs twice, as has been the pattern, to emphasize that the perfect number of angels and trumpets will be used for the next stage in God's display of Lordship over the evil powers. The name *angel* signifies some sort of "messenger," and as the seven blow their trumpets later in the text we will notice that they function merely to announce the various elements of the destruction. God is therefore seen indirectly to be the cause of the punishment, not venting a petty human vengeance upon the enemy, but finally exercising truly righteous and long-withheld wrath. In observing these very acts of displaying Lordship, we realize that the irreproachable Judge has been graciously patient for a long time.

However, these acts of true justice are also responses to the prayers of the saints who have suffered extraordinarily at the hands of their enemies. We recognize this connection because the seer John places the angels with trumpets as a frame (8:2 and 6) around the few verses that talk about the saints' prayers (8:3-5), which earlier had included prayers for vindication (6:9-11).

Another angel appears with the golden censer of prayers. This angel mixes the saints' prayers together with the smoke of his incense. This scene perhaps suggests the intercession of heavenly forces along with the prayers of God's people. We know from the words of Jesus that He intercedes for us (John 17) and from the apostle Paul that the Holy Spirit intercedes for us (Rom. 8:26). Here we are reminded of that great fact — that all our prayers are only supplements to those of the angelic hosts, the heavenly beings, and Christ Himself.

Moreover, our prayer is connected with the silence and with the action of God's wrath in response to the saints' needs. We are invited by this scene, therefore, to connect everything in our lives with prayer — our gratitude for the deliverance from tears promised in the last chapter, our awe at God's majesty, our desire to be freed from our enemies' tormentings. All things are matters for prayer.

The subject of prayer is much too large to pursue in this book. Simply, the beginning of Revelation 8 invites us to enjoy silence in our prayers. Spending time at the listening end enables us to hear God's answers to our intercessions and God's purposes for our lives.

Notice that the other half of the angel's action is to throw the censer's contents to the earth. This image invites us to faithful diligence in prayer disciplines, for it suggests graphically that God takes our prayers seriously and causes momentous happenings on earth in response. Peals of thunder and rumblings and lightnings and earthquakes (four elements again) once more remind us of Mount Sinai and *YHWH*'s appearance there to instruct the covenant people. God indeed comes to us; fire from the altar initiates the theophany.

The images also remind us that by means of prayer we participate in "God's disruptive presence in the fallen world." Prayer becomes the sacrificial offering of ourselves to God (this would have been easily understood by the Jewish Christians, because the incense of holiness in the synagogues of prayer was timed to coincide with the daily sacrifices in the Temple in Jerusalem) to become agents of God's actions in the daily events and situations of life.[1]

Finally, verse 6 specifically proclaims that the angels prepared themselves in order to sound their trumpets. That anticipatory line increases our expectations and fear, for the trumpets warn of God's impending wrath.

We will discuss the results of the trumpets' soundings in Revelation 8–9 in the following chapter. In the Hebrew Scriptures, Israel had used trumpets for their special holiday celebrations and at times to summon the militia together for battle or defense (see especially Num. 10:3-10 and 29:1). Trumpets were also used in the coronations of kings, as in 1 Kings 1:34, 39 and in 2 Kings 9:13. Zephaniah 1:14-16 includes the trumpet blast in its description of the day of the LORD's wrath. Consequently, the references to trumpets in The Revelation might have brought several of these First Testament images to mind for its first readers. God was indeed displaying Kingship, venting wrath, triumphing, ushering in a new age.

Perhaps we should prepare to think about these things with a prayerful half hour of silence.

---

1. M. Robert Mulholland Jr., *Invitation to a Journey: A Road Map for Spiritual Formation* (Downers Grove, IL: InterVarsity Press, 1993), pp. 107-8.

CHAPTER 21

The Persistence of Sin and the Immensity of Grace

(Please refer often to Revelation 8:6–9:21
as you study this chapter.)

I revised this chapter for its first edition the day after, to my great surprise, my best friend proposed. (The discipline of writing was a good
way to keep my feet on the ground at least a little!) It was amazing that
Myron asked me to marry him after faithfully waiting through six years of
friendship (including my four-year stint across the country for graduate
school) and many days of uncertainty about my vocation. Moreover, his
proposal came in a time of confusion and concern over my shattered foot.
In contrast to the usual romantic notions of Prince Charming falling in
love with the most beautiful maiden, he proposed when my whole foot
and leg were ugly red and grotesquely swollen. What incredible love! It has
to be (as Myron first declared) the work of God.

What wonderful timing that on the day I had planned to write about the
immensity of God's grace for a sinful world I should experience its Joy so
richly through the gift of Myron! In this overwhelming love I realize that
human devotion is just one small taste of the infinite love God has for us.

Most people find the description of the trumpets in the eighth and ninth
chapters of The Revelation too gruesome and weird and horrible. However,
if we read carefully, we will see that it is designed to show us — with bizarre
imagery, I admit — how immeasurably boundless God's love is.

To see that love, instead of merely being frightened by what at first
glance seems to be an awful picture, we must very carefully notice some little details. Most important, the accounts of all the trumpets clearly show
that God is in control.

135

As the trumpets sound (beginning in 8:6), various plagues are cast on the earth — fire, hail, blood, a burning mountain, a star that turns the waters bitter, and darkness. All of these affect one-third of the vegetation, the sea and its creatures, the rivers and springs, the sun, moon, and stars. As we move through The Revelation, we will notice that its patterns describing the destructions of God's wrath are like the guide in an art gallery as they continue to restate themes in various styles. The continual literary development in the text does not represent different stages in the historical outworking of God's final triumph. Rather, the details circle around considerably as chapters 6 through 11 progress.

Craig Koester points out how the mounting threats of Revelation 8–9 "show that it is an illusion to think that one can find security apart from God and the Lamb." Readers can't be neutral. As an example, he suggests the contrasting references to blood — that the saints' blood has been shed by the world (6:10) and they are washed in the Lamb's blood (7:14), while the world is spattered with the blood mixed into the hail and fire of the first trumpet (8:7) and "awash in the blood of judgment, as a third of the sea is stained red" after the second trumpet (v. 8). Similar contrasts are noticeable regarding scorching heat (7:16 vs. 8:7, 8, 10), springs of water (7:17 vs. 8:11), and the sun (7:16 vs. 8:12).[1]

The fact that the book of Revelation must be understood cyclically — that is, as restated spheres of literary development — is suggested by the beginning letters to the seven churches arranged in a circle, and by particular literary patterns repeated precisely to show the repetition with variation that characterized God's rebukes (refer again to Chapter 7 of this book). Next we move on to various cycles of scenes in heaven and in battles against evil, emphasizing that as long as this world continues such cycles will continue to be a constant process. Ultimately — as we shall see at the end of The Revelation — God will totally destroy all evil, but in the meanwhile, as history repeats itself, human sin cycles around, deserving God's wrath, but also calling forth divinely patient grace. To the specific venting of God's wrath and the immensity of grace we will now turn.

Chapters 8 and 9 of The Revelation raise a very difficult issue — the question of the relation of evil in the world to God's sovereignty over it. As the various trumpets sound, the forces of evil are unleashed to do their de-

---

1. Craig R. Koester, *Revelation and the End of All Things* (Grand Rapids: Wm. B. Eerdmans Publishing Co., 2001), pp. 98-99.

structive work. Yet we must never forget that the Lord ultimately maintains control, for those forces cannot do their work until God's angels sound their trumpets. God is not the author of evil, but He is sovereign over it.

Divine control is suggested, first of all, by the deliberate confining of the destruction. All the results of the first four trumpets are limited to one-third. Moreover, after these trumpets have sounded and their plagues have wreaked their desolations, an eagle with a loud voice warns the inhabitants of the earth that more of God's trumpets are about to sound.

God's control is even more clear when chapter 9 expands the descriptions of the trumpets. In Revelation 9:3 the seer declares that the locusts "were given power." They had not usurped it for themselves. Their actions come as the result of the fifth angel sounding his trumpet. God's messenger issued the divine command, and the locusts were allotted a certain amount of power.

Secondly, Revelation 9:4 proclaims that their power was specifically limited by restrictions on their actions. The locusts could harm neither the plants of the earth nor the people who had the seal of God on their foreheads, nor were they able to kill anyone. They were given power to inflict pain, but not death. It seems that those people who were not sealed by God were thereby given impetus to think about their lives. In seeking death (but it eludes them — v. 6), they will perhaps think again about the meaning of life.

Now in Revelation 9 we begin to see — in the case of the star who is given the key to the bottomless pit — the ambiguity of the powers of evil, that their forms sometimes imitate God. Although Christ is called the Morning Star in both Revelation 2:28 and 22:16, and in chapter 3 He holds the keys, the "star" in 9:1 who wields the key to the Abyss is probably not Christ. Rather, this star who is given the key in response to the fifth trumpet refers to the star called Wormwood, which in Revelation 8:10-11 was released by the third trumpet in order to fall on the waters and turn them bitter and cause people to die.

Later, in Revelation 12 and 13 (to be discussed in Chapter 24), we will see that the powers of evil imitate the Triune God as they wreak their havoc in the world. Similarly, here the star who is given the key to the Abyss temporarily (since an angel has the key in Rev. 20:1) seems to be a parody of the true Morning Star, who actually holds the keys that cannot be frustrated (see Rev. 3:7). Evil seems to have its way, but its reality is imitation and under the control of the Truth.

This was a crucially important expression of hope for the early Christians being persecuted. Because it must have often seemed that evil was in control, they needed the reminder that God's sovereignty remained supreme over its imitations.

The description of the locusts released from the pit in Revelation 9:4-11 is certainly gruesome, but its bizarre contrasts again enable us to see that its symbolic portrayal makes a momentous point. One certainly couldn't produce an artist's rendition of all the features in this description that would make any sense. However, each detail suggests a factor for our understanding.

First, the locusts look like horses prepared for battle. Obviously, they are being sent to fight the opposition. Furthermore, they wear crowns of gold and have faces that resemble human ones and hair like that of women. These three images perhaps suggest a reference to human authorities or royalty that are sources of evil beyond themselves, especially because the otherwise humanly pictured creatures have teeth like those of lions. The combination of elements is reminiscent of an Arab proverb that the locust has a horse's head, a lion's breast, a camel's feet, a serpent's body, and antennae like the hair of a woman. The picture is unnatural and diabolical — a terrifying picture of cruelty.

The lionish teeth, together with breastplates of iron and the sound of chariots and horses in battle, raise the spectre of ferocious war-making. However, once again limits are put on their power — not only on the severity of their torture, but on its duration. Since five months is actually the extent of the life cycle of the locust, the picture reminds us that evil has a limited life. As we shall see at the end of The Revelation, the God of truth and goodness will someday destroy it completely.

Finally, the description reveals the ultimate character of the locusts' king. He is called the angel of the Abyss, and his names in Hebrew and Greek are Abaddon and Apollyon. These two names mean "Destruction" and "Destroyer," respectively, but for the early Christians to whom The Revelation was first written the latter name would have been much more specific. Indeed, the emperor Domitian (perhaps the one persecuting the first readers of this book) claimed to be an incarnation of the Greek god Apollo.

The next two woes are described at much greater length. Consequently, it is important for us to glance ahead through the whole Revelation to see the overall framework in which we are working. That framework also reinforces our interpretation of this section as one of grace. First, we were introduced to the woes by the crying eagle in 8:13, who warns the inhabitants of the earth about the woes to come. Then, since 9:12 specifically says that the first woe is past, we look for the completion of the other woes and are surprised to find that the second woe (which begins with the sounding of the sixth angel's trumpet in 9:13) ends with the resurrection of the two witnesses, who were also trying to draw people back to Christ (see the following chapter). Moreover, the third woe is declared to be coming soon, but there is no specific phrase in the book at all to proclaim that the third woe has ended. Instead, with the sounding of the seventh angel's trumpet, the heavens break out in praise to God for reigning in justice (11:15-19). Those who are destroyed are those who have destroyed the earth.

Now when we return to the description of the second woe in chapter 9, we again notice many details of divine sovereignty. The voice comes directly from the golden altar that is before God (v. 13); the four angels are called to do their work (v. 14); and God's control shows in the fact that they had been kept ready for this very task at "this very hour and day and month and year." They were to kill a third of humankind — which seems, as does the "third" throughout the sounding of the trumpets, to indicate divine control limiting the amount of destruction.

The troops are huge, numbering 200 million! Once again, the physical description is meant graphically to create an atmosphere. The breastplates of the riders are fiery red, dark blue, and yellow like sulfur, and out of the mouths of the horses come plagues of fire, smoke, and sulfur. Even the horses' tails, which are like snakes, inflict injury — but why?

The key to this whole section comes in verse 20, which informs us that in spite of the two woes recorded in chapter 9 people were still too stubborn to turn back to God. The rest of humankind, those not killed by these plagues, still "did not repent of the works of their hands or give up worshiping demons and idols of gold and silver and bronze and stone and wood, which cannot see or hear or walk" (9:20). How ridiculous to worship such idols, and yet even the warning of the plagues has not sufficed to deter human beings from the vanity of this worship.

Revelation 9 ends with the very great tragedy that in spite of all the different woes God has allowed throughout history (and with enormously long-suffering patience) in order to warn people, human beings have still willed to go their own way. They have not yet repented of all their earthly sins — symbolized by the list of four (murders, sorceries, immorality, and thefts).

The vision of the six trumpets encourages all of us to spend extra time asking ourselves what kinds of trials God has allowed in order to call us back to Himself. Of course, the Triune God does not inflict suffering upon us — the evil and brokenness of this world after the Fall are its cause — but in the Lord's infinite care He knows that sometimes those loved must be allowed to experience discipline. Furthermore, when we turn to God repentantly, the Holy Spirit reminds us again of the blood of the Lamb and the shepherding of His salvation (see Rev. 7:14-17 again).

Every time a new kind of physical affliction assails me I realize that many areas of my life are not yet in tune with God's best purposes. I do not submit willingly to reprimands, and sometimes in my bitterness or rebellion I stray further away and need an even more powerful reminder. (Sometimes it takes a two-by-four to get the mule back into the barn!) The greatest comfort to me in the trumpets of The Revelation is that God always sets limits. No emperor's locust or sulfur-mouthed horse can rage out of the Lord's ultimate control.

We may never judge others and say that their afflictions are meant by God to reprimand them and draw them back. The book of Job certainly teaches us that his friends had no right to condemn him and blame his troubles on his sins. When *YHWH* appeared, He didn't condemn Job, but instead pointed him to a foundation for the world other than the doctrine of retribution that both Job and his friends had espoused.

I dare not judge anyone else, but I know that I personally must join Job in the dust and ashes of repentance. When we have seen God, we all know that we are guilty.

The trumpets of Revelation 8–9 let us see God. The Lord's immense grace allows certain plagues to call human beings to repentance. The Almighty's sovereign control sets definite limits on the forces of evil. The Trinity's ultimate goal is to save.

CHAPTER 22

Asking the Right Questions in Our Suffering: How Long? and Meanwhile?

(Please refer often to Revelation 10:1–11:13 as you study this chapter.)

M any times we deepen our own ethical dilemmas or are prevented from finding answers in them because we are asking the wrong questions. For example, single persons longing to marry often cause themselves problems in their relationships with the opposite sex because they too quickly ask, "Could this be the person I should marry?" — usually out of fear that, if not, they should break off the relationship to avoid causing themselves pain. Instead, they might ask positive questions about Christian love, such as "How can this particular friendship be a means for living out the principles of God's kingdom?" or "How might this person and I be helpful to each other to deepen our relationship with the Trinity and the effectiveness of our respective ministries?" Such questions would free single people to enjoy letting their friendships grow as God would have them grow, without an undue pressure toward marriage or toward the ungodliness of our society's sexual immorality.

Our church communities must more thoroughly teach skills of asking better questions, of learning to think and discern, because our entertainment-oriented society fosters passive acceptance of its usually corrupt values. Christians especially need to ask critical questions — examining the patterns of our society to avoid becoming enculturated in values that do not follow the principles of Jesus, learning how to read the Scriptures in order to apply them appropriately to the issues of our times, and teaching our children to search constantly for the ways of God's kingdom in the midst of a degenerate and twisted world.

The urgency of asking the right questions is especially essential with such a project as reading The Revelation because we can so easily get bogged down in particulars and thereby miss the basic theme of the text. I'm not saying that those specifics aren't important, nor that there aren't sometimes precise historical details that aid us in understanding them, but their function must always be to point us more deeply to the text's purposes. When we get so caught up in deciphering the minutiae that the main thrust is missed, when we atomize the text, we lose the true, practical significance of the Word for forming our daily Christian lives.

In this chapter, therefore, we are going to practice focusing on the main questions that the text addresses and not on the many details of this section of The Revelation. The images of this portion from 10:1 to 11:13 are taken from numerous places in the First Testament, and ferreting them all out would prove very enlightening, but I am confident that you can do that with the aid of a good cross-reference Bible if you are interested. Instead, we need to examine here the larger picture.

The old outlining methods we used in elementary school can be very helpful for finding larger patterns in a literary text. By outlining biblical books we grasp the broad scope of their purposes and themes. If we sketched The Revelation together, we would keep noticing the cyclical pattern that circulates through many places of the whole. The beginning of the book circles through the churches who receive the letters, and now we see cycles of seven seals, seven trumpets, and the seven angels who blow them. A closer look at the pattern, however, also uncovers an interrupting interlude both between the sixth and seventh seals (the two visions of Rev. 7) and between the sixth and seventh trumpets (the two visions of 10:1–11:13).

Each suspension serves a literary purpose — in the latter case to focus on two significant questions: "How long?" and "What is the role of the people of God in the meanwhile?" These two questions, we will continue to discover, form the backbone of The Revelation.

God teaches the saints that their first question is not answered in terms of how long the suffering must yet go on, but with the reversal of this question to them: How long will it be till the Church pursues its duty in the meanwhile? Furthermore, the Church's duty in the meanwhile is revealed as this: to witness to God's sovereignty, which seems to be hidden concurrently.

These are still the primary issues for God's people today. This is the challenge for each of us personally: How can my life manifest God's Lordship, no matter what my circumstances might be? The mission for our church communities is to display that Lordship in these "already-but-not-yet" kingdom times.

For several years my daily meditations focused on the Psalms,[1] and in this project I was repeatedly encouraged to become more theocentrically focused, to turn around that question, "How long?" to ask instead, "Who is God in the midst of this?" This is the lesson of true biblical patience that we have been learning here in The Revelation, too. Such patience does not mean waiting until things change, but learning to wait because of who God is even when the situation doesn't change. Such a change of focus enables us to ask better questions and to search for different answers.

The structure of Revelation 10 seems to underscore the appropriateness of such an approach to this section, because at first we are told of a message from the thunders that the seer was not allowed to reveal. Immediately thereafter the mighty and radiant angel makes it plain that there will be no more delay.

We simply cannot understand all the mysteries of God. Certain things cannot be revealed to us — perhaps because we can't handle them — but this message is unquestionable: there is no more delay. God's purposes must be accomplished now.

The aura of mystery that surrounds this text is wonderfully captured by the composer Olivier Messiaen in his "Quatuor pour la Fin du Temps," for violin, cello, clarinet, and piano, which was inspired by this text. This piece first captured my interest because of its titles. Then a stunning performance (in connection with an Anne Frank exhibit) of its graphic music and the composer's own biblical and mystical comments led me to new questions and a renewed theocentric focus. Written while he was imprisoned by the Nazis in 1941, Messiaen's "Quartet for the End of Time" includes these movements:

1. Crystalline Liturgy
2. Vocalise for the Angel who Announces the End of Time
3. The Abyss of the Birds
4. Interlude

1. This study led to my book *I'm Lonely, Lord — How Long? Meditations on the Psalms,* 2nd ed. (Grand Rapids: Wm. B. Eerdmans Publishing Co., 1998).

5. Praise to the Eternity of Jesus
6. Dance of Fury for the Seven Trumpets
7. Tangles of Rainbows for the Angel who Announces the End of Time
8. Praise to the Immortality of Jesus

Especially in the fifth movement, in which a broad cello melody "magnifies with love and reverence the eternity of the powerful and sweet Word,"[2] the mysterious music of the entire "Quartet" captures not only the rainbow colors of the angel, but also some of the "moments of silent adoration and marvelous visions of peace" of The Revelation. Messiaen himself and three other inmates first performed the quartet on damaged instruments in the prison camp at Görlitz in Silesia. In the midst of persecution and suffering Messiaen was able to rest in the mystery of Christ's sovereignty and offer his music as a witness to "the harmonies of heaven."

That is a critically urgent message for the Christian community in our times. We might not have all the answers, but because of the answers we do have, we must certainly get on with our task of manifesting to the world the undeniable reality of Christ's sovereign Lordship. Even in our imprisonments we can make music!

Consider all the questions about which we are confused. It might not be time yet for us to know any final answers. My favorite assurance is the passage in Habakkuk that reminds us that the vision awaits its time (Hab. 2:1-4). It will not delay, nor will it be too late. If it tarries, we are to learn to wait for it. At the right time God's purposes will be accomplished, even as they were for Israel. Meanwhile, "the just shall live by faith."

When we don't know the answers to all of life's questions, we can ask different ones — questions of how we can best be stewards of this time in the meanwhile. How can we fulfill the purposes of the kingdom with the information that we do have? That makes our approach to life so much easier.

In the example that began this chapter, single people can learn how to deal with relationships. They can look in friendships for how God's purposes can best be accomplished at the moment without knowing what might become of them in the future. The immense pressures toward marriage or sex that are put on friendships by our surrounding culture spoil

---

2. These quotations are Messiaen's own words, translated by Helen Baker for the Musical Heritage Society's recording of the "Quatuor pour la Fin du Temps."

many relationships. Our Christian communities could be a means of support for persons establishing deep relationships in the love of Christ without the added burdens of our culture's pressures.

This is another lesson I learned from my friends Tim and Linden. Years ago I grew to love both of these men more deeply than I could have ever imagined — and I know they loved me that way, too — without romance, though with godly affection, and thoroughly in a growing *agapē* love that will continue to keep us friends throughout life and on into heaven. Though I was alone and lonely at the time, I truly rejoiced when they both found lovely wives — and then they both wrote celebrative letters to me when I became engaged. Asking the right kind of questions freed us thoroughly to enjoy each other's gifts to us when we were all single without spoiling the relationships by romantic games or sexual exploitation.

In Revelation 10:9 the seer is instructed to eat the scroll, which he would find both sweet and bitter, much in the manner of the prophet Ezekiel (Ezek. 2 and 3). Then he is commanded to speak God's Word to all the peoples, nations, languages, and kings. Once again a fourfold typology reminds us that every aspect of earthly existence must be touched by our prophetic message. Furthermore, the inclusion of kings this time emphasizes that God's Word must be spoken especially in the high places, for prophetic judgment and hope both are needed in the halls of government and in the hearts of rulers.

We must always remember, however, that it is a prophetic *word*. Christians are rarely called to be in charge of government, and never dare we force our control on others. Rather, we perhaps might serve in political offices to offer alternatives of justice and peacemaking. Only with utmost integrity may we speak careful prophetic words. Moreover, outside of holding office, we can hold government accountable to its proper duties and just laws. Our primary duty, however, is to live the principles of God's kingdom now, whether or not that matches the ethos of our society.

This is the Church's task. The answer to our first question, "How long?" is that there can be no delay. God's people must be faithful now to proclaim God's message. Furthermore, the answer to the question of the community's task is that we must speak truly the Word the Spirit gives us to proclaim. That is why the second of the two intervening visions introduces the symbol of the two witnesses.

Numerous interpretations have been offered for the vision of the two witnesses in Revelation 11. Scholars debate whether the picture should be taken literally, as a prediction of the rebuilding of the Jewish temple at the end of the age, or whether the temple symbolically represents God's people, so that measuring its inner courts is comparable to the sealing of previous chapters in stressing the protection and security God gives to them.

Too many questions cannot be answered definitively. Do the outer courts that are not to be measured represent the part of the Church that has fallen away in its compromising with the world? Does the message from the scroll that could not be revealed concern the fate of the witnessing Church? How do these visions relate to each other? And who are the two witnesses?

Different commentators suggest various theories including the following for the identity of the two witnesses: Israel and the New Testament Church; the Law and the Prophets; the Law and the Gospel; the Old/First and the New/Second Testaments; Zerubbabel and Joshua; Elijah and Elisha; James and John; Peter and Paul; the churches of Smyrna and Philadelphia which, of all the seven, were not called to repentance; Moses and Elijah; and so forth.

The latter suggestion seems especially likely because of the references to the plagues and the turning of water into blood (Moses and Egypt: Exod. 8–12 and 7:14-18) and to the holding up of the rain for three and a half years and consuming enemies with fire (Elijah: 1 Kings 17:1 and 2 Kings 1:10ff.). Moreover, these two figures had appeared to talk with Jesus on the Mount of Transfiguration, and both had ended their earthly lives in unusual ways — with Moses being buried by God Himself (Deut. 34:6) and Elijah ascending in the fiery chariot (2 Kings 2:11).

Even if we could know absolutely that the two witnesses of 11:1-13 were Moses and Elijah, still we would have to ask these larger questions: Why do they appear at this place in The Revelation? What is their message to us?

Again, we can see them as part of the larger literary whole of the entire Revelation, and once again the key lies in overviewing an important element of the overall pattern. In 11:2 and 3 the numbers *42 months* and *1,260 days* are used — the first number with the negative event of the trampling of the Holy City, and the second number with the positive work of the two witnesses who proclaimed God's message during the same length of time.

These two numbers also occur in chapters 12 and 13 in connection with the story of the pregnant woman and the dragon, and once again 1,260 is used there positively, to describe the fact that the woman was protected by God in a place prepared for her (12:6). The number of 42 months is used again negatively to tell us that the beast was given a mouth to utter blasphemies and to exercise his authority for that length of time. Furthermore, this later section also uses a third figure to represent the same amount of time; "time, times, and half a time" probably means one year, plus two years, plus ½ a year, in connection with the woman's being cared for by God in all God's sovereignty (12:14).

These three figures (1,260 days, 42 months, and 3½ years), equaling the same amount of time, seem to suggest that three different things are happening at once. When we look carefully, we discover that they correspond to the three ideas composing the underlying structure of the entire Revelation. Even though Satanic opposition continues for a time, God is sovereign Lord to provide for us and protect us during that time, so, therefore, the saints can continue faithfully to endure those meanwhiles.

When we apply this basic underlying structure to the story of the two witnesses, we can gain some important lessons. Yes, they are besieged by the enemy who tramples on the Holy City for 42 months. In fact, they are killed by that enemy. Yet they are persistent in carrying out their task for those same 1,260 days. They are patient for the meanwhile and respond to the "how long?" questions with faithfulness to their tasks. Therefore, though they are killed, they are restored by their sovereign Lord.

If the number of 3½ years suggested to the original readers of The Revelation the significance of "time, times, and half a time" in Daniel 7 and then in the history of the people of Israel, all of this becomes even more poignant. From 167 to 164 B.C., the outrageous emperor Antiochus IV Epiphanes had desecrated the temple and reviled the God of the Jews in his vicious campaigns against them. However, after three and a half years the uprisings led by the Maccabee family finally restored some measure of Israelite dignity, and the temple was reconsecrated for its service.

These memories would have made this message of The Revelation clear to some readers in the first century: the ravishings of the present emperor might be severe (as a manifestation of the demonic opposition that characterizes world history), but Christ (the Son of Man in Daniel 7) is still the sovereign Lord, and so we can be faithful to His purposes — knowing that eventually He will vindicate His people and restore the temple. (In fact, as we shall see at the end of The Revelation, there will no longer be a need for the temple, for the presence of the Lord Himself will be all that His people need.)

The message for the twenty-first century is the same: God's ultimate sovereignty empowers our faithfulness. As various empires desecrate our places of worship, cause immeasurable suffering, or mock our faith, we can respond with diligent witnessing — knowing that the sovereign Lord will eventually triumph and vindicate His people.

What is the witnessing task of the Church today? We proclaim the sovereignty of God, not of the nations. Perhaps that might take the form of speaking against the pretensions of nations that would seek to control the world by means of military power and economic exploitation. Perhaps our task is to proclaim to kings the judgment — or hope — of God. Most of all, our task is to live faithfully the ethics of God's kingdom in our own communities, to stand as a witnessing people against the lifestyles of a world that wears the mark of the beast on its forehead and right hand (see the following chapter). We are to be a people marked instead with the Father's name, persons who live in total dependence on Christ. And then, even if we are killed in the process of such a witness, we will be called to come up to heaven, and the world will be astonished at the greatness of the sovereign God (11:12-13).

CHAPTER 23

42 Months, 1,260 Days, and 3½ Years

(Please refer often to Revelation 11:14–12:17
as you study this chapter.)

Long ago, advertisements for some sort of toothpaste utilized a clear plastic shield standing around a great big tooth that was being bombarded by projectiles of decay and plaque. Somehow that image has stuck with me all these years as a singularly appropriate picture of the spiritual life, though, like all analogies, it ought not to be stretched too far.

We are like teeth, highly susceptible to all kinds of spiritual injury and decay. Just because we have become Christians does not mean we won't encounter opposition. However, God has put up a shield around us — invisible to the rest of the world, but durable and impenetrable. Nothing can get through that shield as long as we remain enclosed in it. Of course, we frequently step outside of it. Nevertheless, the shield is always there.

The three key messages of The Revelation are again clear in its twelfth chapter. Moreover, this section also adds some essential insights to prepare us for the primary depiction of the forces of evil in chapters 12 and 13.

We are prepared for something very important by the immediate introduction to the major picture of this section. After the announcement that the third woe is coming and the sounding of the seventh angel's trumpet (11:14-15a), loud voices remind us that "the kingdom of the world has become the kingdom of our Lord and of His Messiah, and He will reign forever and ever" (v. 15b). The elders worship God because Christ has ended the world's usurpation of God's rightful reign; the destroyers are going to be destroyed and the saints rewarded. Meanwhile, the temple in heaven is opened, the ark is revealed (to remind us of God's covenant

149

faithfulness), and the usual signs of God's theophany (lightning, rumblings, thunder, earthquake, and hailstorm) occur. However, these events are all a prelude to the picture of the cosmic battle in chapter 12.

Craig Koester divides The Revelation into two Acts at this point because the elders now sing to the Lord God Almighty, who is and who was. They do not name God as the one who will come, for now the end is beginning.[1]

The seer proclaims that a great sign appeared in heaven (12:1). In both The Revelation and the Gospel of John, the word *sign* carries important connotations. Choosing that word instead of *miracles,* as used by the other three Gospel writers, the evangelist John continually emphasizes with the seven (note the symbolism!) "signs" in his account of Jesus that they point to His divinity. Signs should be accepted as true in themselves — that is, the miracles really did happen — but they are of secondary importance. Most essentially, we must notice to whom the signs point.

Think, for example, of a sign to the beach. The sign is important — it helps us find the beach — but we wouldn't just park our car at it and enjoy the sign. The sign is true, but it is of secondary importance.

This is essential instruction for reading the fantastic accounts of The Revelation: the signs point to something beyond themselves, to which we should pay primary attention.

Our attention in this chapter should be riveted primarily on the two major opponents: Satan and Christ. They are both thoroughly named in verses 7-12, which serve as the center point of Revelation 12.

The major power of evil is named both with all his titles — the great dragon, the serpent of old, the Devil, and Satan — and with the description that he deceives the whole world and, having been defeated, was thrown down to the earth with all his angels. Christ, on the other hand, is named by showing that the forces of evil cannot have their way at all because of what He has done.

A loud voice in heaven proclaims that the salvation, power, and kingdom of God, as well as the authority that God has invested in Christ, have all come and that the accuser has been thrown down. Consequently, the saints can overcome him by the blood of the Lamb Christ.

The vignette preceding this climax also names Christ, by showing that

---

1. Craig R. Koester, *Revelation and the End of All Things* (Grand Rapids: Wm. B. Eerdmans Publishing Co., 2001), pp. 112-15.

God's method for accomplishing the purpose of overcoming the forces of evil was highly unorthodox: sending a child.

The symbolic description of the child's mother is simple, in great contrast to the picture of the harlot in 17:3-6. Clothed with the sun and moon and stars, she carries all the light. The number of 12 stars reminds us of God's children, the covenant people. She is very pregnant, crying to give birth.

We should not try to pin down too tightly the identity of this woman. Many have thought that she symbolizes only Mary because of the description of her child, but she certainly represents more than Mary, for this is not a picture of Christ's birth in historical time. The image also raises thoughts of Eve, who is the bearer of all humanity, as well as of the promised Seed. We will notice other details that expand the symbolism as we work through the text.[2]

Now the powers of evil are introduced — the beginning of a parody that is thoroughly sketched in chapters 13 and 14. The dragon imitates God, having the perfect number (7) of heads and diadems and the complete number (10) of horns (a symbol of power used throughout the Scriptures). This gruesome dragon is bent on destroying the child that the woman is about to bear.

Meanwhile, its tail disrupts a third of the stars of heaven and throws them to earth. This image reinforces our recognition of the cyclical nature of The Revelation as a restatement and development of basic themes, for in 6:13 all the stars fell out of the sky, and in 8:12 a third of them were destroyed again. Here the image certainly underscores the dragon's ferocity and that his efforts resulted in people losing the light.

The main point is that the dragon awaited the birth of the child in order to devour him. However, the portrait immediately given of the child demonstrates that to do so was an impossibility for the dragon. The child, indeed, was to rule all the nations with a rod of iron (see Psalm 2) and was "snatched away and taken to God and to His throne" (Rev. 12:5, NRSV).

This rescue of the child leads to two significant events: the woman

---

2. Koester (*Revelation*, p. 118) identifies the roots of this battle drama in a popular story circulating in John's time about a dragon named Python and a woman named Leto, the mother of Apollo. Roman emperors used that tale, presenting themselves as Apollo, so John reversed the tale to help Christians avoid being assimilated to the emperors' culture.

flees, and the dragon is angry. We saw in the previous chapter how different numbers are used in The Revelation to indicate the same amount of time and several concurrent themes. Here the second use of the 1,260 days indicates that throughout Satan's harassment God's people can know that divine protection is secure. God Himself had prepared the place for the woman, and there she was thoroughly nourished during that time.

Meanwhile, the dragon waged war with Michael and the angels. Of course, the powers of evil are never strong enough to defeat the powers of good, and there is not a place for them in heaven (since they choose to contradict God's purposes), so they were cast out (12:7-9).[3]

Let us pause at this point to notice how untimed this whole account is. We might too simply associate the story of the woman at the beginning of the chapter specifically with Mary's mothering of Jesus, except that this war in heaven is sometimes considered to have taken place before the foundation of the world, or at least at the beginning of time, though other scholars associate it specifically with Christ's defeat of the powers at the cross. Furthermore, in verse 11 we encounter a description of the saints who overcame the powers of evil, and their victory is recorded in a past tense that carries us into the years after the resurrection of Christ.

The perspective of The Revelation is thereby made obvious: we can't take its images literalistically and put them on a future calendar, for they are meant to be understood in an eternal (i.e., timeless) framework. These images show the continued conflict of the forces of good and evil — all the way from the beginning with Eve (perhaps an implication of the sudden shift to the word "serpent" in 12:14-15) — although the end of The Revelation will clearly demonstrate that the powers of good will ultimately triumph.

Satan, who has accused the brothers and sisters before God day and night, is thrown out of heaven (12:10). However, the most significant aspect of the entire story in Revelation 12 is that this Satan can be overcome by the

---

3. A brilliant setting of these three verses, along with the text of Revelation 18:1 and 20:14, can be heard in Part V of *The Company of Heaven,* composed by Benjamin Britten at the time of World War II. The music was lost, however, and was not found again until the end of the twentieth century, so it has been rarely performed. It was a great gift to me at a recent conference in Des Moines, Iowa, to hear parts of this magnificent work about angels performed by the Westminster Oratorio, soloists, orchestra, and organ, conducted by Randal Buikema. A recording of *The Company of Heaven* is available from Virgin Classics conducted by Philip Brunelle with the London Philharmonic Choir and the English Chamber Orchestra.

blood of the Lamb and by the word of the saints' testimony and by their willingness even to die. In a separate book on the concept of the "principalities and powers" I have explicated more thoroughly the biblical description of Christ's conquest of the powers at the cross and the implications of that victory for our daily encounters with the powers of evil,[4] but we can notice at this point that when the Lamb shed His blood and rose again He won a decisive victory over the dragon, which thereby makes it possible for the saints to overcome him, too.

Furthermore, the saints overcome evil by their testimony (which links us to the work of the two witnesses in the previous chapter) and by not clinging to their lives even when faced with death. By this essential reference to their willingness to suffer for the sake of God's kingdom, John encouraged his original readers as they faced the persecutions of their time.

Similarly, as God's people struggle with various physical or spiritual setbacks or challenges, we can also be greatly comforted that our sufferings are part of the overcoming of the evil powers. Sometimes in our personal trials we think that we are being crushed by the powers of evil instead, but this text offers us genuine hope. Though we undergo sufferings, these, too, can be the means for God's purposes to be accomplished. Consequently, we can join the heavens and all who dwell there in their rejoicing (12:12).

However, we must also pay attention to the call of woe given to the earth and sea. Indeed, our earth and seas have suffered tremendously because of the wrath of the evil powers. We might immediately think of such things as pollution of the rivers and oceans, acid rain, global deforestation, and the damage to the ozone layer. These are some of the contemporary visible signs of the cosmic warfare.

We realize that these are effects of human greed and consumption. The prince of evil's major way of working is through the disruption of God's purposes for people, so that people themselves become agents of his destruction. The original readers of The Revelation would have known the suffering of the earth, for example, in the war tactics of various empires, in contrast to God's specific commands to His people to care for the earth — such as the instruction not to harm the fruit-bearing trees in wars (Deut.

---

4. See Marva J. Dawn, *Powers, Weakness, and the Tabernacling of God* (Grand Rapids: Wm. B. Eerdmans Publishing Co., 2001), and also "The Concept of 'the Principalities and Powers' in the Works of Jacques Ellul," Ph.D. dissertation, The University of Notre Dame, 1992 (Ann Arbor, MI: University Microfilms, #9220614).

20:19) or the command to let the fields lie fallow every seven years (Lev. 25:3-5). The powers of evil want to undo God's good creation; the cosmic warfare has earthly consequences.

That is why it is urgently necessary for the Christian community to be concerned about such things as ecological destruction, to do as much as we can to avoid contributing to it ourselves, and to challenge others to change their habits. As one tiny example, our congregation stopped using styrofoam cups during our fellowship hours, since those cups contribute immensely to the pollution of the earth. (If one restaurant chain in the United States each year adds 1,500,000,000 cubic feet of styrofoam waste to our earth's destruction, how much might congregational fellowship hours throughout the land contribute to the load?) We hung up huge mug racks to hold each member's personal mug and several extras for visitors. More importantly, the mugs symbolize, and force us to ask, deeper questions about how the principalities and powers vent their wrath in our world — especially through our greed and violence. Our little habits of carefulness make us more aware of the larger issues at stake in the cosmic battle for all of God's creation and the souls of human beings.

The devil has great wrath because he knows that he has only a short time (v. 12). Certainly we have seen the effects of that in our present society. It seems sometimes that everything is getting so much worse so much faster. Just as a losing ball team scrambles desperately in the last minutes of a game to try to overcome the deficit in points, so the powers of evil are working at full blast because they know their days are numbered.

Especially the dragon wants to get rid of the woman who produced the male child. The rest of this scenario is almost like a James Bond movie — only better because the woman never resorts to any violence or trickery or sexual immorality. No matter what the dragon comes up with to try to destroy her, God creates some sort of rescue.

First, she flies on the two wings of a great eagle to the place which, we remember, God had prepared to nourish her (v. 6). The image of the eagle is used throughout the First Testament to describe the continual care of *YHWH* for His covenant people, so this figure in The Revelation must have been extremely comforting to its readers. Verse 14 also specifically states that she was nourished for time, times, and half a time — the 3½ years that corresponds to the 1,260 days and reinforces our conclusion (see the previous chapter) that, even though the powers of evil rage for 42 months (the same amount of time), they can't overcome the power of God.

Now the serpent (this great deluder changes his form constantly) spews out a river of water from his mouth to try to sweep her away with the flood, but this time the earth comes to her rescue and swallows it up. This picture reminds us that God intervened so that all humanity wouldn't be destroyed by sustaining Noah and his family in the flood through the ark and by bringing the people of Israel through the Red Sea.

Finally, the dragon gave up his attempts to destroy the woman when he saw how thoroughly she was protected, so he turned his attention to her offspring (a statement that again causes us to resist the temptation to identify her solely with Mary). Almost as if to mark the end of this scene with a flourish, the seer describes her offspring more specifically. He proclaims that they are the ones who keep the commandments of God and hold to the testimony of Jesus. In other words, Satan has turned his attention to all of us believers because he was not able to conquer the child or its mother or Michael and his angels.

Thus, he continues to make war. The whole parody will be described more thoroughly in the following chapter, but now we must especially note that the dragon cannot destroy us. God's love and grace will always protect us as we "obey God's commandments and hold to the testimony of Jesus" — by special places of nurture, by the wings of eagles, by the earth and other aspects of God's creation, and, most of all, by the blood of the Lamb and the Word.

CHAPTER 24

Taking the Presence of Evil Seriously

*(Please refer often to Revelation 12 and 13
as you study this chapter.)*

I can't really tell the difference because I do not have such refined taste buds, but my father can immediately tell if the pat on his toast is butter or margarine. One morning during my stay in Wisconsin I enjoyed "Breakfast on the Farm" to help celebrate "June is Dairy Month," and I found it very interesting to listen to folks compare the calories, protein value, nutrition, and other qualities of various real dairy products with those of their imitations and substitutes. However, one has to be educated to know the difference — or else be born a true Wisconsinite!

Spiritually, we have to be born a Christian through the Holy Spirit *and* be formed into the ethics of God's kingdom to know the difference between what is truly of God and what is a corrupted imitation. First, Christ brings us into relationship with Himself and His Father, and His love and grace free us from the control of sin that causes us to choose imitations. Then, the Spirit forms us through the Word and through the Christian community to "have the mind of Christ." Apart from this grace lie the destruction and despair of devilish deceptions.

For example, the problem with a sexual relationship before marriage is that it actually produces the opposite of what the individual is truly seeking. Those who turn to "sex" in order to combat loneliness or to find the protection and loving care that create security discover instead that outside of a permanent covenant commitment a sexual relationship leads to greater insecurity. They never know if they are really loved as persons or if only their bodies are lustfully desired. They can't be sure that they are receiving the deeper commitment for which they long; trust can never be completely grounded. On the other hand, those who turn to genital sexuality only for its immediate pleasure eventually experience that, ripped out of its rightful context, "sex" without meaning is not ultimately thoroughly satisfying.

That is the case with all of the devil's corruptions. The powers of evil take what was originally good in God's design and twist it into the opposite. Leadership becomes dominating power, which often precipitates downfall; hoarding money only leads to greater fears of losing it; possessing fabulous luxury only aggravates the desire for more; achieving the top position introduces greater pressure to stay there. Our society's overabundance of heart disease, high blood pressure, and other tension-related diseases points to the results of these corruptions of that which was originally created good.

But you know that quite well already. What we don't as readily recognize is the very perversion of the powers of evil themselves.

Revelation 12–13 presents us with a repulsive, devilish parody. The dragon and the beasts represent the powers of evil in their corrupted imitation of the real power of God, and the three characters who dominate the scene mock in turn the Father, Son, and Holy Spirit. Notice the following, striking correspondences in the text to what we understand about the Trinity:

the dragon (who covets and imitates the sovereignty of the Lord God Almighty) has the perfect number (7) of heads (for wisdom) and crowns (for dignity and authority) and a complete number (10) of horns (for power)   12:3

the dragon fought with God for His place and was hurled out of heaven as a result   12:7-9

the first beast (who parodies Christ) similarly has seven heads and ten horns (even as Christ is the perfect likeness of the Father)   13:1

like God the Father, the dragon gave his power and throne and great authority to the beast (the Son) and this grouping of three (the divine number) underscores the way these parody God's true power and throne and authority   13:2

the first beast had suffered a fatal wound but had been healed (or "resurrected" like Christ!)   13:3

the whole world was astonished by this and followed after the beast (just as the resurrection caused many to follow Jesus)	13:3
human beings worshiped the dragon because he had given authority to the beast (even as Jesus said His purpose was to lead humankind to His Father)	13:4
the phrase "Who is like the beast and who can make war against him?" parodies Exodus 15:11 and that question asked about God	13:4
the beast was given power and authority for 42 months (approximately the amount of time of the public ministry of Jesus)	13:5
the beast was given authority over every tribe, people, language, and nation (the four elements symbolically represent the whole earth), even as in Daniel 7:13-14 such authority was given to the Son of Man, and just as The Revelation has stressed repeatedly that the sovereignty over all the four corners of the earth belongs to the reign of Christ	13:7
all those whose names are not written in the book of the Lamb will worship the beast, even as Jesus told His disciples that everyone is either for Him or against Him	13:8
the second beast (comparable to the Holy Spirit) exercises the authority of the first beast on his behalf, just as Jesus said the Holy Spirit would come in His place and remind us of what He taught (cf. John 16:13-15)	13:12
just as the Holy Spirit works, the second beast caused the earth to worship the first beast whose fatal wound had been healed	13:12
just like the Holy Spirit, the second beast performed great miracles and signs that would cause the people of the earth to believe in the first beast (the Son)	13:13-14
especially the sign of fire coming down in the presence of others reminds us of the Pentecost event	13:13

the most gruesome of all the parodies is the fact that the   13:16
second beast gives a mark to all the inhabitants of the earth
who follow him, even as Ephesians 1:13-14 talks about
Christians being marked and sealed with the Holy Spirit
for their spiritual inheritance and as Revelation 7:3 spoke
of the sealing of the believers (see also Gal. 6:17)

The mark of this second beast is given on either the right hand or the
forehead. In Jewish thought, hands represent one's deeds — as in the
phrase, "he who has clean hands and a pure heart" (Ps. 24:4), signifying
someone who is upright both outside and inside, in actions/outward behavior and in thoughts/will. Furthermore, the right hand is the symbol for
fellowship in Semitic cultures, so a mark on it suggests that with which the
individual is associated.

To be marked on one's forehead implies one's thinking. That is why on
their forehead and hand the Jewish people wore *tephillin* (plural of the
noun that means "prayer" in Hebrew) — small, square, black cases con-
taining passages from the Torah. These little boxes reminded them to conform their thinking and their behavior to God's designs and purposes.
Even so, the parody of the beast stresses that those who belong to him become like him, accepting his authority over their thinking and deeds.

The fact that the beast's number is 666 has probably raised more speculation than any other symbolic number in the Scriptures. In connection
with my teaching about The Revelation, various people have given me numerous reports about certain documents coming out from computers or
Social Security checks bearing this beastly number. A few people have declared to me that a great computer in Belgium has all the vital data about
all of us in an attempt to take over the world; such rumors scare many seriously devoted Christians who see in these operations the work of the
beast.

Unfortunately, well-meaning Christians get so worried about that future possibility that they miss the fact that the mark of the beast is already
displayed all over our world. That has been the case ever since The Revelation was written.

Biblical numerologists report that in the Jewish system of numbering
the letters in the Hebrew alphabet (the practice is called *gematria*) this
number 666 is equal to the sum of the letters used in spelling in Hebrew
the name of Nero Caesar. For that reason some scholars date the book of

Revelation in correlation with the persecutions of that Roman emperor. That the number might represent him is a very likely possibility, even if the book was written later, for Nero would represent to readers all the persecutions by the Roman state, since his inflictions had been especially gruesome.

Another explanation, however, goes hand in hand with the first. Repeatedly in The Revelation, as we have seen, the number 7 symbolizes perfection, and 3 stands for divinity or godliness/spirituality. In Hebrew thought the number 6 signifies what is less than perfect and, therefore, that which is corrupted or evil. The number 6 is the number of fallibility, less than the perfect 7. To put three 6's together, then, is to divinize that which is not divine, to make sacred what is marred or imperfect. Consequently, anything in our thoughts or life that elevates to the position of a god things that are merely human or actually evil is marked as the work of the beast. The number 666 could thus symbolize all our allegiances to the gods of this world or all the emperors who try to usurp God's place.

When I first began teaching about the book of Revelation many years ago, the Washington state lottery had just been instituted to try to solve the state's financial problems. From the first, I was distressed that many Christians were so excited about the chance to win the lottery — which seems to me to violate biblical principles of earning one's own bread and of stewardship — and I began to see in that system the mark of the beast. Over the years I have seen again and again the subtle and corrupting power of various forms of gambling, the deceptive ways in which Mammon becomes a god.

As part of my doctoral work in ethics, I was stunned to learn from economists the many deleterious effects of lottery systems. They become a regressive tax system because participants tend primarily to come from lower classes, who try desperately to win under the illusion that they can solve all their financial problems forever with just a little luck (the chances of which are terribly slim). Moreover, such systems decrease the normal, taxable revenues of stores, because folks are investing in lottery tickets instead of regular commodities. General income is thus diverted from useful products. Furthermore, if the proceeds from the lottery are used to finance such things as education, often voters will reject the kind of steady tax support that schools need. What bothers me most, however, is that the system merely coats over the real source of a state's financial problems rather than digging to the heart of the matter, assessing the inefficacies of state management, and correcting them from the inside instead of ignoring them and raising finances by such questionable means.

The lottery is just one contemporary example of many (such as Savings and Loan scandals or the collapse of Enron) that we could choose to demonstrate the power of Mammon and the mark of the beast. Jesus warned His disciples extensively about the power of this god. These chapters in The Revelation stir us Christians — who can face life realistically because we know the source of genuine hope — to be on the cutting edge warning the world about the demonic deceptions that we see in various economic, political, social, or other institutional practices and entities. If we speak as prophets, we will not necessarily be heard, but it is our Christian duty at least to speak. As God commanded Ezekiel (see Ezekiel 2–3, esp. 3:18-19), we must warn the people. If they fail to listen, then we are not responsible. But we are held accountable if we haven't warned them.

What other elements of our society illustrate the mark of the beast? When our youth idolatrously think certain brands of clothing are absolutely essential so that they can fit in with the right crowds at school, isn't the mark of the beast on their right hands? When success becomes our only goal, the I-don't-care-whom-I-hurt-just-so-I'm-number-one attitude that dominates our culture, we have marked our foreheads with a 666.

We do not have to be afraid of how the imagery of the mark of the beast might be fulfilled, but let us be vigilant against the ways in which it is constantly displayed whenever we divinize human things in our lives, whenever we let that which might have been good become corrupted and beastly/demonic.

How do things become gods to us? Are we tyrannized by power, prestige, popularity, television, hobbies, music of any sort, clothes, or any other kind of possessions? All these things parody the abundant life that Jesus promised us, a life available to us only when our thinking and way of life reflect the relationship we have with God — desiring the mind of Christ, seeking His Father's kingdom, living the divine purposes by the Spirit's power. All else is a blasphemous parody of the Triune will.

Tragically, the mark of the beast is often evident in our churches. A congregation in my town when I first wrote this book attracted kids to Bible school by offering trips or bicycles as prizes, so that their motivation was to win the world's possessions and not to have the love of Jesus possess them. Too easily some parishes thrive on the world's images of success —

fast growth, the immensity or splendor of the parish facilities, the charisma of the principal pastor, the novelty of programs or the snazziness of innovative technology — rather than the deepening of genuine discipleship. These divinizations of human goals demonstrate the workings of evil powers.

In our Christian communities, instead, let us look for those who can teach us well the danger of relying on human luxuries for our ultimate satisfaction. The elderly, out of their many years of experience, or the physically challenged, who are denied many of the opportunities that able-bodied people routinely have, can perhaps discuss with us what they have learned about the illusions of the beast's mark. My wheelchair-bound friend, Linden, once told me how he had come to see clearly that he would never be able to build the kind of life our culture craves because so much of his financial resources had to be used to hire aides for his personal care. He was grateful that the lures of owning a sailboat, enjoying various sports, or participating in many of the activities of the night life did not appeal to him at all because these idolatries were inherently inaccessible to him. Because circumstances limit him to the simple things that sustain life, he is more aware of the Joy of that simplicity than are those of us capable of attaining more pretentious lifestyles. Similarly, persons with terminal illness often report how imminent death forces them to learn the true value of life. Newly diagnosed with cancer when I first wrote this book, I felt a heightened urgency to concentrate on what is *truly* important.

Again, those who have little are usually much more willing to share than those who hoard their vast possessions. Statistics show that the poor give a much larger proportion of their income to caring for others. This was also demonstrated to me powerfully by some of the poor people who cared for me when I taught in Mexico, Madagascar, and Poland. Those who have little know better how the true value of things is multiplied by sharing.

The idolatries of our culture, symbolized by the mark of the beast, beckon us with illusions of wealth, power, position, and success. In contrast, the Father's love in Christ frees us from the control of these and other gods. Jesus offers us an alternative model of giving, submission, humility, and even suffering for the sake of the kingdom, and the Holy Spirit empowers us to live in those ways that stand against the mark of the beast. In our limitations we learn the Joy of total dependence upon the Triune God, whose mark of ownership is on our foreheads instead.

CHAPTER 25

Songs, Proclamations, and Harvests

*(Please refer often to Revelation 14
as you study this chapter.)*

I n the "Sanctus" of Gabriel Fauré's *Requiem,* there is one phrase that always makes my soul leap with great exultation. Though from its beginning the requiem has primarily been sung softly — marked *piano* and *pianissimo* with only a very few crescendos to *forte* — suddenly the trumpets and French horns enter, and all the tenors and basses sing doubly loud, "Hosanna in excelsis." Then the sopranos enter and also sing the same words *fortissimo.* Before they finish the phrase, however, they have softened back to *pianissimo.* It is stunningly brief, but gloriously bright — a momentary glimpse of splendor that fades into harp arpeggios. Every time I hear it, the heavenly instant catches me by surprise, and I taste exquisite and ecstatic Joy for just a twinkling.

The same sort of brief glimpse of heavenly glory begins Revelation 14. The seer looks and beholds the greatest sight: the Lamb, standing securely ensconced on Mount Zion! (The Greek text uses a perfect verb form for standing, which suggests a firm standing that cannot be changed; the Lamb who had been slain is solidly enthroned on Mount Zion now.) Oh, for such a vision! If we could just *see* the Lamb, victorious, that would give us the kind of sustenance we need for the endurance to which verse 12 summons us.

The Lamb is surrounded by 144,000 saints who bear His and His Father's names on their foreheads. (Again, a perfect verb form emphasizes that the names are unalterably written there and cannot be removed.) The picture is better than our newest multimedia productions, with tones superior to that produced by the finest available audio equipment, for the music sounds as if emanating from harpists and is as rich as the flow of many waters, with the resonance of loud thunder. Before the throne the saints are singing a new song, one that only the redeemed can know — those who satisfy the sacral requirements of chastity for warriors in the constant war against evil. They speak only the truth and are blameless. They are the first fruits of God's harvest of righteousness.

This picture contrasts sharply with the grotesque parody of the dragon and the two beasts in chapters 12 and 13, culminating with the beast's symbolic number 666. The number 144,000 is also symbolic and represents the whole people of God — by means of 12 (the tribes of Israel) times 12 (the new covenant people) times 1,000 (a number of multiplied, thorough completeness).

Not recognizing the symbolism of the number 144,000, the Jehovah's Witnesses have claimed it for their own as the number of their people, though they have had to modify their original insistence that it literally signified them now that the sect has gathered more than 144,000 members. However, the symbolic number stands for all God's saints. Comparably, in all their anxiety over literal 666's coming out of computers, many Christians don't realize that the mark of the beast is constantly displayed in our world.

The Revelation was intended to warn the early Christians (and us) to be alert for all the deceptive ways in which evil works. In the first century, Christians were being tempted to soften their vigilance, to become enculturated in ways that threatened their Christian faith and life. Still today the threat is very real. Christians can easily begin to live for the successes and possessions of the societies around them rather than as participants in, and witnesses to, the kingdom of God. Churches can easily become merely mirrors of the prevailing culture rather than icons of the living God. The dragon and the beasts are still waging war against the children of the woman (12:17).

Similarly, the first verses in chapter 14 continue to be fulfilled. Indeed, God's people bear upon their minds and countenances the radiance of their relationship with God. Every time exhilarated Christians burst out with a new hymn of praise in words or in life, they participate in the songs of the 144,000 before the throne.

The rest of Revelation 14 alternates between verses about judgment and passages of proclamation, repentance, and hope. It has become common in religious circles in the twenty-first century to deny God's judgment and wrath, for God, after all, "desires everyone to be saved and to come to the knowledge of the truth" (1 Tim. 2:4). The Revelation makes it clear, however, that judgment is a necessary element of God's actions (see the following chapter), though the note of urgency and warning in the next several verses makes it clear that God's love is supreme.

Verses 6-7 present several reminders of the fullness of God's grace. The flying angel has an *eternal* gospel to proclaim. (Our English words "gospel" and "proclaim" translate a cognate noun and verb both from the Greek root *euaggeli* and thereby doubly stress the "good news.") Furthermore, this good news is to be announced to every nation, tribe, language, and people. Notice that the terms are four in number to stress universality. God does indubitably desire for all to be saved.

The angel challenges us in a loud voice (so everyone can hear?) to "fear God and give Him glory." In the hour of judgment, our best response is to worship the Creator, who made heaven, earth, sea, and springs of water (another set of four to symbolize everything).

The combination of fearing God and giving Him glory spurs us to consider what this kind of fear might be, since often in The Revelation we are urged not to fear. In chapter 14's mix of warnings and positive proclamations, of first-fruit harvests and harvests for wrath, of calls to endurance and promises of rest with oracles of restlessness for those with the beast's mark, we realize that fearing God is essential. Lest we forget that our salvation lies in none other, that only those who "die in the Lord" are blessed, it is a gift to be fearful of God's wrath. If we really face our true character and discern our sinfulness, we know that we deserve that wrath. Then what a Joy it is to know that we are rescued, that the angel proclaims "an eternal gospel"!

In the midst of the weakness of our human fallibility and fallenness, we know the Joy of grace when we properly fear God. Then, we respond by giving Him glory, for His love is larger than wrath and we are its unworthy recipients.

Lest we dally and think we'll turn to God some other time, the next proclamation by an angel is the death knell of Babylon. She is "fallen, fallen" because she has caused others to drink of her immorality. We won't see details of the sins and end of Babylon until Revelation 18 (see Chapter 27), but the announcement in 14:8 makes it clear that her doom is sure. Christians who think they can play around with the world's iniquities need to realize that they are asking for judgment.

A third angel amplifies the warning in verses 9-11. To worship the beast and join in with the bestial idolatries (i.e., to receive the beast's mark) is also to participate in the torments of God's wrath against all the forces of evil. There will be no eternal rest for those who make that choice.

In contrast, those who "die in the Lord" (v. 13) will surely "rest from their labors." Their deeds will follow them because everything that we have done by means of grace and in grace for God is part of God's gracious work of cosmic reconciliation.

In the meanwhile, until that day when we finally rest in the fullness of God's blessing, we are called to endure, to keep God's commandments, to "hold fast to the faith of Jesus" (v. 12). This is an important call for all God's people in our present circumstances.

I am revising this section of the book exactly a month after terrorists flew three airplanes into the World Trade Center towers and the Pentagon. This is a critical time to distinguish the mark of the beast from God's commandments and the faith of Jesus to which we should hold fast. It is extremely difficult to make the necessary nuances between bringing Osama bin Laden and other terrorists to justice and acting out of vengeance. It requires exhaustive research to combat terrorists without harming innocent civilians. It is tricky to call our nation to repentance for our misuse of the world's wealth without seeming to be indifferent to the immense suffering of families, especially in the U.S. but also throughout the world, whose loved ones were killed in the airplanes' strikes. People of faith have to keep asking better questions in order to be authentic in keeping God's commandments while also avoiding the mark of the beast.

Life that holds fast to the faith of Jesus requires never-ending endurance, for many complexities demand careful nuances. Part of our weakness is that we can never know enough. When we know our own weakness, however, we are more ready to wait humbly for the Holy Spirit's direction. We are more willing to spend time in prayer, to seek the counsel of the Christian community, to obey the commandments of God.

The final two scenes in Revelation 14 depict two harvests — the first by the Son of Man, crowned, and bearing the full authority of Deity (as suggested by three references to the cloud upon which He sat and by the title "Son of Man," which reminds us of the vision in Daniel 7:13-14, in which He is given dominion and glory and kingship by the Ancient of Days). This is a harvest of joy, closely connected to the promise in verse 13 that those who die in the Lord will experience blessing and rest. Verse 4 named the

144,000 as the first fruits of this redemptive harvest. Now the entire harvest of the earth is "fully ripe."

This progression is somewhat similar to that of the sealing in Revelation 7, which also moves from the number 144,000 to a more complete number — in fact, "a great multitude that no one could count, from every nation, from all tribes and peoples and languages" (7:9). So here, those who are harvested are gathered from the whole earth. The saints are found everywhere.

Jesus talked about harvests during His earthly ministry. In Matthew 9:37-38, His comments are tied in with His compassion for those who are as sheep without a shepherd and His urging the disciples to pray for more harvesters since the harvest is so plentiful (as in Luke 10:2). In Mark 4:26-29, His parable includes the surprise that God's kingdom grows without our understanding how. In John 4:35-38 the disciples are invited to rejoice no matter what their part has been, whether sowers or reapers, when the fruit is gathered for eternal life. All these passages imply an abundant harvest, larger than we could imagine, and each contains strong hints of Joy.

The size of the harvest nudges me to think also of Jesus' parable that the wheat and tares grow together until the harvest (Matt. 13:24-30 and 36-43). We don't know who belongs to God's kingdom, and we will certainly be astonished when we find out. My reaction to that is simply to be as committed as possible to sowing and reaping, to participate as fully as I can in proclaiming the eternal gospel to people from every nation, from all tribes, peoples, and languages.

I am all the more eager to be engaged in proclaiming the eternal gospel because Revelation 14 ends with a second harvest, this time a gathering to wrath. We can't ignore God's judgment (as many like to do these days), for it is righteous and just. It will take place, so let us "fear God and give Him glory."

Some newer translations say that the blood that will flow from the wine press of God's wrath will spread for a distance of about two hundred miles. To put this image into contemporary measurements does it a huge disservice, because the point of the image is not to offer a literalistic description of the output from God's press. The original Greek figure is 1,600 stadia and is, no doubt, a symbolic number. A universal four and the number of completion (10) are both squared; this might suggest that those who deserve God's wrath also come from all over the earth. Or perhaps the figure signifies the squaring of 40, which throughout the Bible is the traditional number signifying trials or testings. We can't know precisely, but any of these interpretations simply intensifies my desire to proclaim the eternal gospel and to urge my hearers to look to the God whose love is stronger than wrath. More than anything, may we who bear witness, along with the angels (especially in 14:6-7), do all we can to urge our listeners to heed the gracious warnings that The Revelation gives and respond with repentance and perseverance in faith.

Even as in the time when The Revelation was written, today Christians are tempted to let slide our vigilance against the incursions of the evil powers into our lives. We are constantly allured by our society's attractions and beckoned away from steadfast faithfulness. We need the strong pictures in these chapters to bolster our wariness against the ways in which evil entrances us, then enthralls and enraptures, and finally ensnares us.

The Lord God Almighty continually warns and chides us to save us from such deadly peril. How can we not see that as an immense work of grace?

May we be stirred to respond with repentance and renewed commitment. And may God be glorified through all that you and I do to help our neighbors throughout the world to love and fear God, who warns and harvests and blesses those with steadfast faith.

CHAPTER 26

We Wouldn't Want Love without Holiness

(Please refer often to Revelation 15–16
as you study this chapter.)

I remember a time in elementary school when I was given a lower grade than another student even though I had done better work. Even at that young age I knew it was unjust and questioned the unfair assessment.

In contrast, a few years later a music competition judge gave me the only low score I'd ever received on solos even though I had practiced my clarinet diligently. I didn't question that rating, however, because I recognized my deficiencies and aimed to correct them with future practice. The judge's assessment was just.

On a much larger scale, many people question the justice of God. The text of Revelation 15, which lies before us in this chapter, makes it clear that, even when God vents his wrath, God's judgments are always both just and loving.

We are warned by the opening sentence of this scene that we are about to encounter a very important event. The seer tells us that he saw another sign in heaven, great and marvelous, and that the seven plagues which the seven angels held were the last because in them God's wrath is finished (15:1).

Before we see that final venting of God's wrath, however, we hear a song of praise for God's justice. The exaltation of the song is heightened by the preceding description of those who sing it. All of them have come away victorious from the beast's work, from his image and from the number of his name. Furthermore, they stand on a sea of glass seemingly mixed with fire. Finally, even the harps they hold are given to them by God. Every element in this description, especially because each one echoes previous passages in The Revelation and in the First Testament, heightens our awareness that these saints truly are God's people, committed to Him and faithful in His service.

Moreover, the songs they sing are those of Moses, God's faithful bond-servant, and of the Lamb. Perhaps these titles are meant to indicate the whole counsel and entire Word of God, since Moses certainly represents God's covenant with Israel, even as the Lamb represents God's work of reconciliation with the whole world. Certainly the song that follows is composed of bits and snatches from many portions of the Scriptures, both Hebrew and Greek. We won't trace all of those connections here (since you can readily find them yourself in any good commentary or cross-reference Bible). Rather, the important note for our purposes is that the song exalts the righteousness, the truth, the justice of God's ways. That is certainly the reminder we need before we encounter the scene of God's final wrath.

We have to hear this content of the song especially because people in our times often object that they can't believe in a God who punishes people. "I believe in a God who loves everybody," they say. "Certainly you can't believe that there is a hell. If God is really loving, then doesn't God want to save everyone?" Such comments demonstrate the common problem of reducing the complexity of God's dialectical character to a single attribute. If we recognize God only as loving, we will forget that the Trinity is also just and holy. If we concentrate only on divine justice, we might lose the Lamb's grace in overemphasizing the Almighty's wrath.

God is both loving and holy. Certainly divine love pervades divine justice (as we shall see in the following pictures of God's wrath), but holy justice must be weighed nonetheless, or else ultimately everything would be unfair. Even my childhood insight prevented me from accepting unfairness; those who want only a loving God would reject that one-sidedness, too, if they seriously considered its ultimate implications.[1]

Instead, the song of all those who had conquered the beast exults that

1. For a summary of First Testament teaching concerning God's wrath, see the section titled "Historical and Prophetic Visions of God's Wrath" in chapter 5 of my *Unfettered Hope* (Louisville: Westminster/John Knox Press, forthcoming 2003). This summary is based on Terence E. Fretheim's superb (as yet unpublished) paper, "Theological Reflections on the Wrath of God in the Old Testament," presented at the American Academy of Religion/Society of Biblical Literature annual meeting in Denver, Colorado, on November 18, 2001.

when the nations genuinely see the righteousness and truth of God's ways, they will come to worship the Lord, who is indeed King of the nations (15:3-4). This song gives us a model for dealing with those who want only a loving God. When we listen to people who decry God's wrath, we do not need to defend Triune wisdom. Rather, we want to show them how the righteousness of the Lord's ways has already been revealed.

In 15:5-8 the descriptions of the angels who undertake the task remind us again of God's holiness and purity in divine actions of wrath. First, we are told that they came out of the temple of the tabernacle of testimony in heaven (a pictorial stacking that certainly underscores the holiness of their origin). Next, they are robed in clean, bright, pure linen and golden sashes. Finally, the bowls they are given are golden.

Most important, their description is undergirded with the themes of the character of God. The angels deliver the wrath of the One who lives forever and ever, the One whose glory and power fill the temple with smoke (a reminder of the scene in Isaiah 6, to which the prophet responded with a sense of his uncleanness because he had seen the holy God).

The same theme of the righteousness and justice of God's acts is carried into the description in chapter 16 of the first three plagues and the response they elicited. Verse 2 insists that when the bowl of the plague was poured out upon the earth it became a loathsome and malignant sore only upon the ones who had the mark of the beast and had worshiped his image. As Craig Koester points out,

> The mark of the idolatry through which people accommodate evil and seek to escape affliction, is now matched by a sore that brings affliction. Painful though it is, however, the sore that God inflicts upon the followers of the beast is less severe than the death that the beast inflicted upon the followers of the Lamb. Like the sores that came upon the Egyptians before the exodus (Exod. 9:10-11), it presses people to repent of their oppressive practices (Rev. 16:9, 11).[2]

Let us pay close attention to three insights in Koester's comments. The grace of the sore matches its source in a gracious God. It is less severe than

---

2. Craig R. Koester, *Revelation and the End of All Things* (Grand Rapids: Wm. B. Eerdmans Publishing Co., 2001), p. 149.

the evil done by those who experience it. And, again, it provides another call to repentance. How many chances will the Lord continue to give those who rebel against God?

Another element of this passage that is crucial for our understanding is that it is not intended to explain why the innocent suffer and perish. Instead, these chapters are intended to press a related question, "Why do the ungodly survive?"[3] The second and third bowls of wrath add to the urgency of people's chances to repent as God limits the sufferings (Koester calls it "a strange restraint in the justice of God") and yet matches them to the evil deeds of those who worshiped the beast.

However, as the text proceeds, there is no sign of repentance yet. Instead, after the second and third plagues, both the angel of the waters and the altar offer another hymn of praise for the righteousness of God's judgments (16:5-7). In addition, the judgment they praise resembles the blood plague in Egypt and would no doubt have reminded The Revelation's initial readers of the righteous significance of God's intervention there in the Israelites' lives.

With the pouring of the fourth bowl the theme of repentance is specifically introduced. The responses to both the fourth and fifth plague are similar, though their slight differences as a literary technique draw us to pay more attention to them. Meanwhile, their repetitiveness underscores the importance of this point: human beings responded to God's efforts to draw them to repentance with curses. The blasphemers resented the fact that God had power over these plagues and themselves; instead of letting that power draw them to infinite divine love, they did not repent and give God the glory.

Their responses (vv. 9 and 11) call each one of us to repentance. How easily we resent the Almighty's power, instead of seeing that it is always used for the purposes of Triune love! Sometimes we feel backed into a corner — with no way out except God's way — and we rebel because we don't have more choices.

To write this makes me feel ashamed of my stubbornness. How long I have fought some of God's purposes in my life because I keep wanting to do things my way. Even as my husband waited through six years of friendship (including my graduate study far away from him) for me to recognize and accept his devotion and commitment, so (multiplied infinitely) God

---

3. Koester, *Revelation and the End of All Things,* p. 149.

waits immeasurably long for the people of the earth to repent and be drawn to the Lord's forgiveness and salvation.

The sixth plague, however, makes us realize that God won't wait forever. Finally divine judgment must come.

The beginning of the description of that plague, however, contains a mysterious little verse (like so many in The Revelation) that stirs up our curiosity and invites us to deeper reflection. When the angel pours the bowl, the waters of the great river Euphrates are dried up in order to prepare the way for the kings of the east (16:12). One wonders why these dignitaries were singled out, except that the only other use of the phrase "of the east" (literally, "from the rising of the sun") occurs in chapter 7, just before the sealing of all God's elect.

Furthermore, the idea of the drying up of the Euphrates would remind the original readers of The Revelation of God's promise in Isaiah 11:15-16 and 44:27-28 that the river would be dried up and a way made for the LORD's people to return from the Babylonian captivity. Cyrus himself (a king of the east!) would be a shepherd to fulfill God's purposes of restoration. Similarly, the Roman powers that oppressed people at the time The Revelation was written feared invasion by the Parthians from east of the Euphrates. Thus, in the midst of these descriptions of the plagues is another promise that the LORD will gather in the covenant people and care for them.

The plague itself is actually initiated by the powers of evil, for out of the mouths of the dragon, the beast, and the false prophet flow three unclean spirits like frogs — a vivid image for their peskiness and pervasiveness. These, we are told, are the spirits of the demons, the ones who perform signs and gather the kings of all the world for the war with God.

Our concentration is pulled away from their gathering, however, by the reminder that Christ is coming soon (v. 15). We must pay careful attention to this literary emphasis, which underscores my point about the whole book of Revelation. We ought not to hate the book or be afraid of it, for it does not primarily emphasize gruesome wars and horrible creatures.[4]

---

4. I was thinking of this after seeing the new movie version of the first part of J. R. R. Tolkien's *Lord of the Rings* trilogy. The first book, *The Fellowship of the Ring,* confines the violence to a few short pages at a time and emphasizes instead the landscape, the people, their friendship, and, most deeply, the good power that undergirds everything. In contrast, the movie highlights and focuses on the violence; it contains

We are not allowed to focus here on the gathering of the kings for war against God, nor on the evil spirits who call them. Rather, they are gathering for the war "of the great day of God, the Almighty" (16:14). That phrase resets our bearings, as does the second half of verse 15, which reminds us that those who are waiting for Christ's coming are blessed. They are not naked and ashamed if they are awake and watching. Rather, they will thus have kept their garments to be ready for Christ's coming.

Certainly we have all heard various theories about the great battle of Armageddon. During the most critical years of the Cold War between the U.S.S.R. and the U.S., some people thought, and even today some still think, that Armageddon will take place in a nuclear war. Such theories totally miss the point of the name.

The name literally is *Har-mageddon,* and it is an oxymoron, a figure of speech in which contradictory terms are combined.

Ancient Megiddo was located in the Plain of Esdraelon and was the famous site of several important battles in Jewish history. It is also mentioned in a number of Egyptian and Assyrian texts, so it most likely would have been immediately recognized by those who first read The Revelation as a place of conflict. However, they might also have been taken aback by the prefix *Har,* for that Hebrew word signifies a mountain, whereas the plain of Megiddo is the flattest land in Israel. What could this mean — the Mountain of the Battle Plain?

Since the seer John has consistently used Hebrew names in The Revelation symbolically, this oxymoron reminds us not to put these illustrations of the conflict of good and evil into literalistic, physical human terms. The book of Revelation is not trying to teach us how the world will end. Rather, it seeks to comfort us in our struggles with the hope that, in the end, evil will ultimately be vanquished forever.

This emphasis is reinforced by the fact that the name *Armageddon* is never mentioned again in The Revelation and by the seventh plague, which is depicted with all the elements from a First Testament theophany, or appearance of God. Flashes of lightning, peals of thunder, and severe earthquakes all remind us of God's descent to Mount Sinai (which we then con-

---

horribly gruesome characters and spends a great deal of time picturing them and their actions. Similarly, people want to accentuate the plagues and judgments of The Revelation instead of noticing how often those are interrupted by grace and how profoundly the main focus of the book is the Lamb, the Christ, who delivers us.

nect with this symbolic Mount of Megiddo). These images reinforce the notion that the end of the world is not going to be brought about by any warring between the earth's kings or nuclear weapons or terrorist attacks, but by the mighty coming of God.

Furthermore, the preparation for the kings' warring is not the cause of anything that happens, for the loud voice from the temple has already said that "it has come to pass" (16:17) — and the Greek verb tense emphasizes that what has already come to pass remains. God's justice and righteousness have already had their way. Evil was destroyed at the cross and empty tomb, and now we will only see effected what Christ already accomplished there.

The images of the next few verses reinforce this point. The cities of the nations fall; God's cup of wrath is poured out upon Babylon, which is split in three; the islands and mountains flee; and huge hailstones fall.

However, the scene ends with this tragic declaration that the whole picture was meant to make more poignant to us: even though all these events happen to warn human beings and to call them to repentance, still they respond only with more blasphemy. This time the verse does not even contain the comment that they refused to repent. It did not even enter their minds that this was the reason for all their agony.

How terribly disturbing it is if Christians get excited about this chapter and happily anticipate an Armageddon, merrily declare that nuclear war will bring the world to an end, or express gladness that God will punish all the evil people in the world. No, instead we must leave this chapter with subdued hearts and grief for those who continually resist. Let us also remember how easily we, too, blaspheme God and do not repent.

How have I failed to heed all God's warnings? What calls is the Lord giving me now to which I'm not paying heed? In what areas of my life am I being rebellious? How do I deserve God's wrath — and yet I know that Triune grace enfolds me? How can this be, that in my failures and weaknesses and doubts and sinfulness Triune grace still enfolds me? How can I spread the message of that grace more effectively? How can I urge my neighbors to repent and learn the Lord's love?

It drives me to my knees in gratitude — this overwhelming grace and righteous justice of God!

CHAPTER 27

Fallen! Fallen Is Babylon the Great!

*(Please refer often to Revelation 17–18
as you study this chapter.)*

One of the most painful Gospel narratives we read or hear is the account of the rich man who asked Jesus what he must do to inherit eternal life. In the ensuing discussion Jesus tells him to sell all that he has, to give it to the poor, and to follow Him. The rich man walks away sad, so possessed by his possessions that he cannot obey. Poignantly, Mark's account includes the momentous statement, "Jesus looked at him and loved him" (Mark 10:21). How Jesus longed to deliver that rich man from the snare of Mammon! He yearned for him to turn back in repentance and contrition. God certainly delights when Triune grace leads us to recognize our sin and turn to the Lamb in sorrow.

As the Hebrew prophets frequently show and as Revelation 17–18 makes clear, the power of Mammon is extremely tenacious. The Holy Spirit repeatedly calls us through both messengers and the Triune Word to repent, but eventually God must judge those who reject divine grace and continue in their idolatries.

In 1988 sexual scandals surfaced in connection with televangelists Jim Bakker and Jimmy Swaggart. As we Christians face the cynicism of a world that already looks askance at our Christian beliefs, we must realize that these men fell morally long before they were caught in explicit sexual immorality. The demonic power of Mammon had ensnared them as well.

A few years ago a Christian "think tank" in the Pacific Northwest sponsored a "Spiritual Roundtable," in which we discussed the nature of our society and the dangers to Christians of becoming enculturated, both personally and corporately, in the world's economic patterns, which are contrary to those of the Gospel.[1] For example, Christians might be tempted by our culture's elaborate ostentation in weddings — when families spend such inordinate amounts of money on gowns, tuxedos, flowers, receptions, and gifts that the ceremony focuses on glitz rather than on the meaning of marriage. Corporately, throughout history various Christian denominations have been characterized by a spirit of accumulation rather than generosity, by exploitation of the Two-Thirds World rather than economic support, by seeking after economic power rather than siding with the poor and the oppressed. Recent theological and political developments have caused church bodies in general to reassess our character — though individuals and movements have questioned Christian economic policies in various times ever since Constantine first joined the "faith" with the Roman empire.

The Hebrew prophets fervently warned Israel of the idolatry of wealth. Jesus warned us, too. About one-sixth of His sayings in the Synoptic Gospels relate to the dangers of the god Mammon. Here The Revelation culminates all these warnings that economic temptation is the undoing of the world, that the principality we have most to fear is that of Mammon.

Out of all the judgments depicted by the bowls of wrath, chapters 17 and 18 now focus on the particular judgment of the city of Babylon. Of course, this name does not refer only to that specific city, for it has stood throughout the Scriptures as the name for those who oppress God's people. To the original readers of The Revelation it stood for Rome, but Jacques Ellul makes an effective argument for understanding Babylon as the archetypal city, the focus of sin, one of the powers that exerts its influence on the present world.[2]

At first we might think that the city's most serious problem is its sexual depravity, because an angel summoned the seer to show him the great harlot, "with whom the kings of the earth committed acts of immorality." However, the Hebrew prophets had set the biblical precedent for using the title "harlot" to denote more than sexual immorality; especially Hosea in his life and words repeatedly warned Israel against going "awhoring after

---

1. See also my book on this subject, *Unfettered Hope* (Louisville: Westminster/John Knox Press, forthcoming 2003).

2. See Jacques Ellul's *The Meaning of the City*, trans. Dennis Pardee (Grand Rapids: Wm. B. Eerdmans Publishing Co., 1970), for his very powerful argument and warning.

other gods." Now the entire description of Revelation 17 and 18 exposes the treacherous lure of Mammon in luxury and economic injustice.

The beast on which the harlot sits is full of blasphemous names and has symbols of authority and power in the perfect and complete numbers (seven heads and ten horns). This reminder of the first beast in chapter 13 points to the demonic power that exerts its influence on the world through her.

The beginning description of the harlot herself unveils her excessive luxury. She is clothed in purple and scarlet and adorned with gold, precious stones, and pearls — all symbols in the ancient world of wealth. Her cup is gold, but its contents begin to show us three other things that we must notice about her at this point.

First, this description is loaded with scathing satire, as Craig Koester points out superbly well.[3] It is like a caricature in a political cartoon. At first she seems to be elegant in her wealth, but the gorgeous cup from which she sips is filled with the vile sewage of her abominations, her uncleanness and immorality. She is a ludicrous and contemptible buffoon, a "debauched courtesan," clinging to an outrageous beast.

Second, her name is very complete (written across her forehead as in a cartoon) and seemingly self-explanatory — "Babylon the Great, the Mother of Harlots and of the Abominations of the Earth" — and yet it is specifically called a mystery. That word warns us not to think that we can pin her title down, that we can reduce it to some simplistic understanding. She does not merely stand for Rome (in the time of The Revelation) or some decadent city in our present age. Evil pervades everything. We dare not think it is only focalized in a particular city, race of people, or type of sin.

Third, she was drunk with the blood of the saints and the witnesses of Jesus. Many Christians throughout history have lost their lives in the battle against the power of Mammon. Consider, for example, the many martyrs in Central and South American countries whose Christian faith directed their work among the poor and powerless — and led to their arrest and torture and assassination. Moreover, many Christians have found that there is no point in giving in even slightly to this world's powers in the hope that we can preserve our own life. As believers in Eastern Europe and

---

3. Craig R. Koester, *Revelation and the End of All Things* (Grand Rapids: Wm. B. Eerdmans Publishing Co., 2001), pp. 146, 155-59.

the former Soviet Union found out, raw Mammon kills Christians, including those who try to accommodate.

Here in the United States the killing might take less obvious forms, such as what happens to persons of integrity like employees who refuse to obey criminal business practices. We are also warned by these chapters to be vigilant against, and to continue to resist, extreme luxury, which leads to economic injustice that actually kills.

At the seer's wondering (17:6), the angel proceeds to tell him all about the mysteries of the woman and the beast (vv. 7-18). Various interpretations of this story have falsely pinned down its details, greatly to the destruction of its point. The ten kings have been identified with the Common Market of Europe; the seven mountains on which she sits are correlated with Rome.

It is true that the description in the text most likely raised up various associations with the city of Rome for the first people who read The Revelation, and we do well to locate its initial meaning there. However, the danger is to take that kind of specific identification into the future and declare that we can associate these descriptions with particular people and places in the twenty-first century. In doing so, we violate major rules for reading the Bible.

Our procedure throughout this book has been to locate the meaning of a text in its history at the time of writing, when the Christians were being persecuted by Imperial Rome and/or their neighbors and needed hope and comfort. Now, however, that kind of geographical locating is not possible, for there are Christians everywhere being persecuted by all kinds of governments. We have become a global community, and our persecutors sometimes are people who claim the heritage of a "Christian nation." What matters, then, is to note the sins of which the harlot is guilty, to see how those sins have pervaded our lives, and to be called to repentance and new strength to stand against the powers that draw us to false values and actions.

The very language of 17:8-18 makes us realize that we run into trouble if we reduce the image to only one specific figure. The beast is drawn as the "one who was and is not, and is about to come." These phrases remind us of the parody in chapters 12 and 13, in which the powers of evil imitate the God "who is, who was, and who is to come," a description by which the Lord Almighty is named throughout The Revelation. This particular scarlet beast, whose heads are various kings, might represent any demonic line of government or dynasty of emperors.

The seven kings, of which five have fallen, probably referred originally to specific Roman emperors (since Rome sat on seven hills), but that very identification and the inability of scholars to agree on which leaders might be signified warn us against trying to match the kings up with specific people now in order to date the end of the world precisely. Instead, the situation in first-century Rome shows us this tendency: how the principalities and powers of the earth rise and fall.

The language of 17:10-11 is quite mysterious, though it probably had specific connotations for the original readers of The Revelation. The phrase "the beast which was and is not, is himself also an eighth and is one of the seven" might help us to understand that the power of evil manifests itself in particular forms in our world and yet is a principality outside of human influences. Though we do not know the particular identifications, we can certainly know that the beast is headed for destruction. We saw in chapter 13 that the beast is an imitation of God, that the demonic principalities usurp a power that is not theirs. We must be wary of all the forms these principalities take in our modern world.[4]

Five essential items of the description that closes Revelation 17 must be noted. First, these kings and powers all receive their authority from someone else (v. 12). They serve one purpose, and that is to give power to the beast. All the evil influences in our world serve one end — to contradict and destroy the work of God and to draw humankind away from God. Ultimately, as The Revelation repeatedly shows us, there is but this one conflict in the cosmos: between the purposes of Satan and the purposes of God.

Second, we must note that all these kings, beasts, horns, and whatever are not going to be able to accomplish anything in the end. They might seem to cause a lot of trouble now, to get all sorts of people to live under their sway and to act on their power. In the final war against the Lamb, however, He will overcome them all because, let us never forget, He is Lord over every lord and King of all kings and everything else.

Third (wonder of wonders!), we are named right there with Him. The

---

4. Many of the works of Jacques Ellul discuss this topic of the biblical concept of the principalities and powers and their contemporary manifestations and influences. See, especially, *The Humiliation of the Word*, trans. Joyce Main Hanks (Grand Rapids: Wm. B. Eerdmans Publishing Co., 1985), and *Money and Power*, trans. LaVonne Neff (Downers Grove, IL: InterVarsity Press, 1984).

ones with the Lamb are the "called and chosen and faithful." These names appear repeatedly in The Revelation and throughout the entire New Testament. They give us enormous hope for the future. The Lamb who will ultimately triumph keeps us securely right by His side. We are not going to be left behind. He has called us; He has chosen us. Are we faithful in response to such grace?

Fourth, we must notice that an awful lot of people get sucked up into the deceptions of the powers. A slightly different set of four summarizes the universality of their influence over peoples, multitudes, nations, and tongues. The four corners of the earth and everything else in between are harassed by the actions of the powers. No place on earth escapes the demonic working of evil forces.

However, none of this is out of God's control. Verse 16 reminds us of this fifth and final point: the powers of evil betray and destroy themselves. The ten horns and the beast turn on the harlot, just as those lusting after power in our world make use of people only until they are no longer needed and then turn their machinations against them. The manipulation and exploitation of one another always characterize the demonic powers and their cohorts. Ultimately, however, even these demonic turnings accomplish God's purposes. Evil wreaks its own havoc, which serves God's purposes of demolishing it. God's righteous wrath and justice allow evil eventually to annihilate itself.

From the perspective of Christ's victory over the powers, evil is indeed already destroyed. Meanwhile, until His victory is thoroughly manifested at the end of the world, evil continues to carry within itself the seeds of its own destruction. God's purposes of good cannot be thwarted — the last enemies were exposed and defeated in the cross and resurrection of Jesus. That is why chapter 18 begins with the declaration that Babylon *has* fallen. The angel who bears this message is described in a way that underscores his authority — even the earth is illumined with the glory of that authority.

Babylon is already fallen. The angel announces God's judgment that she has doomed herself because many participate in her sins (specifically the acts of sexual immorality and the excessive luxury of her sensuality) and because she is a dwelling place for evil powers.

All of chapter 18 is quite self-explanatory. After the declaration of the reasons for the harlot's fall (vv. 1-3), there is another call to repentance. People are urged to come away from the sins with which she is imbued. They are warned not to participate in her iniquities and sensuality, for she will surely be tormented to the degree that she has glorified herself and lived without concern for others.

This is underscored by the use of the word "woe" (*ouai* in Greek) in verse 10. This word is better translated in The Revelation as "alas!" — an exclamation of mourning — for the statement is not a curse, but a lament. In Revelation 12:12 the dirge is genuine, but here in 18:10, a passage in the genre of a city lament, it is satirical because of Rome's exploitation of the whole world.[5] The merchants and sailors who cry, "Alas!" are not really weeping for Babylon, but out of their own self-concern and worry over lost wealth. The root problem with opulence is that those who enjoy it care for no one but themselves.

Especially noteworthy in all of this is the point made at the beginning of this chapter: Babylon's major sin is not so much sexual immorality as the sensuality of wealth. Notice the long list of kinds of luxury related to the city. All the rest of chapter 18 is composed of various elements that make up the god of Mammon: luxury goods, exploitation of other human beings, sensual pleasures, empty hilarity, self-absorption in music and crafts and festivals without any concern for the call of God. Commodification spreads out from goods to people.

Certainly the text is not criticizing music or crafts, cinnamon or ivory, money or parties per se. What is wrong is the deception, the greedy amassing of material possessions, hilarity without meaning, self-aggrandizement without care for the rest of the world, the killing of the saints, the idolatries.

Perhaps one reason our age has been so busy making up lurid interpretations of The Revelation is that we have not wanted to face how much this eighteenth chapter condemns us. In a world of gross inequities, we are reproached for our accumulation of silver and silks and spices. We are rebuked for our enculturation into a society that has fallen to the power of Mammon.

We dare not read The Revelation to find out who to blame as a beast having ten heads. We can read it only to know our own idolatries and sins and to repent for them with humility and grief.

---

5. I thank Barbara Rossing of the Lutheran School of Theology in Chicago for insights included in this paragraph from her paper, "'Fallen Is Babylon': The City-Lament Genre in Revelation 18," presented at the American Academy of Religion/Society of Biblical Literature annual meeting in Denver on November 19, 2001.

It is not a book for the mighty — those who think they are better than others because they have not fallen to the sin of sexual immorality, like those prominent Christians caught in scandals. It is a book for the weak — those who know they have fallen and need redemption and grace.

CHAPTER 28

Preludes and Wedding Songs

(Please refer often to Revelation 19:1-21
as you study this chapter.)

A fter the wild frenzy and dense darkness of the storm, the brilliantly hued double rainbow was all the more dazzling. In contrast to the wracking pain of the day before, the genuine calmness in my body was most refreshing. After the frantic pace of the previous day's activities, the leisure and pleasant visiting of my Sabbath day were a welcome relief. Many of the positive experiences of our lives are made all the more delectable by the sharp contrast between them and whatever preceded them.

In Revelation 19, the virtues of the bride, viewed from a heavenly perspective, are made all the more magnificent by their extreme dissimilarity to the vices of the harlot in the previous chapters as she was viewed from the perspectives of earth. Whereas the harlot was characterized by sin, corruption, mourning, doom, death, and sorrow, the bride is portrayed as righteousness, purity, singing, victory, life, hope, and Joy.

Besides these elements contrasting to the prostitute of corruption, that great city Babylon, several aspects of the literary form focus our attention on this bride. For example, chapter 18 includes a series of three laments about the doom of the city Babylon, to be contrasted now with the three songs of praise and victory at the beginning of chapter 19 (in vv. 1-3, 4, and 5).

Another element of the literary form is that the elders and the living creatures, who appear again in 19:4, vanish after this incident. All along they have served to point to the Lamb, and in the process we grow rather fond of those characters in the drama; but their disappearance from the scene is necessary at this point so that full attention can be given for the rest of the book to the final victory of the Lamb and His marriage with the bride. In order for us to appreciate the immensity of the victory, all elements of the story now point to it rather than to other characters who have participated in the drama thus far.

There is also great dramatic splendor in the announcing of the marriage feast. The addition of such elements as the voice of the great crowd (from Dan. 10:6), the sound of many waters, or the loud peals of thunder (from Ezek. 1:24 and 43:2) heighten our anticipation for the announcement that will proclaim the Lamb's feast.

As another example of God's delightful timing, while I was first writing this chapter on The Revelation's thundering voices I was enjoying the sounds of a good old Midwestern thunderstorm. I grew up liking them — probably because my mother had first calmed me with the assurance that the thunder was the voice of God. (On days when I'd been really naughty that was a rather terrifying thought, but on most days of my childhood the idea of God's loving voice was comforting.) Now living on the West Coast, I have sorely missed the strong thunderstorms, so I thoroughly enjoyed the crashes and drummings of the storm while working on this chapter. This experience served, as does Revelation 19:6, to heighten my anticipation as we prepare for the grand finale of the book of Revelation.

All of this proclaims a momentous change of perspective. For several chapters The Revelation has focused on the corruption of Babylon and the way she has corrupted the earth. Anyone who is not in touch with the reality of sin and its social, economic, and political corruptions will grasp them more easily if he or she thoroughly pays attention to the evil of these chapters. Now in 19:2-4 the fall of Babylon is announced and praised.

We must be very careful, however, to note in the praise of verse 2 a critical distinction between our humanly marred revenge and God's righteous condemnation. The great harlot is not destroyed "to get even." Rather, God's vengeance on the city comes from divinely "true and just" judgments. With total holiness and truth God condemns the great prostitute and vindicates the Lord's bondservants by avenging their deaths.

We must be very fearful of any theologies (including some liberation theologies) that resort to violence and power. When they do so, the motive for victory seems to become revenge, rather than restoration of God's true justice. We can't justify violence as a means to an end, for the character of the end must also determine the means. We won't restore truth if we use false means to attain it; if our goals are peace and justice in the world, we will not bring them about by methods that are unjust or that inflict pain on others.

My friend Linden provides a good model of this correlation of means and ends for asserting truth. I have never seen in him any violence against others; he is not capable of inflicting violence upon anyone. Rather, he accomplishes his purposes by gentle forbearance and careful suffering. I call it "careful" because it is not masochistic. We do not choose to suffer, just for suffering's sake, if it is not necessary. However, if our faithfulness to God's purposes involves suffering, then we willingly bear that cross of suffering for the mission of the kingdom.

The various references in The Revelation to Babylon's corrupting influences upon the kings of the earth (see 14:8; 17:2; and 18:3) show the great extent to which her evil has been perpetrated and why the salvation that the triumphant believers experience is such a great source of Joy. The final "Amen. Hallelujah!" of the elders and living creatures (19:4) reinforces this image, especially because the phrase echoes Psalm 106:48, which marks the end of the fourth book of the Psalter and serves as the climax of a tremendous poem proclaiming the ways in which God has taken note of the distresses of His people and restored them in remembrance of the LORD's covenant with them.

Revelation 19:5-10 ties together several ideas that summarize many of the main points of the New Testament. The passage talks about praise, celebration, equality under God, the Lord's reign, blessedness, rejoicing, the righteous deeds of the saints, the purity of the bride, and testimony.

One aspect of this chapter in The Revelation that is especially important in light of the purposes of this book is the equality mentioned at several points. In verse 5, the great voice declares that all the Lord's bondservants are to praise God, both the great and the small. Later, when the seer John falls at the feet of the angel to worship, the latter reprimands him with these words: "Do not do that; I am a fellow servant of yours" and of the brothers and sisters (19:10). All of us together are servants (literally in the Greek, "slaves") out of love for the Lord; all of us equally need to praise Him; no one among us deserves honor, for all the glory belongs to God and to God alone. Everything else is reduced to equality — even between angels and humankind — because of the surpassing magnificence of the Lord's greatness.

All the servants of God, all the ones who fear the Lord, are invited to participate in the celebration and the praising, for, as was announced in 19:6, the Lord our God, the Almighty, has indeed reigned. Though most English translations render this verb in the present tense, the original Greek verb was in the past tense. The difference is important, for the proclamation in the past tense helps us to recognize that the Christ has been Lord even when that was not apparent. His was the triumph even before we saw the destruction of Babylon. Therefore, we can rejoice and be glad and give Him the glory because the Lamb's wedding feast has come and His bride has prepared herself.

The doubled phrase translated as "rejoice and be glad" occurs in only one other place in the New Testament, and that parallel to this text is most interesting. In Matthew 5:12 the expression is used when the cause for such rejoicing is the greatness of the heavenly reward awaiting those who have been reviled and persecuted for the cause of Christ. That passage occurs at the end of the Beatitudes. Here in The Revelation the expression is followed by the fourth of the seven beatitudes in the book of Revelation (1:3; 14:13; 16:15; 19:9; 20:6; and 22:7 and 14). Rejoicing and being glad are not necessarily associated with human happiness, but they are appropriate reactions to the griefs we experience in God's service, for fulfilling God's purposes is its own reward. We are indeed blessed to be participants in Christ's sufferings (see Col. 1:24).

We must also notice that Revelation 19 stresses the purity of the Lamb's bride, since the Scriptures elsewhere focus more on the bride's failure — especially in the book of the prophet Hosea, where the bride Israel is represented by his prostituting wife Gomer. Nevertheless, as Hosea 3:1 shows, the LORD promises a husband's protection and care to the recalcitrant bride, the people of Israel (cf. also Isa. 54:5-7). Of course, the well-known portrait of Ephesians 5:22-33 gives the most positive image of Christ's bride.

The bride in Revelation 19 is dressed in white linens, which are defined as the righteous deeds of the saints. We must read that description in the light of the whole chapter, lest we think that those righteous deeds earn her salvation. All the other images of the context — God's victory over the corruption of the harlot, the rejoicing and blessedness given to the saints in this celebration — are very important, for they prevent us from creating a false conflict in this passage between faith and obedience. Rather, the true Church is obedient in her faith, and a submissive Church is faithful in that obedience. Verse 8 does not deny justification by grace, but it stresses instead that a transformed life is our Spirit-created response to the call of the bridegroom.

A similar combination of the truths of justification and sanctification is found in Ephesians 2:8-10, where the great hymn about faith being a gift (and definitely not of works lest any one might boast) is followed by the assertion that we are God's workmanship, created to do the good works the Trinity has designed beforehand in order that we might walk in them. Here the picture is the same: the linen garments have been prepared for the bride. She definitely puts them on and is involved in the righteous deeds that God has planned, but they are not the works of her own creation. Revelation 19:8 emphasizes instead that it has been *granted* to this bride to be clothed in them.

How blessed it is, then, to participate in the marriage feast. We are reminded of the great parable of Jesus in which He declares that, when those who have been invited refuse to come, the Lord of the supper invites all the lame and blind and helpless from the roadsides to come to the feast. All are made welcome except the one who has refused to accept the wedding garment that would have been provided for him if he had not rejected it (Matt. 22:2-14).

Once again the importance of our own weakness is emphasized. God doesn't invite us to the feast because we are worthy; we cannot come out of our own capabilities. Rather, we truly come to the wedding supper when, out of our helplessness, we joyfully receive the gifts of God's gracious banquet.

As we recognize our humble station along with the seer John, we, too, would fall to worship the angel who has brought the good news of the supper, but the angel continues to remind us that we are equally all servants who need to direct all our worship to God and not to each other. It is the testimony of Jesus that must always draw forth our response of praise.

Often the main emphasis of self-proclaimed "miracle workers" is on what they have done. They dress with finery and live in luxury and proclaim the wonders of God working through them. Those who faithfully follow Jesus in the sufferings of illness offer a significant contrast to these faith healers who try to "fix" them. The former give better testimony to Jesus in their humble submission to God's best purposes, even when they include suffering.

Notice again the necessity of theocentrism, God-centeredness. We can truly know our place only when we are focused upon the Lord's glory and recognize His preeminence.

That is illustrated graphically by the following passage (19:11-16) about the warrior on the white horse going forth to the final battle (which we have already considered in Chapter 17). He is described in terms of majesty and carries the title of "the faithful and the true." Notice the emphasis on His justice with which He both judges and fights. All that He does is eminently right.

Again, as in chapter 1, His eyes are described as flames of fire and He is crowned with many crowns and an unknowable name. He is also called the Word, and He leads the armies of the hosts of heaven to engage in the last battle against the evil opposition that has controlled the world till the end. And now the great and final destruction of God's enemies will begin.

The overall literary construction of this segment is dramatic. Craig Koester points out this chiastic arrangement:

Satan thrown from heaven to earth (Rev. 12)
    beast and false prophet conquer (Rev. 13)
        harlot rides on the beast (Rev. 17)
        harlot destroyed by the beast (Rev. 17)
    beast and false prophet conquered (Rev. 19)
Satan thrown from earth into the abyss (Rev. 20).[1]

Specifically at this point in the proclamation, the great destruction of the harlot Babylon is declared, the bride of the Lamb is introduced, and the wedding supper is announced before the final scene of battle in order that we might anticipate the victory as well as participate in it.

Such an expectation has dominated the whole book of Revelation. All along we have known that God would be the triumphant Lord. Though we have agonized over the persecution of the saints and the opposition of all the satanic forces, yet all along we have known the assurance of the victory. The bride has been getting ready. In the hymns of praise throughout the book, we have acknowledged God's reign and looked forward to its consummation.

This is the attitude that prevails in a theology of weakness. In spite of the sufferings of the present moment, in which all of us are reduced to equality before the Lord whom we worship together, we have tasted of the final victory. And that gives us courage to put up with the pain of the meanwhile.

---

1. Craig R. Koester, *Revelation and the End of All Things* (Grand Rapids: Wm. B. Eerdmans Publishing Co., 2001), p. 174.

CHAPTER 29

The Ultimate Defeat of the Powers of Evil and the Present Reign of Christ

*(Please refer often to Revelation 20:1–21:8
as you study this chapter.)*

There are a lot of things that I (stupidly) worry about, but what I should do when having an insulin reaction is not one of them. The first time I ever had one I was terrified, not understanding why my body was suddenly becoming so uncoordinated and clammy. I was a teenager, formerly very athletic and active, but suddenly a diabetic because of the destructive effects of a measles virus. I rang for the nurse and anxiously explained to her my symptoms. She calmly introduced me to the reasons for, and treatment of, insulin reactions. My fear of them was pretty well killed that day.

I hate them. I want like crazy to avoid them. But I don't have to fear them as I did that first day because I know that what I need is a good dose of sugar — and fast!

That illustration is, of course, totally inadequate to describe the significance of the first and second death, but it is a simple case in which, having conquered the fear when a reaction occurs, I no longer have to be alarmed. The nurse's patient instruction freed me to go into my future with insulin without terror about what to do when my dosage is too strong.

Any illustration would be inadequate. Incredibly more powerful is the freedom of those who have a part in the first resurrection and therefore will not ever have to fear the second death, for it can have no power over them (Rev. 20:6). This verse is the key to our understanding the difficult problem of the thousand-year reign of Christ in the book of Revelation, and it will help us better to understand the ultimate defeat of Satan.

The twentieth chapter of The Revelation causes the most extraordinary speculation because too often the number 1,000 is understood in a literalistic sense. All the other numbers in the book are symbolic numbers, and surely this one is, too. Ten (the complete number) multiplied by itself three times (the divine number) certainly suggests that this 1,000-year reign is divinely complete or powerfully long. But when will Christ reign for 1,000 years? It is critically important for us to understand the phrase appropriately because otherwise we forfeit the Joy that can be ours in experiencing in the present His sovereign reign already begun. We can delight in it now already, even as we still acknowledge and grieve the pain and suffering yet present in the world.

Often our struggles with limitations can help us to understand the presence of Christ's reign more thoroughly than when everything seems to go well for us. When we suffer intense afflictions, we might believe at first that evil will overcome us. Then in the midst of affliction we discover, by God's gracious provision, that Christ rules and that the evil, though terrifyingly and threateningly present, cannot triumph over us ultimately.

When I was finishing the revisions of the first edition of this book, I was simultaneously going through such a learning time. After almost thirty health complications in the previous dozen years (including bowel resectioning and foot reconstruction, frequent unhealable wounds inside my leg brace and bouts with intestinal disorders, a hysterectomy, and several surgeries on my hands and eyes), I was finally able to walk and see again — only to discover lumps that were cancerous. My first reaction was to scream, "God, it isn't fair! I've had more than my share of physical suffering!" I needed God's reminders that evil cannot overcome us. And those reminders came — in the truths of The Revelation as I worked on this book; in other Scripture readings, hymns, sermons; in the care and cards of friends, the flowers in the yard and the beauty of creation; and mostly in the Lenten worship services that reveal that God's love on the cross triumphs over all the powers of evil and our enemies of suffering and death.

The apostle Paul knew profound suffering, too, and asked God to deliver him; but, after receiving the assurance from God that grace would always be sufficient, he learned that evil cannot ultimately overcome us. He declares this triumphantly in one of my favorite parts of the second letter to the Corinthians. After noting that we hold a treasure in old clay pots to show that the transcendent power belongs to God and not to us, he describes the near miss of Satan's wiles against us in these terms:

We are afflicted in every way, but not crushed; perplexed, but not despairing; persecuted, but not forsaken; struck down, but not destroyed. (2 Cor. 4:8-9)

J. B. Phillips paraphrases these verses in this way:

We are handicapped on all sides, but we are never frustrated; we are puzzled, but never in despair. We are persecuted, but we never have to stand it alone; we may be knocked down, but we are never knocked out!

Sometimes the more tightly we get hemmed in, the more we learn of God's Lordship over it all. During a difficult period in graduate school when a developing allergy to animal insulin caused great delays in its functioning and I woke up in the middle of night after night with severe insulin reactions, God gave me still a deep sense of His protection and care. What if I hadn't awakened and my blood sugar had continued to plummet too far for me to escape a coma? Since I was single and lived alone, who would have found me? Such questions crossed my mind — and yet each time the Lord woke me up. In the affliction I rejoiced that I was never physically or emotionally crushed.

Similarly, one of the most Joy-full times of my life was during a period of being teased and persecuted for my Christian beliefs. My faith was strengthened more at that time than ever before, and I delighted to see God at work in the situations that developed. Those who harassed me most became more open to the good news of Christ's forgiveness and love. Meanwhile, members of a Bible study group I was leading gave me strong support, and the experience of such Christian community showed me that, though persecuted, I was never spiritually abandoned.

It is this sense of God's sovereignty — in spite of evidence to the contrary — that is underscored by the message of The Revelation concerning Christ's reign and the ultimate defeat of the evil powers. At the end of the nineteenth chapter, the false prophet and the beast are thrown into the lake of fire, and the armies of heaven wage war against all the kings of the earth and their forces of evil. The heavenly forces are victorious by means of the sword of the Word. Notice that there is no battle at all with human weapons; the only weapon used to end everything is God's Word!

However, the twentieth chapter begins with the binding of Satan for

1,000 years, and questions always arise whether this occurs before or after the "rapture" and the "tribulation," before or after the second coming of Christ, and so forth. The problem lies in our trying to pin down chronologically and literalistically events that are part of the cyclic symbolism and multi-layered mystery of The Revelation. If we read Revelation 20 very carefully, we learn all that can be known about the eventual triumph of God's reign. The most important aspect is when that ultimate victory begins.

One key can be found in the combination of these two verses, which structure the text literarily and theologically:

> Blessed and holy is the one who has a part in the first resurrection; over these the second death has no power, but they will be priests of God and of Christ and will reign with Him for a thousand years. (20:6)

and

> But for the cowardly and unbelieving and abominable and murderers and immoral persons and sorcerers and idolaters and all liars, their part will be in the lake that burns with fire and brimstone, which is the second death. (21:8)

These two statements structure very clearly a theology that recognizes Christ's reign beginning at His (the first) resurrection and continuing until the end of time, when the second death finally separates His own from those who have rejected Him. That sequence is developed in Revelation 20 and 21.

The first essential point in this theology is that God's reign was instituted in Christ's cross and resurrection. The New Testament frequently proclaims Christ's triumph in His crucifixion over the powers of separation, death, and Satan. (See, for example, Eph. 2:13-16 and Col. 2:13-15.) Furthermore, the saints' reign is declared in 1 Peter 2:5 and 9, as well as earlier in The Revelation (see 1:6 and 5:10). Moreover, the apostle Paul constantly stresses that believers participate in Christ's death and resurrection and thereby reign with Him. (See, for example, Gal. 2:20 and Rom. 8:9-11, as well as Eph. 2:4-6.)

Of course, Christ's Lordship is not honored by everything and everyone yet. However, His reign began when He defeated the political, economic, and even religious principalities and powers on the cross and when He burst from the tomb triumphant over the last enemy, death. His present rule is evident in the fact that since His resurrection the gospel has continued to draw people to the Trinity and to spread hope and faith throughout the world.

Indeed, Christ is already making His people into participants in His kingdom. Those who have been martyred for the gospel, for example, are assured that their sacrifice was not in vain, but that they actually share in Christ's reign during this time. Those who have rebelled against God's ways have rejected the first resurrection, and thereby do not participate in the present Joys of Christ's thousand-year reign. Meanwhile, one of the marks of the times is that Satan does not have ultimate power to deceive the nations. He was bound by Christ on the cross and will try, at the end of time, to gather the world for war against God, but he will immediately be defeated and cast into the lake of fire (20:2-10).

These verses in Revelation 20 circle around the basic facts that the Lord's people are secure in God's sovereignty even though Satan is doing his utmost to wage war against the Almighty. Those who participate with Christ in the first resurrection do not have to fear the second death at the end of time when all the powers of evil are destroyed. We know that there will eventually be a decisive showdown at the end of the world in which the forces of Satan will be totally devoured and the devil himself perpetually tormented. What we do not know is the timing of that final defeat.

It will indeed be ultimate. Furthermore, the defeat will be accomplished entirely by God's hand. Notice that the text says the enemy will surround God's people, but the former will be annihilated by fire that will come down from heaven (20:9).

This is urgently important for us to note because too many Christian groups try to prepare for the last battle — as if there were anything we could do about it. At the height of the Cold War, many wanted to stockpile nuclear arms to prepare for the Armageddon of a third worldwide conflict. This theology was usually coupled with the notion that we must possess the power to demolish God's enemies — namely, the U.S.S.R. Such an attitude has no basis in the biblical account (and did not take into consideration the millions of God's people living in "enemy" lands!). The Almighty's fire will destroy the enemy. The Lord's people might be surrounded, but in their weakness they will experience God's true triumph.

Verse 11 introduces the scene of judgment. Because of this sequence, it makes more sense to think of the reign of Christ as happening now. Satan has been bound so that he is not in complete control, but his cohorts are still at work causing trouble in the world. Then, when Satan is released for his final fling, cut short when God's fire destroys his forces, all that has taken place in this meanwhile time will be judged. The powers which have thoroughly rejected the Lord, disregarded God's constant warnings, and fostered the evils of the 666 will be brought up from death and hell and Hades and finally thrown into the lake of fire. At that point — the time of the judgment, the second death — all evil will be totally obliterated from the presence of those whose names are written in the book of life.

Next, chapter 21 promises the new heaven and the new earth — a heaven and earth unmarred by the presence of any of the evil powers, for they have all been thrown into the lake of fire. This is especially emphasized in the text by the assertion that there is no longer any sea, for earlier in The Revelation the sea was associated with the dragon and his beasts (13:1). Already in the First Testament the sea had symbolized vicious forces. Since there were no natural harbors along the Israelite coastline, the Jews had never become much of a seafaring people. No wonder that to them the sea represented terror and death.

Now we see the heavenly Jerusalem, prepared as a bride, beautifully adorned for her husband (21:2). Throughout our study of the seer's vision, let us remember that it is not describing the New Jerusalem so much as a *place,* but as a metaphor for *God's people,* in whose midst God will someday dwell — even as the old city of Zion metaphorically stood for the whole people of Israel, who longed for the coming of the Messiah, while the Temple represented and demonstrated the LORD's presence. Now the New Jerusalem encompasses all the believers, and, most wonderful of all, the tabernacling of God with His people is announced as an actual reality (21:3). (Remember that in Rev. 7:15 it was still seen as a future hope; refer to our discussion in Chapter 18.)

Now in God's eternal presence everything is new, and all that is associated with evil is done away with forever. Tears and suffering and pain will not have a place when God culminates His reign with His covenant people, for the old order, these first things, will have passed away (21:4-5).

Note that the old order had not been demolished during the thousand-year reign, so we can't postulate a millennium only at the end of time when Christ's reign is complete. It is an already-but-not-yet reign, taking place now, during which the old order still continues to exist, though it cannot have ultimate authority because Satan himself has been bound. However, he has not yet been totally defeated — that remains for the end of time — so he and his under-demons are still continuing to wreak their havoc in the world.

Eagerly we look forward to the time when God says, "It is done." The Lord is the beginning and the end, and someday He will fulfill His promise of drink to all who are thirsty (notice again these images from Isaiah and the Gospels). Furthermore, God promises all these gifts as an inheritance to those who overcome (a phrase reminding us of all the promises given in the seven letters of Revelation 2–3). The overcomers will be God's sons (with all the rights and privileges that sonship signified for both women and men in the first-century Church), for indeed God will be their God.

When the old order passes away, however, all that is of that order will no longer have any place. Those who have backed down from the faith (the cowardly), those who have rejected the faith (the unbelieving), and those who have not accepted the wholeness of salvation in its power to transform our way of life (the abominable, the murderers, the immoral persons, the magicians, the idolaters, and the liars) will not have a place in the new order. They will be destroyed by the second death (21:8).

On the other hand, those who have participated in the resurrection — to use Paul's terms, those who have died with Christ and, thereby, have died to sin and risen to new life in Him — will not be harmed by this second death. This death does away instead with all that is related to sin.

The list of those persons who will be harmed by the second death not only speaks of the time of judgment and ultimate defeat of evil but also gives us an urgent warning. To participate in God's kingdom is to resist the temptation to engage in such attitudes and activities. Modern Christians must pay more careful heed to all the aspects of this warning.

We can see by the combination of sins on the list that no dimension of our ethics is trivial. We would probably all readily agree that it makes sense that those who are idolaters should be cast out of the kingdom and into the lake of fire, but we might wonder if lying is so terribly wrong.

This text indicates that it is. So is sexual immorality — and murdering of all kinds, including the many times that we murder each other with snide words and rude glances, violent attitudes and hostile actions.

If we meditate on this text with utmost seriousness, each of us will find aspects of our present behavior opposed to the kingdom's principles. Sins of distorting the truth, for example, are just as destructive of God's purposes as other idolatries, such as greed, or the sin of killing someone.

I have been especially troubled the last thirty years by the terrible increase of sexual immorality in our culture and the related symptoms of broken marriages, abortions, children growing up without nurture, fractured homes, and juvenile delinquents. So many of these problems feed into each other and multiply each other's effects. Moreover, many of the problems stem from this same root: a blatant rejection of God's authority over our bodily life. Those who think they can do what they please with their sexuality are shaking their fist at God's creation of their wholeness and the divine design for committed relationships. These sins are terribly destructive, yet Christians often do not stand firmly enough against them.[1]

The Revelation's warning about the second death and its invitation to participate in the present reign of Christ and the future of His kingdom after the judgment force us to think carefully about our personal and social ethics. The Christian community continually seeks God's guidance for faithfully living out the reign of Christ's kingdom at this time.

His thousand-year reign will last for the perfect length of time — to complete thoroughly all God's purposes to reconcile the cosmos. This reign began at the cross and the empty tomb, when Christ defeated the powers, and will continue until the final assault and defeat of Satan. In the meanwhile, however, we manifest Christ's reign to the world by living out the purposes of His kingdom. If He has made us priests in that kingdom and enabled us to rule in it, then we are invited to be models of that alternative way of life right now. Believers in Christ are a people who are marked, not with the 666 of idolatrous evil, but with the sign of the Father's name on our foreheads. We must always be asking ourselves if Christ's reign is evident in all that we are and say and do and choose.

I ponder this question with great sadness. We are all sinners, subject to temptation; we easily let idolatries control our lives. Various immoralities and murders are constant temptations to us. However, The Revelation keeps urging us constantly to seek to be faithful to God's best purposes because we know that Christ's reign has begun in our lives and that the Holy

---

1. For an explication of the goodness of God's purposes for our sexuality, see my *Sexual Character: Beyond Technique to Intimacy* (Grand Rapids, MI: Wm. B. Eerdmans Publishing Co., 1993) and *Is It a Lost Cause? Having the Heart of God for the Church's Children* (Grand Rapids, MI: Wm. B. Eerdmans Publishing Co., 1997).

Spirit within us empowers us to demonstrate the kingdom's truths and purposes in our everyday existence.

I want the reign of Christ to dominate the way I choose, the values I espouse and demonstrate, the behaviors that characterize my way of life, the methods I use to build peace in the world. I want to participate in the thousand-year, divinely perfect reign as much as possible. Moments when that reign is not evidenced in my life are my fault.

Those Christians who focus on a literal 1,000-year reign of Christ at some time in the future — though all the numbers in The Revelation are symbolic and though Christ tells us we can't know anything about the future calendar — miss the whole message of this section of The Revelation. Surely it calls us to notice how Christ governs in this present time so that we more deliberately choose to live out the purposes of His kingdom in daily life.

To understand His reign as a present, though not thoroughly culminated, reality makes a huge difference in our perspectives on life. We do not have to be defensive about our faith because we will remember that we are already involved in the kingdom and its rule. We will instead seek to live according to the principles of the kingdom in every aspect of our lives and to invite others into the Joy of Christ's present reign.

Such a perspective will influence the way we handle all of our daily affairs — our sexual ethics, our avoidance of magic arts and lies, our desire not to murder anyone with words or actions. Everything that we are and do becomes an important indication of whether or not the life of the kingdom characterizes our existence and choices.

Most important, Christ's present reign enables us to be overcomers in times of suffering and trouble. When we feel the force of the assaults of evil powers — in sickness or doubts or any other sort of spiritual pain — we will cherish the unfailing hope that someday this old order will have passed away. Someday our tears will be gone, so in the meanwhile we can carry on.

CHAPTER 30

The Beautiful City: An Agent of Healing

*(Please refer often to Revelation 21:9–22:7
as you study this chapter.)*

Once when I was a not-very-rich graduate student, I received the gift of a plane ticket from Indiana to the state of Washington to spend some restful time with my former secretary and her family. As the plane circled around the city of Seattle, my heart soared with the love of that place. How beautiful the city seemed to me — more captivating than ever before. Of course, my ecstasy was deeper because its source was in the unexpected gift of being with people I loved.

Indeed, absence makes the heart grow fonder. Expectant longing deepens our pleasure. For that reason those who struggle with physical limitations or other trials often long more for the beauty of heaven than do those who are well and so thoroughly involved in the things of this present life that they do not want to give up what they are doing now to go on to a better life in God's presence.

Once (ironically, more than twenty years ago) Tim and I were talking about the depth of love in our friendship, and he suddenly said, "I wonder what our friendship will be like in ten years." I answered that I probably wouldn't live that long, and he responded, "I probably won't either. Just imagine what our friendship will be like in heaven!" What an exciting thought! At last we will have enough time to do all the talking for which we yearn. At last we won't struggle anymore with low blood pressures that make us dizzy and deficiencies that debilitate our bones and nerves. Most important, at last we will know Jesus face to face! How thrilling to look forward to heaven where all is beautiful to the extreme!

Revelation 21–22 portrays the bride of Christ with such glory that we hardly need to comment on the various dimensions of her beauty. We need no special theological expertise to see in the description a poet gone wild with delight in all the loveliness of this vision. (I even began to write poetry for the first time in a long while as our plane swooped over Puget Sound and the city of Seattle spread its panorama before my weeping eyes.) However, several characteristics of the glorious fulfillment of God's great promises to us are lessons desperately needed in our churches and community relationships.

First, we note that the Holy City comes down from God and shines with the Lord's glory. In other words, the beauty is derived. Nothing inherently worthy in God's people makes them fit to be the bride of Christ, but we are transformed by His relationship with us and made into the jewel that The Revelation describes.

This emphasis is underscored by the frequent use of the symbolic twelve in these verses, for that number always stands for the people of God. The LORD had made the twelve tribes of Israel His people by His special election and not because they were so worthy. They were a weak nation, not very successful, and not large in numbers, yet God chose them to call them His own (see, for example, Deut. 7:7-8). The derivative nature of our beauty as Christ's people is an important part of our future — and of the present.

The more we recognize the derivative beauty with which God endows us, the more thoroughly we can enjoy it now and appreciate it ardently. There is no place for pride in the Church, for all that our communities accomplish is by God's hand among us and through us. However, when we recognize that the Lord is really present in each of us, we can find greater worth in all the participants in our community. We can learn more deeply to value the weak and infirm among us — those whom the world would not call beautiful — because we can see the beauty in them that God bestows already, though not yet fully.

Quite mistakenly, some modern biblical translations and paraphrases try to put the measurements of the Holy City into literalistic modern figures. Changing the stadia into miles or kilometers, however, drops the significance of the number 12,000 — a number that represents the people of God (12) times a number of thoroughly (and divinely) multiplied completion (1,000). Furthermore, the thickness of the wall is 144 cubits or 12 times 12 — a doubly reinforced emphasis that this is indeed the city of God's people. Moreover, throughout history walls have been constructed for protection and security. Such a 12 by 12 wall, then, suggests God's great care for His people, His thorough protection and possession. To modernize that figure into 216 feet or 72 yards (as various translations and paraphrases do) makes it just seem ludicrous to have a wall so thick or a city that is so incongruously cubed.

Notice again the use of all kinds of precious stones (some of which can't even be precisely identified anymore) and the predominance of gold and pearl. This piling up of glorious images gives us the opportunity to enter with the seer into his attempt to comprehend a beauty that is not comprehensible. How could we describe that which is beyond description?

For the past dozen years I have tried to tell people how wonderful my husband is. Words always fail me, though, so I usually have to end lamely, "You should meet him — then you would know how gracious he is." In the same way, we can hardly begin to imagine the incredible splendor of the presence of God Almighty until we get to the "place" (*with* Him!) that Christ has prepared for us.

Through all of this someone might object, "But this is really old-fashioned. I don't believe in some sort of glorious city to which we are all going when we die. The place wouldn't be big enough to hold us all anyway." Many modern thinkers reject the images of The Revelation because they are not reasonable. Unfortunately, our hyper-rationalism steals from us the sense of mystery that these pictures are intended to convey.

Too easily we Christians let our society's way of thinking determine ours — and such scientific quantifying (to turn the symbolic cubits into feet, for example) destroys the truth of the symbol. Whatever description we might offer of what it means to be in the presence of **GOD** after our death will be grossly inadequate. It is not the *place* we are interested in, after all, nor some sort of spectacular final event. It is our encounter with the Person, the Lord of lords and King of kings. All our feeble, finite attempts to comprehend the greatness of a relationship with God Himself (unmarred by human sin and evil's corruption) can only stir up longing in us for the final fulfillment of its promise.[1]

There is a joke about a man who can't accept the idea of a life after

---

1. Surely one of the best descriptions of the Joy of heaven in all of literature is found when the children are finally at home with Aslan at the end of C. S. Lewis's children's tale, *The Last Battle* (New York: Macmillan, 1956), pp. 158-74.

death in the presence of God. He says to a believer, "Do you mean to tell me that there is really going to be a city where the streets are paved with gold?" His believing friend answers, "I just know that when we are finally with God all the right values will be restored. Do you think gold is important? After we die and learn the true meaning of it, we're just going to walk on the stuff."

That joke illustrates well how we must understand the descriptions of The Revelation. What does it mean that the streets are paved in gold? They signify stunning magnificence certainly, and they invite our imaginations to run freely as we contemplate the wonder of life in God's presence. They invite us also to realize that our conceptions are grossly inadequate and that our human values someday will be put into proper perspective. What we think most worthy of praise now is but a mere (and marred) foretaste of the true reality of God's creative glory.

All the dimensions and jewels and gold of the beautiful city prepare us for this central climax: there is no need for a temple in the New Jerusalem because the Lord God Almighty and the Lamb are its temple. The seer's use at this point of such a full name for God reminds us not only of the Lord's fulfillment of the First Testament covenant and of the Almighty's power over all that is, but also of the suffering of the Lamb whose sacrifice makes it possible for us to be in the city — that is, with God and His people — at all.

These names reveal why a temple is not required. We will no longer need a place to worship, nor a time set aside explicitly to focus on what our God is like. Rather, we will be enjoying the Lamb's very presence and can join the living creatures and the elders and the angels in falling at the foot of His throne. Similarly, not even the natural lights of the heavens will be required, much less human means of enlightenment and artificial fixtures, because all darkness will be gone — cast into the lake of fire — and the radiance of God's presence will illumine the city, and the lamp of the Lamb will enable us to see clearly and to understand.

Once again let us pause to reflect on the significance of this message for our times of suffering and for our relationships with the weak and afflicted in our midst. This time my reflection is stirred by the constant echo in my mind of an exquisite choir anthem based on this text. In a delicately simple setting that begins with the invitation "Peace be to you" and ends with words from Revelation 21:23 and 22:5, the composer Paul Manz poured out his soul onto coffee-shop napkins while nearby in the hospital his infant son lay dying. In the darkness of his anguish Manz yearned intensely for the victory of the Lamb and for a clarity of hope — so he called for Jesus quickly to come and bring him the light of His presence.

By the time his composing had poured out his pleas, his son had taken an unexpected turn for the better — and grew up to become a pastor. Meanwhile, the father's vision of the meaning of eternal life — born out of the pain of his helplessness — remains in his stirring music and gently invites us all to a deeper appreciation of the Lamb's light when we get too attracted to the neon ones.[2]

Revelation 22 begins with the pictures of the river of life, the tree with its twelve months of fruit and its leaves for the healing of the nations, the presence of God to remove the curse, and the constant ministering of those who are the Lord's servants. They are able at last to see God's face, and they carry the Lord's name on their foreheads as they reign forever in the Lamb's light.

All these images work together to create a tremendous hope and to stir up longing in us for the abundant life. It is a life thoroughly nourished, well watered, healed. All the conflicts of the past are over, and now people live together equally serving God in His presence. Pictures such as these inspire our work in this present world. If this is what the kingdom is going to be like when we experience it fully in God's own presence, then our life now, which is to be a reflection of Christ's reign at this time, must seek the same ends. Our work as God's people, in our present imperfect service, is to receive the nourishment of God's living water and fruitful tree of life, to be counteracting the curse, and to bring healing to the nations.

Sometimes there is a tendency among Christians to focus so much on heaven that we lose sight of God's commands for life now in this world. Certainly it is right for us to look forward to the day when we will know Jesus face to face — but in the meanwhile there are many ways in which we can participate in His purposes to bring healing to the nations. Nourished by His present reign in our lives, we are challenged to be ambassadors of His kingdom and bearers of its reality. What aspects of our present environment urgently need our witness to the governance of Christ's kingdom?

For example, the invitation to bring healing to the nations causes us to couple our witness to salvation in Jesus Christ with careful efforts at peace-

---

2. Paul Manz, "E'en So, Lord Jesus, Quickly Come" (St. Louis: Concordia Publishing House, 1954).

making. Our words about God's grace are more easily perceived as true if our lives seek to manifest that grace faithfully.

The picture also intensifies my concern for the hungry of the world. God purposes to nourish people spiritually with the water of life, as well as to provide for their material needs — to provide food for them rather than weapons of the curse. Because Jesus commands us to love and feed our enemies, it grieves me that our world spends so much of its wealth on weapons of destruction when so many people are dying of starvation and malnutrition-related diseases. If God's kingdom determines our priorities, we are empowered to live the gospel in ways that bring the reality of that kingdom to our world. Our ethics are an integral part of growing to understand the meaning of salvation and eternal life, for Christ's reign is not some far-off future event. It begins to take place now in the kingdom work of His servants.

We don't dare dismiss too lightly the words that close this section of The Revelation. Right after the beautiful pictures of the new city, the holy Jerusalem, the seer records this message from the angel: "These words are faithful and true," for "the Lord, the God of the spirits of the prophets, sent His angel to show His bondservants the things which must shortly take place" (22:6). In the first century those words called suffering Christians to new hope and renewed action in living out God's kingdom in spite of persecution. In our time, similarly, they urge us to live the truth of God's promises now. The angel has been sent to twenty-first-century servants, too, so that we might know what is soon to take place and how we can participate in it. (We recall our questions from Chapter 22 — for the "How Long?" is changed by the answer to "In the Meanwhile.")

The strong challenge of The Revelation to continue faithfully doing the Lord's work is heightened by the potent contrast between the beautiful city in these final chapters with Babylon in previous chapters. Craig Koester emphasizes that the seer's "Tale of Two Cities" was intended to give its first readers confidence and motivation to pursue the Lamb's way of life and faith in the midst of their present, difficult circumstances. He summarizes,

> The contrasts between Babylon and New Jerusalem, between the harlot and the bride, seek to alienate readers from powers that oppose God, while drawing them more firmly to a vision of life with God. Readers are called away from Babylon (18:4) and toward the New Jerusalem. There will be no reason for a bride and groom to rejoice in

Babylon (18:23), but there will be celebration at the marriage feast of the Lamb in God's city (19:7, 9). Babylon will be a dwelling for demons (18:2), but the New Jerusalem will be the dwelling of God (21:3). The harlot may exhibit a splendor that comes from the exploitation of people (18:12-13), but the bride manifests the glory that comes from God (21:11-21). Nations are corrupted when they seek to amass wealth for themselves by trafficking with the harlot, yet God calls the nations to a vision of the bridal city, where they will bring their glory into the presence of God and the Lamb (21:24-26). Babylon is filled with impurity and deception (17:4-5; 18:23), but there is nothing impure or false in the New Jerusalem (21:27). The harlot makes the nations drunk on idolatry and sin (17:2; 18:3), but the bride invites the nations to drink of the water of life and to be healed by the leaves from the tree of life (22:1-5).[3]

Can we, too, learn to see more clearly the impurities and deceptions of the world around us, so that we are alienated from them and drawn instead to participate more fully in the life of God's people?

Immediately after the angel's words about truth and trustworthiness, the Christ Himself speaks and promises that He is coming quickly. How blessed are the ones who heed the words of the prophecy of this book. As we wait for His coming, then, our time is not to be spent in useless speculation about how and when He will come or how to literalize the thousand-year reign and the tribulation. Rather, we are to be busy keeping the words of the book — following the warnings sent to the seven churches and still applicable to situations in our times; recognizing the presence of evil in this world, but praising God for His Lordship anyway; faithfully enduring with biblical patience the tribulations we must suffer in order that we might participate in the suffering work of the kingdom; and serving as priests for the world.

The trouble throughout centuries of history has been that Christianity has not found the proper balance between heaven and earth in its perspectives. To be too heavenly minded is to be no earthly good. If all we do is

---

3. Craig R. Koester, *Revelation and the End of All Things* (Grand Rapids: Wm. B. Eerdmans Publishing Co., 2001), p. 196. Koester cites Richard Bauckham's *The Theology of the Book of Revelation* (Cambridge: Cambridge University Press, 1993), pp. 131-32, as his source for these comparisons.

speculate about what it might be like when we finally get to the holy city, we will not be involved in the present work of the kingdom. The question must rather be, How are we to *be* the holy city now?

In our day perhaps we are more likely to err on the other side — to get so involved in trying to remedy the situation of this world, which will someday pass away anyway, that we lose track of the heavenly city, and most of all its Temple, for which and Whom we are headed. If the relationship with God does not motivate our present service, then it will not last. We will have lost our first love. But if we serve out of adoration and genuine worship of the Lord God Almighty and the Lamb that was slain, then our hatred of false doctrine and our patience and our works will be commended.

Blessed are those in the process of keeping the words of this book — those who faithfully live according to the kingdom as they wait for its grand fulfillment.

CHAPTER 31

"Come!": Living Now in the Coming Victory

*(Please refer often to Revelation 22:8-21
as you study this chapter.)*

I needed a place to finish the rough draft of this book. There was a possibility that I could stay alone in my grandfather's home while my parents took him on a brief vacation, but the neighborhood wasn't very safe, and I was a bit worried because my health was not too stable. It is terribly hard for me to ask for help, but finally I turned to some dear friends from the first congregation I had ever served. Hesitantly requesting to work in their home for a few days, I was greatly relieved to hear their enthusiastic, "Come."

I especially appreciated the gift of that invitation a few nights later when winds of 90 miles an hour lashed the Wisconsin countryside, and a tornado just 25 miles away killed 8 people, injured more than 50, and destroyed an entire town. Throughout that night I thanked God that I was not alone, but had friends to awaken me and take me to the basement for safety.

So many other times, too, the word "come" has brought immense "come-fort" or relief from pain — like the time when I desperately needed an encouraging hug and one of my graduate school professors opened his arms wide and gently said, "Come." We all need to belong, to be accepted, to be invited, to be desired, to be welcomed, to be loved, to be cherished — and the word "come" speaks to all those needs. In all our eccentricities (like my strange, restless habits and frequent outbursts on the piano while I'm writing rough drafts), in all our pain (when we need a hug), in our confusions (over who to be and what to do), the word "come" invites us to peace and hope and strength.

Our last section of The Revelation focuses around the invitation "come." In response to the announcement of Jesus that He is coming quickly (22:7, 12, and 20), that precious word is spoken by the Spirit and the bride, by the ones who hear, and by the seer who announces that all who are thirsty are welcomed (v. 17). Finally, on behalf of all the longing saints, the seer cries, "Come, Lord Jesus" (v. 20).

Truly, when we are burdened and persecuted, we learn the depth of the word "come." When we are defenseless, we must be careful whom we invite to come; when we struggle endlessly with simple tasks in life, we look forward eagerly to the invitation to come to rest. Sometimes if we lack the human resources to meet our basic needs, we become more aware of the thirst that yearns to be satisfied and waits to be bidden to come.

Our section begins with the seer so overwhelmed with gratitude for the gifts of these visions that he falls down at the angel's feet to worship the one who had shown them to him. His action and the angel's response, which are similar to the scene in 19:10, renew again that previous warning to keep our gratitude properly directed. (This reminds us afresh of the necessity of theocentrism with which this book began.) Too easily we turn to the human agents who bring us comfort or take care of us and thereby do not appropriately recognize the source of all good things in God. I do not mean, of course, that we should not be grateful to the Trinity's human representatives, but we must watch lest our relationships with them get idolatrous. The Lord alone we are to worship, not the creatures God made and empowered for His service. Once again we are reminded that together all of us are equal bondservants and equally in need of constant reorientation so that we keep worship focused where worship is due.

In contrast to the instruction given to Daniel (Dan. 8:26), the seer in The Revelation is told to keep the words of the prophecy open and available to God's people, for the time is near (22:10). Verse 11 does not mean that human beings are fated or doomed to continue in their wrongdoing or filthiness or that they can gloat in their righteousness or holiness. Rather, we must continually recognize that our deeds issue from the kind of character we are developing. We cannot be satisfied with our present state of holiness, but we will want faithfully to keep practicing the principles of God's kingdom now already during Christ's present reign.

Such an ethics of character, let me emphasize, is not fatalistic, as if we had no choice about whether we select right or wrong. Rather, the text reminds us that each of our choices reinforces the character that is developing in us. If grace reigns and we make virtuous choices, then we will continue to develop habits of virtue. On the other hand, our bad attitudes and actions reinforce the unfolding of evil. Thus, if we continue to do wrong, our character will become more and more vile.

We can all recognize this state of affairs in our lives when we fall out of habits of letter writing or exercise or whatever. When we stop staying in touch with our friends, we find it terribly difficult to get back into the habit. When we've broken our disciplines for physical fitness, it is hard to force ourselves back into the pain it will require to get into shape again.

That is why it is so important that we recognize the present reign of Christ — His 1,000-year reign that has been going on now for about 2,000 years. Unless we know the profound importance of each act as worthy of our participation in the kingdom or a violation of its ethics, we will not take seriously the task of our constant faithfulness and deliberate intentionality in this present world. Are we choosing the kingdom values whenever we shop? in the way we use our leisure time? in our selection of occupations? in our attitude toward the community of saints in which we are growing?

While in graduate school, I especially appreciated the opportunity to participate in a vibrant Mennonite congregation. The people in the parish demonstrated profoundly the meaning of Christian community in the way they prayed for each other, pursued Jesus' way of life, and cared for those in need. Steeped in a rich tradition of faithful attention to the Scriptures, their deliberate commitment to following Jesus as peacemakers and justice builders nurtured the kind of Christian character that I long to exhibit, too.

All this is hinged, remember, on the One who is coming soon. All that is good must necessarily be seen as the work of His hand through us. Consequently, when He brings His reward, He will give to each according to what has been done. After all, He is the alpha and omega, the first and last, the beginning and end, the One who makes it possible for us to choose all the good that comes from Him. The ones who are blessed are the ones who have washed their robes in His blood, who have been given by His grace the right to eat of the nourishing fruit of the tree of life, and who are thereby strengthened for the tasks He gives. These are the participants in the new city (22:12-14).

Once again, however, we are reminded in 22:15 that such things as magic arts, sexual immorality, murder, idolatry, and falsehood have no place in the kingdom. This is the constant testimony of Jesus, who calls us to an alternative way of life not patterned after these sins that characterize the society around us. To be involved in such things puts us outside the kingdom of Christ.

The combination of this list of sinners who have no place in the city (v. 15) and the proclamation by Jesus that He has sent His angel to testify these things for the churches (v. 16) urges us again to recognize the importance of the Christian community. The positive purpose of church discipline is to remind the members of Christ's body that certain actions lie outside the realm of the kingdom. Discipline is not intended to push people out for sinful behavior; rather, it is meant to declare that certain actions do not characterize the people of God. The Church invites everyone to choose whether or not they want to participate in the moral life of the community. Those who do not — those who persist in idolatry, sexual immorality, magic arts, murder, and falsehood — have chosen to belong to a different sort of society from the community of the bride who says, "Come."

These verses comparing those who have washed their robes and therefore eat from the tree of life with those who practice the five sorts of sins that lie outside the kingdom remind us that we are constantly involved in the spiritual battle that has dominated the entire book of Revelation. Jesus is indeed Lord, but, as long as the forces of evil continue in opposition to Him, we will have to endure constantly the struggle of our sainthood.

In Revelation 22:16 Jesus suddenly refers to Himself as "the root and the offspring of David and the bright morning star." The images come from Isaiah 11:1 and Numbers 24:17, where the contexts emphasize the sevenfold spirit that was given to the offspring of the root of Jesse and the fact that Balaam could not curse God's chosen people. These images underline the truth and wisdom of the testimony of Jesus, and they remind us that His first coming was long foretold, even by enemies of Israel. Now again the promise of His second coming brings hope for a brighter day and the ending of the darkness.

The two images also carry us back to earlier portions of The Revelation. In 5:5, the name "Root of David" was used when the Lion-Lamb was first introduced. We are reminded, then, that Jesus is the one able to break the seals and to reign. The idea of the morning star recalls Christ's promise to the church at Thyatira that He would be with them (2:28).

We are eager, therefore, to respond to the Spirit's invitation to come.

God's people have continued throughout the ages to be the bride saying, "Come." We enter into her tradition and join "all the ones who hear" in passing on the summons to others. We respond both by coming and by swelling the chorus of those saying, "Come."

The invitation to each one who is thirsty, to all who desire to receive the free gift of the water of life, reminds us of the stunning chapter in Isaiah where these phrases are first used. Let us note here several appropriate aspects of Isaiah 55:1-2.

First, by means of an unusual combination of singular words for "each" with verbs that are plural, the prophet Isaiah literally says in Hebrew, "let each one/all of you come." We each accept God's invitation as individuals, and yet we come together as a community. We need each other for the coming, though no one can receive God's gracious gifts for another.

Furthermore, the Isaiah text develops its point by proclaiming that we can come and "buy without money and without price." To offer us the gift of the water of life was costly for God — it required the sacrifice of the Lamb who was slain. The gift had to be purchased, but the money for us to buy it is provided. We dare never take it for granted, therefore, as if the gift were worthless, but we also must not get caught up in our own efforts as if we could earn the gift or deserve it or pay God back for it.

This is especially important when we bear in mind the previous verses in Revelation 22 about our deeds and moral character. The paradox is that all these things are gifts to us, to be received with total thanksgiving and in absolute weakness, yet we do have the ability to choose the direction of our character development and to reject the gifts God would freely give us.

We might refuse to listen to the bride's calling — maybe we don't like the way the Church has borne its tradition. We might refuse to acknowledge our thirst — perhaps we think that the pleasures of the world satisfy it well enough. Or we might refuse to drink the only water that will quench it — probably we are afraid of the plunge into commitment it asks of us. All these are our own choices for response. On the other hand, if we accept the gift of life-giving water, it is through no merit of our own, no great ability to choose that which is right, for this ability, too, is a free gift from God. That is why the word "Come!" is so precious. It simply invites us into Christ's waiting and welcoming arms.

Penultimately, we are warned about the seriousness of The Revelation's prophecy. We are admonished not to take anything from it, lest we lose our place in the holy city, nor dare we add anything to it, lest God add to us the plagues. This rebuke takes us back to the emphasis on theocentrism with which we began our study together. We dare not presume to be God by adding to what the Spirit has to tell us about the Lord's purposes.

This warning is especially urgent when so much effort is being invested in adding to The Revelation a specificity about the end times. Jesus commanded us not to chase after such things. To add such interpretations when we have no biblical basis causes us to deserve the plagues poured out on those who act rebelliously against God's reign.

Moreover, we are not to take away from the words of life, because then we will not be able to be nourished by them. This caution is singularly appropriate when many contemporary believers want to give up the vision of the heavenly city. Certainly we must recognize the vision's symbolism — that none of us can really know what form, ultimately, our relationship with God will take. However, we dare not mislay the hope of the final defeat of the Satanic opposition and the eventual triumph of God's purposes. Those truths nourish us and create in us the ability to continue patiently and faithfully in the struggles of our temptations and suffering.

Certainly God isn't up in heaven threatening, "Now you'd better behave or I'll punish you for sure." Rather, the Spirit wants us to see that to read The Revelation with anthropocentric eyes causes us to miss some of its blessings and to add to ourselves plagues of worries and fears that we do not need to carry. We are most blessed when we can simply accept all that we can learn from The Revelation of God's purposes and not try to subtract anything that we don't understand or add what we think and want to make it more specific. In short, we are blessed when we bow before the mysteries of God.

Appropriately, then, The Revelation ends with a statement of longing. For the third time Jesus promises that He is coming soon, and the hearts of His people cry out, "Yes, it is true — Amen. Come, Lord Jesus." In the context of the first-century Church, those phrases no doubt were a request for Him soon to exert His Lordship over the entire world and to rescue His people from the sufferings they were presently undergoing. That is why the plea is followed by the assurance that in the meantime grace is sufficient to sustain us in the struggles. Truly it is so: the sufficiency of the grace of Jesus as He exerts His Lordship in this time will enable us to wait until He comes.

Only when we are weak and do not rely on our own strength are we able to keep this paradox in the best balance. Consumed with longing for the coming of Jesus, we can yet know that in the meanwhile grace will be sufficient to sustain us. We develop this balance only if we submit our whole lives in utter dependence upon the One who is coming.

I have written many of these comments about the lessons to be learned in our weakness because in my own struggles I have not learned them very well. Mentors like Tim and Linden and others who have entered my life over the years continue to teach me the need for weakness and the sufficiency of grace as we wait for Jesus to come. All of us in the Christian community need to learn in our various sufferings how to say, "Come," and how to respond by coming.

While we are waiting, these are the invitations: Come. Trust. Be graced. Long for the coming of Jesus and His ultimate triumph over evil. And, in the meanwhile, know His Lordship in your weakness.

Qualities for a Theology of Weakness: Perspectives from The Revelation on Suffering

We live in a world that makes a god of strength and power, of being most important and best. Tragically, our churches have become so caught up in our society's success and victory philosophy that U.S. Christians rarely speak a prophetic word to the world around us. We do not stand as an alternative community, offering a model of a different way of life under Christ's Lordship.[1] Individually and collectively, we have chosen too often to go after the chariots of Egypt rather than relying on the victory of God (see, e.g., Isa. 30:15-18 and Matt. 5:3-16). We have forgotten that God's Word still applies today, to be lived and proclaimed. We are called, as were the earliest Christians, to live by depending only upon God — resisting the idolatries of the world around us and yet compassionately offering the citizens of that world a message of hope.

The book of Revelation, written to God's people suffering in a time of persecution, has offered us clear guidance for such a life of dependence. Let us summarize the lessons that we have learned from The Revelation about the theology of weakness so critically needed to resist our world's idolatries.

1. First of all, we have gained from The Revelation a deeper sense of the

---

1. This is, to a great extent, due to our enculturation into the world's patterns of power and "success." See especially chapter 3, "Churches Being, and Acting as, Fallen Powers," in Marva J. Dawn, *Powers, Weakness, and the Tabernacling of God* (Grand Rapids, MI: Wm. B. Eerdmans Publishing Co., 2001).

sovereignty of God, the Lordship of the Christ. He has been proclaimed as the King of kings and Lord of lords. We have seen the Almighty's power and ability to defeat Satan and all the forces of evil. Though Satan is even released to vent his final fling, his last assault on God's people is easily crushed, and he and all his hosts are sent forever into the lake of fire. The Revelation offered to first-century believers the profound assurance that, in spite of all appearances to the contrary, God was still in control of world history. We desperately need to recover that assurance and confident hope in our time. The secret to its recovery lies in turning our perspectives away from the anthropocentrism with which we are dreadfully infected and in becoming again, more like the saints of old, a people characterized by theocentricity, God-centeredness.

2. Next, we have gained a deeper awareness of the intensity of the battle. C. S. Lewis's old dictum that we can make two mistakes about Satan — either to take him too seriously or not to take him seriously enough — is most certainly true. Our first lesson about the effective sovereignty of God enables us not to take the powers of evil too seriously, for we know that in the end God will triumph. This second lesson enables us to take them seriously enough. We must acknowledge that we are in a strenuous and continuous battle against the hosts of evil. The principalities and powers might have been bound at the cross so that they cannot fully control things, but Satan and his cohorts are busily at work, wreaking havoc in this world, corrupting that which is good, deceiving the people of the earth and leading them astray into all kinds of false values and idolatries, rebellions and self-centeredness. We must be vigilant against all forms of evil oppression and be conscious in our daily decisions that we choose between the purposes of God's kingdom and the misleadings of the Satanic hosts. Every action will tend toward one or the other.

3. A third lesson stems from the combination of the first two. Because Jesus is Lord in spite of the powers of evil, we yearn for a greater willingness to endure suffering patiently. We have learned a new meaning for patience in situations that cannot be changed. Because biblical patience invites us to look for the Lord's presence even in our contrary circumstances, we do not just ask how long it will be till things are different, but we seek to learn who the Lamb is and how He enables us to respond in the midst of our suffering.

4. We have learned, therefore, the value of our sufferings and of being weak — of accepting that weakness in order that we might more thor-

oughly learn to depend upon the sufficiency of God's grace. We have recognized that Christians do not faithfully perform our tasks by seeking to be powerful and to overcome the opposition of the world around us by force. Rather, we are called to a new gentleness, a submissive humility, a gracious integrity that enables us to stand true to the principles of God's kingdom — not opposing the world's values in an obnoxious way, but in the compassionate offering of a better alternative, a way of life that awaits its eventual vindication.

5. Of necessity, these first four lessons have led us to recognize the importance of the Christian community and each one of its members. We have seen our need to learn these lessons of weakness from whoever might know them best. We have appreciated the importance of encouraging everyone — including the handicapped, the infirm, the elderly, and the poor — to offer to our communities their gifts of insight and spiritual patience, their ability to transform the struggles of life into periods of hope, and their understanding of Christ's Lordship in the midst of afflictions. We have also seen the vast failure of our communities to make use of everyone's gifts, to nourish the equality of all of God's servants among us, to concentrate seriously on the wholeness of Christ's body and the integral relationships of all its parts.

We have learned from the suffering Church of the first century our great need for each other. The letters to the seven churches, which deal with seven different kinds of problems that we all evidence in greater and lesser degrees, remind us that we always need each other to find a better balance of love and clear doctrine and moral purity. Especially we need the gifts of those who depend on God in their limitations so that we might learn to be a Church of weakness, effectively participating in the sufferings of Jesus in a culture of power.

6. As we learn to live such a theology of weakness, we must walk a careful line between the dangers of cynicism and despair. Concentrating too much on the second lesson — the opposition of Satan and the forces of evil — will foster great cynicism. We will never expect any good to come out of anything. Concentrating only on the difficulty of our third lesson — the task of patience in the face of all this opposition — will lead to despair. How can we keep on going if we will never be able to accomplish God's purposes, to bring the Lord's kingdom to bear on this world?

The solution to keeping the necessary balance is to remain carefully theocentric, to concentrate on the hope that is ours because Jesus is Lord.

Such a hope can never be disappointed. It does not look for immediate victory, but it does acknowledge the perfect power and wisdom of His sovereignty. In His time and according to His best purposes, all evil will ultimately be defeated. For that end we continue to yearn — and to work, since we have been given the task of witnessing to His sovereignty in the meanwhile.

7. Finally, we have seen that such a theology of weakness creates a life of great Joy. Even in the midst of the direst of sufferings, we can know the Joy of the sovereign Christ's infinite love for us and of our relationship with Him. We have sung with the elders and the living creatures many new songs of praise. We have exulted in the Lamb's worthiness to receive all honor and glory and power and thanksgiving and strength and wisdom and might into the aeons of the aeons. AMEN! it shall be so — and in the assurance of that Amen we rejoice with an exceedingly great Joy, which our human existence cannot otherwise know.

Such Joy characterizes the Christian community that knows its place and eagerly awaits the consummation of its visions. Such is the Joy of those who recognize that the dwelling of God will someday be with us thoroughly, but that now, in the meanwhile, Christ tabernacles among us in our weakness. Such is the Joy of those who love their King and submit willingly to His sovereign presence — His 1,000-year reign — in their lives and struggles.

These are the characteristics of a theology of weakness. Our world mocks such a theology — but that does not in the slightest detract from its truth!

For Further Consideration

Books and Articles

Boring, Eugene M. *Revelation*. Louisville: John Knox Press, 1989.

Botts, Timothy R. *Doorposts*. Wheaton, IL: Tyndale House Publishers, 1986.

Browning, Don S., Bonnie J. Miller-McLemore, Pamela D. Couture, K. Brynolf Lyon, and Robert M. Franklin. *From Culture Wars to Common Ground: Religion and the American Family Debate*. Second edition. Louisville: Westminster/John Knox Press, 2000.

Chilton, Bruce, and J. I. H. McDonald. *Jesus and the Ethics of the Kingdom*. Grand Rapids: Wm. B. Eerdmans Publishing Co., 1987.

Clapp, Rodney. *Families at the Crossroads: Beyond Traditional and Modern Options*. Downers Grove, IL: InterVarsity Press, 1993.

Dawn, Marva J. "The Concept of 'the Principalities and Powers' in the Works of Jacques Ellul." Ph.D. dissertation, The University of Notre Dame, 1992 (Ann Arbor, MI: University Microfilms, #9220614).

―――. *I'm Lonely, LORD — How Long? Meditations on the Psalms*. Revised edition. Grand Rapids: Wm. B. Eerdmans Publishing Co., 1998.

―――. *Is It a Lost Cause? Having the Heart of God for the Church's Children*. Grand Rapids: Wm. B. Eerdmans Publishing Co., 1997.

―――. *Keeping the Sabbath Wholly: Ceasing, Resting, Embracing, Feasting*. Grand Rapids: Wm. B. Eerdmans Publishing Co., 1989.

―――. *Powers, Weakness, and the Tabernacling of God*. Grand Rapids: Wm. B. Eerdmans Publishing, 2001.

————. *Reaching Out without Dumbing Down: A Theology of Worship for This Urgent Time*. Grand Rapids: Wm. B. Eerdmans Publishing Co., 1995.

————. *A Royal "Waste" of Time: The Splendor of Worshiping God and Being Church for the World*. Grand Rapids: Wm. B. Eerdmans Publishing Co., 1999.

————. *Sexual Character: Beyond Technique to Intimacy*. Grand Rapids: Wm. B. Eerdmans Publishing Co., 1993.

————. *Truly the Community: Romans 12 and How to Be the Church*. Grand Rapids: Wm. B. Eerdmans Publishing Co., 1992; reissued 1997.

————. *Unfettered Hope: A Call to Faithful Living in an Affluent Society*. Louisville: Westminster/John Knox Press, forthcoming 2003.

Dawn, Marva J., and Eugene H. Peterson. *The Unnecessary Pastor: Rediscovering the Call*. Grand Rapids: Wm. B. Eerdmans Publishing Co., 1999.

Ellul, Jacques. *Apocalypse: The Book of Revelation*. Translated by George W. Schreiner. New York: The Seabury Press, 1977.

————. *The Humiliation of the Word*. Translated by Joyce Main Hanks. Grand Rapids: Wm. B. Eerdmans Publishing Co., 1985.

————. *The Meaning of the City*. Translated by Dennis Pardee. Grand Rapids: Wm. B. Eerdmans Publishing Co., 1970.

————. *Money and Power*. Translated by LaVonne Neff. Downers Grove, IL: InterVarsity Press, 1984.

Gunton, Colin E. *The Actuality of Atonement: A Study of Metaphor, Rationality, and the Christian Tradition*. Grand Rapids: Wm. B. Eerdmans Publishing Co., 1989.

Gushee, David P. "Race." In *Christian Ethics as Following Jesus*, edited by Glen M. Stassen and David P. Gushee. Downers Grove, IL: InterVarsity Press, forthcoming.

Hauerwas, Stanley. *Suffering Presence: Theological Reflections on Medicine, the Mentally Handicapped, and the Church*. Notre Dame: Notre Dame Press, 1986.

Koester, Craig R. *Revelation and the End of All Things*. Grand Rapids: Wm. B. Eerdmans Publishing Co., 2001.

Kreeft, Peter. *Making Sense Out of Suffering*. Ann Arbor, MI: Servant Books, 1986.

Lazareth, William H., ed. *Reading the Bible in Faith: Theological Voices from the Pastorate*. Grand Rapids: Wm. B. Eerdmans Publishing Co., 2001.

Lenski, R. C. H. *The Interpretation of St. John's Revelation*. Minneapolis: Augsburg Publishing House, 1963.

Lewis, C. S. *The Last Battle*. New York: Macmillan, 1956.

Mounce, Robert H. *The Book of Revelation*. Revised edition. The New International Commentary on the New Testament. F. F. Bruce, general editor. Grand Rapids: Wm. B. Eerdmans Publishing Co., 1998.

Mulholland, M. Robert, Jr. *Invitation to a Journey: A Road Map for Spiritual Formation.* Downers Grove, IL: InterVarsity Press, 1993.

Nouwen, Henri J. M. *In the Name of Jesus: Reflections on Christian Leadership.* New York: Crossroad, 1989.

O'Connor, Elizabeth. "Learning from an Illness." In *Cry Pain, Cry Hope: Thresholds to Purpose,* pp. 114-29. Waco, TX: Word Books, 1987.

Solzhenitsyn, Alexander. *Stories and Prose Poems.* Translated by Michael Glenny. New York: Farrar, Straus and Giroux, 1971.

Tolkien, J. R. R. *The Fellowship of the Ring.* Part One of *The Lord of the Rings.* Boston: Houghton Mifflin Company, 1955.

————. *The Return of the King.* Part Three of *The Lord of the Rings.* Boston: Houghton Mifflin Company, 1955.

————. *The Two Towers.* Part Two of *The Lord of the Rings.* Boston: Houghton Mifflin Company, 1955.

Ugolnik, Anthony. *The Illuminating Icon.* Grand Rapids: Wm. B. Eerdmans Publishing Co., 1989.

Vanier, Jean. *The Heart of L'Arche: A Spirituality for Every Day.* New York: Crossroad, 1995.

Walhout, Edwin. *Revelation Down to Earth: Making Sense of the Apocalypse of John.* Grand Rapids: Wm. B. Eerdmans Publishing Co., 2000.

Wallerstein, Judith S., Julia M. Lewis, and Sandra Blakeslee. *The Unexpected Legacy of Divorce: A 25-Year Landmark Study.* New York: Hyperion Press, 2000.

Music

Britten, Benjamin. *The Company of Heaven,* Part V. Virgin Classics recording. Performed by the London Philharmonic Choir and the English Chamber Orchestra. Conducted by Philip Brunelle. (Musical score published by Faber Music of London, 1990.)

Fauré, Gabriel. *Requiem.* Performed by the Academy and Chorus of St. Martin in the Fields. Conducted by Sir Neville Marriner. Soloists: Sylvia McNair, soprano; Thomas Allen, baritone. (Other fine recordings are also available.)

Manz, Paul. "E'en So, Lord Jesus, Quickly Come." St. Louis: Concordia Publishing House, 1954.

Messiaen, Olivier. "Quatuor pour la Fin du Temps." Musical Heritage Society recording. Program notes by the composer translated by Helen Baker.